SIXTY YEARS OF LUXURY
The Dorchester

Louis Stanley

PEARL & DEAN PUBLISHING LTD
LONDON

Published by:
Pearl & Dean Publishing Ltd,
27 Sale Place,
London W2 1YR

© Copyright Louis Stanley

First published 1991

ISBN 0 948308 10 9

This book was designed and produced
for Pearl & Dean Publishing Ltd by
A. H. JOLLY (EDITORIAL) LTD
Yelvertoft Manor, Northamptonshire NN6 7LF.

Printed in Great Britain by
JOLLY & BARBER LTD, RUGBY, WARWICKSHIRE

Contents

FIELD MARSHAL THE LORD BRAMALL

Foreword

Louis Stanley is indeed a man of many parts with a wide range of interests and an even wider circle of eminent friends and acquaintances in many different fields of activity. His own expertise ranges from ceramics to motor racing and broadcasting to golf; and he is also well known as a writer of many books in which his penetrating analyses of characters and situations and his anecdotes about people and events provide a fascinating commentary on life, as well as often throwing new light on his subjects.

I am therefore delighted that such an authoritative author should have elected to focus his spotlight and attention on *The Dorchester* which, after nearly sixty years in the limelight as one of the leading hotels in the world had, in 1989, to close its doors for a complete and fundamental renovation and modernisation, and has now reopened with its famous dignified luxury fully restored, but now augmented by the latest technology and advanced facilities to bring it up to the requirements of the 21st Century.

Louis Stanley is, of course, immensely qualified to write an anecdotal history of the Hotel. Not only has he visited and stayed at *The Dorchester* over a great many years but, being a much travelled man, there is hardly an International Hotel of note with which he is not acquainted. He is therefore very conversant with the standards, idiosyncrasies and foibles of the world of the 'Grand Hotel'. Moreover, since any Hotel is really only as good as its staff and indeed revolves around people – those that work there, those that manage and those that come as guests and clients – there is plenty of scope for his penetrative powers of observation and his fund of stories to bring alive the personalities and the 'goings on' in *The Dorchester*'s history, which has seen many dramas as well as great and stirring events.

A new offering by Louis Stanley which is linked to the reopening of something which has become a national institution is an event indeed, and I am confident that his enormously well researched yet entertaining book will give much pleasure and enjoyment, not only to those who have loved and loyally supported *The Dorchester* over its sixty years of existence, but also, to all those who are intrigued by the whole mystique and atmosphere of a great Hotel and what 'makes it tick'.

Bramall

FM

Chairman of the Board of The Dorchester Hotel

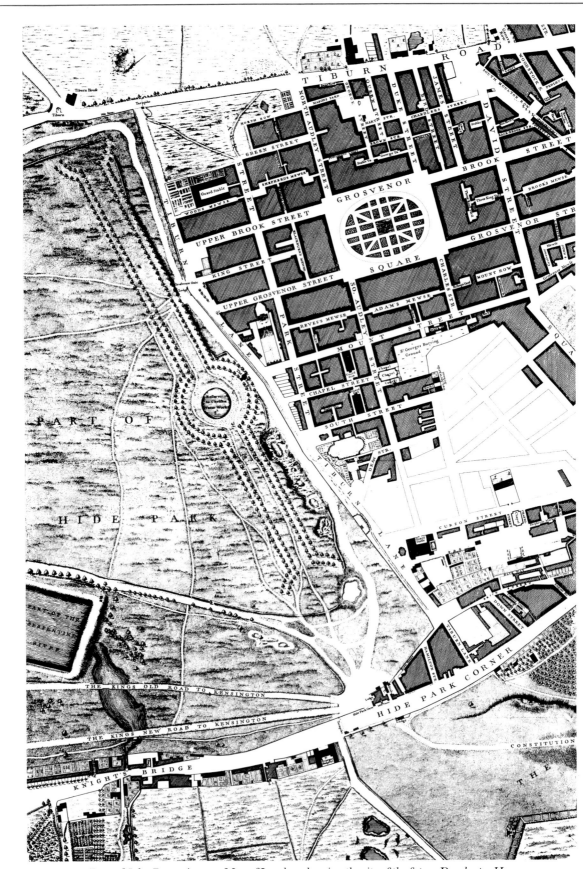

1. *Part of John Rocque's 1746 Map of London, showing the site of the future Dorchester House*

In the Beginning

I n medieval times when justice was more arbitrary than in later years, upwards of 200 petty offences were punishable by death from hanging. At the northern end of Tyburn Lane, once the boundary of Hyde Park, a towering three-sided gallows stood for over 500 years. Its forbidding appearance gave the name of Tyburn Tree to gallows throughout the land; until 1783, when Newgate took its place, it was the clearing-house for offenders of both sexes and all ages, the staple supply being highway-men, pickpockets and petty thieves. It also witnessed scenes of ceremonial floggings and torture.

Procedure seldom varied. The condemned were taken past St Stephen's in a tumbril, with final farewells at the Blue Boar Inn, Holborn, where 'goodly amounts of ale were drunk and much wailing'. The procession continued down Tyburn Street (now Oxford Street) to the gallows. Prayers were said, the noose fixed, and the cart driven from under the prisoners leaving them hanging and lifeless.

Eye-witness descriptions make horrible reading. It is hard to credit the insensitivity of the onlookers, many of them aristocrats and ladies of fashion. Executions were accepted as box-office spectacles, with grandstands encircling the gallows. There was no shortage of victims. Samuel Rogers recalls a cartful of young girls executed merely for being present when houses were burnt in the Gordon Riots (1780); they died in batches. Horace Walpole described how in 1792 seventeen men were strung up in groups. Claude Duval's execution, recorded by Macaulay, lacked the public appeal of Jack Sheppard, the prison-breaker, who amused an audience of several thousand by stealing from the chaplain's pocket, not a prayer-book, but a corkscrew which he clutched as the rope tightened. The last peer to be hanged, Earl Ferrers in 1760, insisted on a silken rope being used, the privilege of nobility. Two of the judges of Charles Stuart had a similar fate. The

2. *The execution of Earl Ferrers at Tyburn, 5 May 1760*

first anniversary of the Restoration was observed in a bizarre fashion. The bodies of Cromwell, Bradshaw and Ireton were disinterred from their graves in Westminster Abbey, dragged to Tyburn on hurdles and left dangling until sunset. Violent death became macabre titillation.

In those days Tyburn was a landmark in a rural setting, with only a few houses, from one of which the sheriffs watched the executions. The only reminder of the brutalities to survive is a small brass plate on Marble Arch. These grandiose gates, designed in 1828 by John Nash after an arch in the Roman Forum and made of marble taken from the Michelangelo quarries in the mountains of Carrara, were the main gateway to Buckingham Palace until the year of the Great Exhibition when they were moved to their present position. It was an unfortunate decision; even in those days the traffic was overwhelming. In 1908 the flow was rerouted and Marble Arch became an island with gates that are only ornamental features.

From here the Dorchester saga begins. It was part of the Manor of Hyde given by William the Conqueror to Geoffrey de Mandeville, who in turn granted it to the Abbot and Convent of Westminster. It remained ecclesiastical land until acquired by Joseph Damer, who became Earl of Dorchester in 1792, giving the name Dorchester to the building erected on the site. Damer lived from 1718 to 1798; the first mention of his name occurs in the rate books for St George's Parish, Hanover Square, in 1751 as owner of a house of small consequence. Over a period of years the rise in rates indicates that substantial improvements had been made. Damer married Caroline, daughter of the first Duke of Dorset, a Whig who had the temerity to oppose Horace Walpole. In 1808 on the

3. *Portrait of the third Marquess of Hertford in the*
Wallace Collection

death of his son, the second Earl of Dorchester, the title became extinct and the house passed to another branch of the family.

As London expanded its boundaries and titled gentry moved away from the congested city, their requirements for grand houses eventually turned this small, dirty lane into an elegant avenue. The neighbourhood became known as Mayfair and Park Lane emerged. The Damer property was taken over by the third Marquess of Hertford, one of the richest men in England, whose reputation as an art expert was acknowledged when the Prince Regent commissioned him to select some of the best canvases in Buckingham Palace. Hertford's personal collection laid the foundations of the Wallace Collection in Manchester Square. As a Regency Buck he was a calculating gambler, said to have won £40,000 in a night's play at cards. It was an age when cheating was commonplace, and Hertford did not escape. He fell victim to an ingenious trick: the Prince Regent had introduced an elegant blue coat for Court wear at the Brighton Pavilion, a feature being the large polished steel buttons. After repeatedly losing to the Prince Regent, Hertford suddenly realised that the buttons mirrored the cards in his hand. Complaining that the room had become unbearably hot, he undid his coat, hid the buttons and continued to play, but never again played cards in the Pavilion.

There was another side to Hertford's nature. He was an incorrigible womaniser and boasted a collection of over a hundred miniatures of young women he had seduced. At 22 he married Maria Fagnani, the illegitimate daughter of the fourth Marquess of Queensbury, a union of convenience that lasted forty years, mostly spent apart. There were three children, two undoubtedly his, the third popularly regarded as the son of Napoleon's Marshal Junot. After his father died in 1872, Hertford inherited an annual income from tenants' rents of £100,000 and an estate worth several million. An extravagant life-style was assured. The last parental restraint on debauchery went when his mother died. Dalliances were common; to cope with mistresses, a small house was built in the garden of Dorchester House. His valet, Nicholas Suisse, dealt with awkward situations. Attractive young women would arrive unexpectedly from the Continent; accommodation had to be found in Clarges Street, a private gate in the garden of Dorchester House being used for discreet exits into the street.

In his closing years, Hertford paid scant attention to personal appearance. Partly blind, the unfortunate fellow lived in only two rooms, the library and the dining-room. Ignoring convention, a particular extrovert pleasure was driving round London in a carriage full of prostitutes. On the last day of February 1842, he decided to spend the day at his Richmond villa and set off in the early morning with a noisy assortment of women. The trip was disastrous: even champagne did little in a damp, cold house with fireless rooms. He returned in the evening to Park Lane, speechless and wretched. The next morning he died, leaving £2 million in a rambling will of 16,000 words complicated by twenty codicils that baffled legal experts. A sad end to a flamboyant, wasted life.

The next occupant was Robert Staynes Holford, who purchased the freehold of Dorchester House, previously known as Hertford House, from the Dean and Chapter of Westminster Abbey. Architect's records show that Holford's original intention was to repair and alter the old house, but in 1849 he decided that a completely new structure would be more sensible and commissioned Lewis Vulliamy, the Italian architect, to carry out the work in rich classical style, a design influenced by the Italian Renaissance palaces. The choice came up to expectations. Born in 1790, the eldest son of D.L. Vulliamy, the watch and clockmaker, Lewis had gained experience from extensive travels in Greece, Italy and Asia and was responsible for the design of the Law Institution in Chancery Lane as well as churches in Woburn Square and Ennismore Gardens. The correspondence and notes of discussions with his patron relating to the new house, begun in 1849, show a leaning to Peruzzi's Villa Farnesina in Rome.

By this time the image of Park Lane had noticeably improved, accelerated by the spate of rebuilding and increase in value as well as by improvements to Hyde Park under the superintendence of Decimus Burton and John McAdam. Residents approved the substitution of iron railings for the former high wall that blocked their view of the park. They also benefited from the relocation in 1811 of Grosvenor Gate, their main access into the park for the drives and promenades so fashionable at this time. By 1845 it was possible for an advertisement of a small house close to the corner of Upper Grosvenor Street to recommend its situation as 'one of the most *recherché* in London, enjoying the varied Scenery of the Park, the distant hills of Surrey and the salubrious air therefrom, while at the same time it is placed in the Centre of Fashion'.

Dorchester House was to be the last of the great Italianate aristocratic London private houses of the nineteenth century, built primarily for entertainment and displaying a superb

4. *Vulliamy's Dorchester House*

5. *Dorchester House: The Library*

6. *Dorchester House: State room*

collection of paintings. It was set in a triangular forecourt enclosed by a massive stone wall where Deanery Street now meets Park Lane. Magnificent in conception, with state room after state room, its life belonged to the nineteenth century and the first part of the twentieth. The chemistry between Holford and Vulliamy was right, apart from a slight headache over the owner's concern about the heating arrangements. Correspondence in the autumns of 1851 and 1852, when Holford was in Scotland, dealt with the design of functional objects. Italian Renaissance palaces on which the new Dorchester House was to be modelled rarely had visible chimneys. Eventually a compromise was reached. There

7. *Dorchester House: The dining-room chimney-piece by
Alfred Stevens*

also seemed disinterest in bathrooms. There were only four: two for the owners, one for guests and another for servants. Architect and patron agreed that Dorchester House should be richer in effect than Bridgewater House, designed in 1845 by Sir Charles Barry for the first Earl of Ellesmere, but Holford would not let Vulliamy go over the top. He wrote to the architect in 1851: 'I agree with your criticisms pretty generally, but you will find that the World, more usually will admire large spaces treated as simply as to become unified, rather than appreciate clever intricacy, though possessing much pictorial effect.'

When the family was installed in 1856, the interior was far from complete. The staircase was under construction from 1856 until 1863. Some of the painted decorations were carried out by Sir Coutts Lindsay, the builder's brother-in-law; others were executed by Morant and Boyd of 91 New Bond Street, the parent firm of Lenygon and Morant who were to be involved with the décor of the hotel seventy years later. The first important rooms to be finished, about 1860, were the libraries on the ground floor. (It is interesting that panelling from one of the libraries was preserved on the eighth-floor main lift lobby of *The Dorchester*.) Holford's personal attention to every detail of the new house is shown by the fact that it was he, not the architect, who selected the artists and

8. *Dorchester House: The Staircase*

craftsmen who worked on the project. One of the principal causes for the delay in completion was his decision to have the decorative work done by Alfred Stevens, one of the most remarkable and fascinating artists of Victorian England, whom he met through John Morris Moore. As an art connoisseur, Stevens was instrumental in creating the Holford Collection that included Titians, Velazquez and Van Dykes. The house was completed in 1876. The contractor's final building account amounted to £131,400, to which was added Vulliamy's fee of £6573.

Dorchester House as such lasted only seventy years and was owned throughout by the

Holford family. At this point it is interesting to recall what life was like in Mayfair and Park Lane during those years, to catch a glimpse of its social life and fashions. The gold of the last century was perhaps never more than gilt, but life was full of glitter. There was complete assurance and a leisured air about the beauties of those days as they drove round Hyde Park in regal victorias and barouches with coachmen bewigged and powdered footmen, or the choice might have been a private hansom in place of a carriage-and-pair.

Ladies of fashion who knew Dorchester House and the adjoining Park Lane mansions lived up to their reputations in dresses with bodices so tight they might have been poured into them, with skirts rustling over countless beribboned and lace-flounced petticoats. The dresses were elegant and feminine charm was cluttered with a flurry of parasols, feather boas and hanging vanity bags. They were proud, self-contained and reserved, but all was not perfect. That age may have been one of restless luxury, but it was also vulgar to a degree. The long years of the mournful widowhood of Queen Victoria gave place to the social life of dinner parties and balls. Money rather than social rank was the key to recognition. Robert's father, Peter Holford, who died in 1803, was Governor of the New River Company, which supplied water to London and designed its water supply system. He was able to give the family multi-millionaire status, making possible the building of Dorchester House and the acquisition of a collection of Old Masters. His case was exceptional; in general, life lacked simplicity and style, like the hard glitter of their new electric lights.

There was abundance of leisure, but many moments of monotony for a young man of means. Immaculately dressed, he would ride or walk in Rotten Row for about an hour, then change into frock-coat and tall hat for lunch at the Club. Ladies might drive sedately in the Park or stroll in fashionable Eaton Square. In the afternoon there were concerts, perhaps by Lady Radner and her band or Lady Downe singing or Alec Yorke giving a recitation. A young man might be fortunate enough to be invited to a Saturday afternoon party at Holland Park or Syon, but on Sunday morning the ritual would be the traditional parade in Hyde Park. Luncheon would be memorable if he received an invitation from Lady Dorothy Nevill or Lady Jeune. He would then be certain to find himself in the company of statesmen and men of letters. He might even go to one of the musical receptions given by Mrs Ronalds with the assistance of Sir Arthur Sullivan, or opera at Covent Garden on a Reszke night, perhaps a theatre show with Connie Gilchrist or Arthur Roberts as the attraction: a Ball at Marlborough House or Dudley House, even a reception at Dorchester House.

Bric-a-brac vignettes are endless after a stay in one of the best houses – and, of course, all Park Lane houses were the best, with innumerable routine observances. The commotion on Sunday mornings as to who should ride to church in the landau, who in the wagonette, who in the victoria, who in the brougham, who should walk, as so often was the case when the church was St George's in Hanover Square, a landmark to the memory of Joseph Damer. Built and designed by Turnbull, its spire and portico look so like American colonial. Inscribed on the balcony panelling are the names of aristocratic churchwardens, many known in Dorchester House and the later hotel, particularly in

9. *A ballroom in the 1880s, from a drawing by Hugh Thomson*

10. *Riding in Rotten Row, Hyde Park, 1889*

11. *A Hyde Park 'church parade' during the London season, 1892*

connection with fashionable weddings. It was here that Sir William Hamilton and Emma Hart came, likewise George Eliot and Mr Cross. Theodore Roosevelt wrote in the register that he was '28, widower, ranchman'. When Mr Asquith married Margot Tennant, it was signed by a Prime Minister in office (Rosebery), a retired Prime Minister (Gladstone) and a Prime Minister-to-be (Balfour). It was not a coincidence that St George's was voted by Parliament to give Park Lane the air of a Christian country.

After the death of Sir George Holford, the son of Robert who built the house, it passed to his nephew, the fourth Earl of Morley. Then followed a succession of occupants. In 1910 it became the American embassy during Whitelaw Reid's term of office. The First World War saw it converted into a hospital for wounded officers. It might have been the Italian embassy and nearly became a National Art Centre. There was change in the air. John Harris recalls that in 1909 a drop in property values had become so marked that 'only an exceptionally attractive house would have any chance of finding a purchaser'. The recession marked the decline of the great houses.

12. *Ex-President Theodore Roosevelt leaving Dorchester House in 1910 when it was the American embassy*

In 1927 details were released of a hotel and a gigantic block of flats to be built on the site of Grosvenor House in Park Lane. Gloucester House had been built for the Cholmondeley family in Tyburn Lane in the 1770s. Lord Elgin bought it and stored there the Elgin Marbles which he brought back to England in 1802. It was purchased by the Duke of Gloucester on his marriage to Princess Mary, though critics said the house looked more like a seaside villa than a London town house. Upon the death of the Duke's uncle, George III, the house was sold to the Grosvenor family along with its site of two and three-quarter acres and became known as Grosvenor House. In 1926 it all came down and gave way to plans for the massive blocks of flats and a hotel of the same name.

Hard on its heels came rumours that Dorchester House was also to be demolished. The news brought storms of protest. Two issues of *Country Life* in May 1928 carried illustrated features of the exterior and magnificent interior of the house. Regrets were expressed at the possible letting of contracts for demolition, describing it as a grievous loss of a 'monument of individualism'. In the early 1920s Sir Malcolm McAlpine and Sir Francis Towle had discussed the idea of building in London an hotel which would give the most modern facilities, quietness and comfort without the annoyances experienced in other hotels. In 1929 that opportunity presented itself, the ideal position for such a project.

In July that year the site was bought jointly by Sir Robert McAlpine and Sons Ltd and Gordon Hotels, then one of the largest groups of hotels in Europe. The price was £500,000. Within twenty-four hours of the purchase, arrangements were made for the disposal of the Dorchester House fitments. On 12 August 1929 an auction was held, attended by hundreds of buyers and sightseers. At the time Sir Malcolm remarked, 'It is unfortunately the lot of the builder to destroy as well as to create. The destruction of the old Dorchester House was unpleasant for all concerned.' A fortnight's grace was allowed for purchases to be removed. The handsome marble staircase, originally costing £30,000, was installed in a Scottish mansion, later being sold in 1965 to an American, Paul Knight of Dallas, who moved the 59-foot stairway in sections to Texas. One of the choice fireplaces went to the Victoria and Albert Museum.

By 1 September the building had been cleared for the contractors to start work. Every possible use was made of the waste materials, such as old bricks, steelwork and lead; about 30,000 tons were dismantled and marketed in the short space of seven weeks. Mechanical excavators next removed some 40,000 tons of earth from below the level of Park Lane to make way for the underground part of the hotel – the garages, kitchens and Turkish Baths, which covered an area equal to one-third of the building visible above the ground.

The choice of Sir Owen Williams, a civil engineer, as designer of the hotel was an imaginative appointment. He specialised in reinforced concrete design and was acknowledged as one of the country's earliest experts in this field. His engineering achievements in the planning and lay-out of the British Empire Exhibition at Wembley in 1924 was rewarded with a knighthood. The Dorchester commission followed the withdrawal of the original architects, Wallis Gilbert and Partners, late in the summer of 1929. Work began on site before Williams's radical proposals were disclosed to any outside body.

The essence of the design was to treat the public rooms on the lower-floor levels and the bedroom accommodation on the eight upper floors as separate structural systems. This required an intermediate structure at first-floor level, allowing loadings from the cellular-plan units of the upper floors to be transmitted to the large spanning concrete-

13

14

15, 14, 15. *Stages in the construction of* The Dorchester: *site-preparation, foundations and steel work, and the building of the walls*

15

16. The Dorchester *under construction. The reinforced-concrete raft at first-floor level had been completed*

frame arrangement at ground and basement levels. The advantage of this was that it provided flexibility in the planning of both zones. The solid concrete roof over the public rooms left large areas without pillars, though considerable skill was required to reconcile the different design parameters associated with each.

The radical scheme created considerable controversy and led to the client having second thoughts. Williams asked if he would allow the architect, Curtis Green, to add architectural embellishments to the elevations and interiors. He refused, resigned, and despatched all his drawings immediately to Green's office by taxi. By this time the building had emerged above ground level on site.

Curtis Green's brief required an open form of bedrooms, superimposed over large public rooms below, which filled the whole site area. The use of reinforced concrete allowed a definite change of structure to be achieved at ground-floor ceiling level, a solid raft three feet thick supporting the bedrooms, the concrete walls faced with pre-cast terrazzo panels. It was a significant breakthrough, not only for Curtis Green but for architectural expression in England. For the first time the main classical stream had responded to the needs of new construction and materials, not for reasons of dogmatic or philosophical theory from which the seeds of the Modern Movement sprang, but from the requirements of the brief which Curtis Green did not originate. In *The Dorchester* he was able to express the structure in a way that stemmed from his arts and crafts roots.

An outstanding feature of the hotel was the method employed to eliminate noise. Every bedroom was isolated from noise by the floor and ceiling having a lining of compressed seaweed, which was a perfect non-conductor of sound. The outside walls had a lining of cork and the interior walls were double with an air space between. The

17. *Construction continues, 1930*

question of construction and expansion of the structure had to be carefully evaluated. No expansion joints in the ordinary sense were provided but certain precautions were taken which, to some extent, affected the appearance of the hotel. The contraction of the various bedroom floors, particularly that of the first floor which covered a large area, and their expansion when the hotel was heated, were known to be possible sources of trouble. It was expected that some movement would take place and, to direct this positively to the corners of the building, walls at these points were stopped short by the introduction of a flexible coupling. These metal bay windows, though primarily for structural reasons, proved to be one of the outstanding elevational features of a simple and well-disciplined façade.

The hotel was so constructed that it enabled anyone to occupy as many rooms as desired and to go from one room to another without ever having to enter the corridor. Every room had a private lobby while the suites had private halls as well. As far as the original décor was concerned, the builders sought to decorate it as nearly as possible to the lines of the best English private houses. The flexibility of the structure had made it possible for Curtis Green and his engineers, Considere and Partners, to make alterations, sometimes only hours before it was due to be put in hand. Green's contribution to the design was principally restyling the elevational treatment and decoration of the interior spaces. This restrained classical decoration has been an identifying feature of *The Dorchester*. When the hotel was opened it claimed to be bomb-proof, earthquake-proof and fire-proof. In the Blitz it was undoubtedly one of the safest public buildings in central London. Under the concrete umbrella, the Grill Room became a popular place to spend an evening.

The first floor was completed by September 1930, and the hotel rose at the speed of a complete floor per week, the roof being completed in November 1930, a speed never before attempted. It caught the public imagination, progress being followed from Hyde Park. At the peak of building, McAlpines had a labour force of some 1700 working on the project. Statistics give some indication of the scale of the task. In the construction 50,000 tons of sand and gravel were used; the reinforced concrete required 2000 miles of steel rods; 20,000 cork slabs, 2 inches thick, were needed to line the external walls; water, drainage and radiator systems used 20 miles of pipes; electric light, telephones and bells had 160 miles of cable; 140,000 square feet of polished marble concrete blocks were built into the work; more than 24,000 square feet of glass was used, approximately half an acre; 2500 doors went into the construction. Altogether it was a mammoth undertaking, executed with precision.

18. *Decorators pose outside the building in April 1931 – 331 of them*

The fact that *The Dorchester* was so architecturally advanced, with a construction unique for the Thirties, held particular interest for Ove Arup. He had a rare distinction. For over a century the RIBA has recommended to the Sovereign that its annual Gold Medal for Architecture should be given to a specific architect. Only on two occasions has this tradition been broken: in 1960 it went to Pier Luigi Nervi, the Italian engineer; some years later the award was given to Arup, the consulting engineer, for significant contribution to modern architecture. It is difficult to think of anyone on the British building scene who has exercised such influence.

A frequent visitor to the hotel, it is sad that this lean, aesthetic-looking Dane with powerful profile and great domed head could not have seen the renaissance of *The Dorchester*, for much of the planning and design work would have been in accord with his convictions. With a rare facility for getting to the meat of a problem, Arup liked to raise questions that are never completely resolved: rhetorical questions over a meal that in substance have cropped up during planning sessions for the rebuilding programme. He would ask what is the fundamental difference between the architect and engineer, if any. When does an engineer become an architect and vice versa? How should architects and engineers collaborate? Should the engineer's loyalty be to the client, to the architect, to Architecture with a capital A, or to his own engineering principles, if any?

He would argue that the engineer's role is that of a technical adviser to the architect; he should look after stability and advise the architect about the cost of alternative

19. *Sydney Opera House under construction*
20. CENTRE: *John Harris*
21. RIGHT: *Ove Arup*

structural solutions. But there were occasions when the engineer ought to declare the project too silly for words. On the other hand, how does he know it is silly. It might be Art. In that case, what role should Art play in architecture, a question that splits the architectural profession and architectural critics into several factions. Whilst architects see themselves as master-builders, Arup worried that great architecture was too often produced by people who didn't care a damn about sensible building. They became excited about Corbiere visions, Miesian aesthetics and Louis Kahn's towers, but few seemed interested in whether they worked or were concerned about the people condemned to live with or in their masterpieces. He divided architects into Art-boys, the System-boys and the One-off boys. It didn't matter. It was all about the same thing.

Both Owen Williams and Curtis Green had much in common with Arup. He regarded their difference of opinion as an instance of the time-old clash between civil engineers and architects. Any major work requiring flexibility between the two professions was invariably dicey. Williams would have been the first to applaud Arup's imaginative flair that won the contract for the Sydney Opera House, its most prominent feature being the series of forty-six concrete shells which billow over the auditoria like sails. I have given some impressive statistics regarding the building of *The Dorchester*. It is interesting to compare them with the build-up for Arup's preparations. About sixty engineers worked in London on the project, with 250,000 man-hours of work behind them. Extensive use was made of computers to calculate how to draw the rounded shapes of the shells, which rise as high as 179 feet, on flat sheets of paper. Arup worked out a system for prefabricating the shells out of pre-cast concrete units by designing them all as segments of one large theoretical sphere. This way the shells could be broken into rib units resembling segments of an orange. The various shells were all constructed from similarly shaped basic components which only had to be varied in length to make larger or smaller shells. It seemed simple enough once somebody had thought of it – until the scale of the job was realised. The largest shell is vast enough to enclose a 12-storey block of flats. Without Arup's calculations, it is speculative whether the plans would have succeeded.

Had the opportunity presented itself, Arup indulged in wondering how the final design of *The Dorchester* might have varied had he been involved. It would certainly have been architecturally advanced and ahead of its time. I am also certain his theories would have been in harmony with the plans of the present architect, John Harris, senior partner of the John R. Harris Partnership, who has let the humanity of art permeate the cold economics of efficient building by encouraging closer understanding, interchange of ideas and collaboration between the two professions.

On a lighter note, Ove Arup would have appreciated the new Oriental Restaurant that combines the cuisine of various Far Eastern countries in a setting of simple Oriental clarity. He would have been in his element. Engineers usually carry slide-rules in their breast pockets. Arup was different; a pair of chop-sticks protruded. Whenever the food lent itself to this custom, he preferred to eat with them and wickedly enjoyed watching his guest struggling to master these table weapons. I admitted defeat and settled for conventional tools.

State Occasions

THE Monarchy provides a basis for political continuity so that, whilst parties can change, the essence and theory of government continues. It provides the titular authority under which the executive, the law and the military can function on a day-to-day basis. A serene and unruffled Constitution, it presides over and softens the acerbities of change, offers a union with the past that does not block the future and embodies qualities that leaders of other countries admire and envy. Her Majesty the Queen epitomises the human expression of society and is the symbol of continuity and tradition.

When Royalty or Heads of State are invited to England by the Queen for a State Visit, they are her guests for a few days at Buckingham Palace or Windsor Castle. When the stay ends, the visitor by tradition gives a return Banquet in honour of Her Majesty. Occasionally the venue is their Embassy, but if not spacious enough to accommodate the large guest list, a hotel is chosen. *The Dorchester* has enjoyed this privilege on several occasions. In 1985 the Queen and the Duke of Edinburgh were entertained there by Sheikh Khalifa bin Hamad Al-Thani, Emir of the State of Qatar, at the completion of his State Visit to the United Kingdom. Other members of the Royal family who attended were the Prince and Princess of Wales, just returned the previous day from a tour of Australia and the United States, the Duke and Duchess of Kent, and the Duke and Duchess of Gloucester. The 270 guests included the Prime Minister, the Lord Chancellor, the Governor of the Bank of England, and their ladies, the Diplomatic Corps and Civic representatives. The Ballroom had been transformed with cascades of flowers. Equally glittering was the setting for the Banquet given in 1984 when His Highness Sheikh Isa bin Sulman Al-Khalifa, Amir of the State of Bahrain, entertained the Queen, the Duke of Edinburgh and other members of the Royal family following his State Visit and stay at Windsor Castle. The Amir, a frequent guest at *The Dorchester*, invariably sat in the centre

22. *Queen Elizabeth II and Prince Philip are welcomed by the Emir of Qatar*

23. *The Queen with the Amir of Bahrain at a State Banquet*

of the Promenade enjoying coffee, surrounded by a watchful entourage. An immense admirer of the Royal family and conscious of English traditions and way of life, the Amir expressed delight of the Castle and the surrounding countryside, the massive buttresses of grey stone at Eton, the beauty of the Thames and the dominating fabric of the Castle.

State Banquets at *The Dorchester* are organised with quiet efficiency; the décor is outstanding and the cuisine meticulous. Such smooth planning does not happen by chance. The routine is programmed by professionals with the emphasis on teamwork. One man in particular has played a prominent role, Oliver Ford, for many years consultant designer to the hotel. His distinctive taste has enriched the hotel, and he has done the same in a similar capacity for Queen Elizabeth the Queen Mother in her homes at Clarence House and Royal Lodge at Windsor. His rare skills were recognised by *The Dorchester* chairman, Sir Malcolm McAlpine, in the Bahamas where he was decorating the Nassau Country Club. He was invited to apply his skills to the hotel. The brief is best described in his own words: '. . . to achieve a general order of decoration in good English taste, not by spending vast sums of money on ostentatious opulence but by creating a tasteful backdrop for some of the world's beautiful and discerning people who enter through The Dorchester's doors.'

State Banquets added a fresh dimension to his approach. This was demonstrated in the Banquet given by Ayub Khan, President of Pakistan, in 1966 in honour of Her Majesty the Queen and other members of the Royal family. Ford concentrated on a Durbar theme in which 400 yards of gold lamé with green and white silk were used. The Queen, the Duke of Edinburgh and the President were seated on a dais over which hung a canopy of gold lamé. An enormous vase of white lilies was in the centre of the Ballroom on a floor made of white carnations and green leaves, whilst pyramids of yellow carnations were positioned round the room. Overall more than 10,000 white and yellow carnations were used.

The Banquet given by King Faisal of Saudi Arabia inspired similar imaginative treatment. The design included arabesque arches based on authentic copies of Saudi Arabian buildings of historic interest: silhouette forms outlined by skilful lighting. Guests walked on a red carpet bordered with gilded magnolia leaves. A string orchestra played from a bandstand of arabesque arches erected at the end of the Ballroom farthest from the Royal table. At the Royal table high-backed chairs upholstered in gold lamé bore the coats of arms of the guests who sat upon them. The Saudi Arabian colours of red, white and green were emphasised by the use of over 2000 yards of material that transformed the scene; chairs at the tables followed a green and white colour scheme in alternate placings. The Saudi Arabian emblem of a palm tree and crossed swords formed a focal point above the Royal table.

Highly original was the preparation for the Banquet given by King Hussein of Jordan and Princess Muna. A 65-foot pool was laid out in the centre of the Ballroom with water plants, waterlilies, and goldfish transferred from the pond in the hotel forecourt. Exotic plants were set in moss-covered banks. The reception rooms were decorated by a thousand white carnations interwoven in bay-tree pyramids. An enormous horseshoe table was arranged with 2000 red and white roses. A coat of arms was set between the flags of Jordan and Great Britain and hung at the back of the principal table. Light music was played by a 35-piece band of the Arab League, whilst Arab pipers paraded round the room.

Credit for such themes rightly belonged to Oliver Ford, but were dependent on the skill of *The Dorchester* team of fourteen florists who worked through the night to achieve such brilliant effects. Banquets are dependent on the skill of those who prepare them. *The Dorchester* has been fortunate to have the role of Maître Chef des Cuisines held by such men as Eugene Kaufeler and Anton Mosimann. The menus they produced for these State Occasions confirmed the axiom of Auguste Escoffier: 'Good cooking is when food tastes of what it is.'

Possibly Eugene Kaufeler and Anton Mosimann were fortunate not to have lived in a different period, when Royal Banquets were more robust affairs. When Henry VIII met the French King, François I, near Calais on The Field of the Cloth of Gold, he took with him not only Queen Catherine of Aragon, but hundreds of courtiers, soldiers, servants and entertainers. It was the most ambitious banquet of that century. Cardinal Wolsey was in charge of the catering, no mean feat for the shopping list included 700 conger eels, 2014 sheep, 26 dozen heron, a bushel of mustard, and one penny worth of cream for the King's cakes. Music and a pretty face were equally important, Henry turned musician and composed the ballad sweetly sung by Anne Boleyn, the Queen's scheming lady-in-waiting.

Gargantuan appetites also marked a banquet at Versailles in the reign of Louis XIV attended by the Duchess of Orléans. Records show that the king was served four plates of soup of different kinds, a whole pheasant, a partridge, a large plate of salad, two thick slices of ham, a dish of mutton in a garlic-flavoured sauce, a plateful of pastries, followed by fruit and hard-boiled eggs. It was hardly surprising that the monarch required the attendance of 498 employees of the 'Service de la Bouche'.

24. LEFT: *The Ballroom decorated for the State Banquet given by King Faisal of Saudi Arabia in 1967*

25. ABOVE: *The Ballroom decorated with a 65-foot lily pond for the State Banquet given by King Hussein of Jordan in 1966*

26. *Maître Chef Eugene Kaufeler*

27. *Maître Chef Anton Mosimann*

28. *Maître Chef Eugene Kaufeler at mid-morning conference with Banqueting Manager Max Colombi*

Even though guests in those days were only expected to sample about half of the dishes, I question whether the combined skills of Kaufeler and Mosimann could have coped with such quantities. Dedicated attention to detail must have been blunted. Etiquette required rose water proffered in silver bowls by servitors to rinse sticky fingers. Maybe some dishes would repay research for future banquets. Some items had exotic names like Nomblys de Roo, Pety perueis, Mammenye and Lèche Lumbarde. Intriguing, but silent as regards taste. Other delicacies bore the name of the celebrity who created them, like Potage à la Conde, Poulets à la Villeray, Chartreuses à la Mauconseil and Gigot à la Mailly. Certain members of the aristocracy would be delighted to achieve such gastronomic fame.

Banquet for the Amir of the State of Bahrain

Consommé de Volaille à la Reine

—

Ragoût de Sole au Safran
Grains de Siam Pilaff

—

Rosette de Boeuf Sauté aux Fruits des Bois
Pommes de Jersey Poêlées
Légumes du Marche

—

Soufflé aux Fruits de la Passion

—

Menthes

—

Fruit juices served throughout

Maître Chef Anton Mosimann

Banquet of King Hussein of Jordan

Corton Charlemagne Ancien 1965	La Langouste Belvedere La Sauce Verte La Sauce Mayonnaise
	—
Château Pichon Longueville 1955	Le Poussin du Printemps à la Derby Les Haricots Verts Fins
	—
Charles Heidsieck Royal Champagne 1955	La Surprise à l'Orientale

Le Panier des Friandises

Maître Chef Eugene Kaufeler

Banquet of Ayub Khan, President of Pakistan

Le Turban de Sole à l'Orientale
Le Riz Pilaff

—

Le Suprême de Volaille Lucullus
Les Têtes d'Asperges Fraîches
La Mousseline Clamart
Les Pommes Olivettes

—

La Poire de Comice à l'Orange
Les Petits Fours

—

Wines: Gewurtztraminer and
Bollinger champagne.

Maître Chef Eugene Kaufeler

Banquet of King Faisal of Saudi Arabia

Le Homard Froid à la Czarina
La Sauce Verte

—

Le Consommé Royale
Les Palmiers

—

Le Filet de Boeuf aux Morilles, Sauce Perigourdine
Les Légumes du Paradis
Les Pommes Olivettes
Le Coeur de Laitue

—

Les Fraises et Oranges à l'Orientale
Le Parfait Glacé Pistache
Le Panier de Petits Fours

—

Fruit juices served throughout

Maître Chef Eugene Kaufeler

Cultivated Palates

THE Maître Chef des Cuisines at *The Dorchester* has always been a chef of international ranking. Chef Ferrant began the tradition in 1931 when he came from the Mayfair Hotel. Four years later Anton Bon, the Managing Director of *The Dorchester*, enticed Emile Aymoz out of retirement in France to take charge of the kitchens, an appointment cut short when war was declared on 3 September 1939. Aymoz, on holiday abroad, was unable to return to England. His misfortune was Eugene Kaufeler's gain. After working in *The Dorchester* kitchens for three years, he had gone to the Norbury House Hotel in Droitwich Spa. Bon's dilemma found a sympathetic ear; Kaufeler was persuaded to forget his commission in the Swiss Army and begin a new career in *The Dorchester*. Jean Baptiste Virlogeux, Restaurant Chef at the Savoy, was the next Maître Chef, holding the post until March 1950, eleven years when standards were maintained in spite of war years austerity, rationing, and the enforced restrictive charge of five shillings for a three-course meal. On 1 April 1950 Kaufeler was made Maître Chef and continued until 1975. Credit for a steady expansion of demand was equally due to the acumen of Max Columbi as Banqueting Manager, and the fact that by removing the sliding divisions between the Ballroom and the Ballroom lounge it was possible to seat over 1000 guests, other diners being switched to the Orchid Room.

Kaufeler, approaching seventy and anxious that *The Dorchester* culinary reputation should be retained after he retired, gave thought to a possible successor. Choice lay between Richard Shepherd, a young chef he had trained, and Anton Mosimann, of similar age and highly praised in Switzerland. The decision went in favour of Anton. He worked as sous-chef for a year before being promoted Maître Chef, Eugene becoming Executive Chef. The other candidate, Richard Shepherd, had a short training stay in France, joined the Capital Hotel in Knightsbridge, then entered into a successful partnership with the actor Michael Caine and the ill-fated Peter Langan in Langan's Brasserie.

29. Emile Aymoz, Maître Chef in the Thirties   *30. Maître Chef Jean Baptiste Virlogeux*

Mosimann's appointment was an imaginative challenge to the ambitious young man, who helped his parents as a lad in the family restaurant and began apprentice work at the age of fifteen. Two years later he became the youngest person to win the Swiss Diplôme de Cuisine and was only twenty-three when appointed head chef for the Swiss Pavilion at the World Fair at Ottawa. After another two years Anton set a new record as the youngest chef to gain the Swiss Chef de Cuisine diploma. The World Fair in Japan had additional significance for also working in the Swiss Pavilion was Kathrin, a pretty girl later to become his wife. Anton's stay at *The Dorchester* was stimulating, at times revolutionary. He established the reputation as an exceptionally creative culinary artist. His personal signature was on every dish that left the kitchens. Improvements behind the scenes included the provision of a kitchen next to the Grill and a similar facility by the Terrace Restaurant. The old practice of heating everything in the kitchens became a thing of the past. Anton employed a team of 120 chefs and directed operations with military and courteous efficiency. Staff relationships were excellent. His skill as manager and teacher was reflected in the number of his protégés in top jobs as head chefs or chef proprietors.

31. *Anton Mosimann with his predecessor Eugene Kaufeler*

In a specialised creative profession Anton introduced a touch of imaginative genius. He restored natural flavours to food, vegetables retained freshness and the vitamins so often lost through overcooking. Elaborate garnishings were avoided. Instead artistic presentations on black octagonal plates highlighted intriguing visual effects with swirling sauces. An element of unpredictability was created by his 'Menu Surprise' which became a feature of the Terrace Restaurant. It lived up to its name: six choice courses were presented with an explanation of their contents by waiters always carefully briefed beforehand. Few diners expected such dishes as brill with sea-urchin sauce, soup covered with gold leaf, or foie gras with a purée of bananas and walnuts, but not all dishes were so exotic. He extended his range of influence in developing people's enjoyment of food beyond *The Dorchester*, particularly on the BBC television series *Food and Drink* when he cooked Sunday lunch for a family of eight in Sheffield within the budget ceiling of £10. He shopped with them, cooked on their small kitchen stove, served fricassee of chicken followed by bread-and-butter pudding, at a cost of £9.88 including wine. The series was an unqualified success.

The Terrace

Diner

Salade de Foie Gras Chaud aux
Haricots Verts Fines
(AN AUTUMN SALAD OF WARM GOOSE LIVER
AND GREEN BEANS)

Suprême de Turbot à la Façon
du Chef
(POACHED TURBOT ON A BED OF VEGETABLES
IN A BUTTER AND BASIL SAUCE)

Trois Medaillons d'Agneau Poelées
au Thyme
(PIECES OF LAMB WITH THYME AND MARKET
VEGETABLES)

Parfait aux Fruits de la Passion
(PASSION FRUIT PARFAIT)

Café

Délice des Dames

£29.00 PER PERSON, INCLUSIVE OF SERVICE & V.A.T.

Menu Surprise

Six delicious light courses of
fresh produce from the Market

£70.00 FOR TWO PERSONS
INCLUSIVE OF SERVICE CHARGE AND V.A.T.

Pour Commencer

Aiguillettes de Faisan sur   £8.20
un lit de Feuilles d'Automne
(SLICES OF WARM PHEASANT ON A BED OF SALAD)

Saumon d'Ecosse Mariné   £9.90
(SCOTTISH SALMON MARINATED WITH
HERBS AND YOGHURT DRESSING)

Parfait de Foies de Volaille   £5.80
aux Truffes
(DELICIOUS CHICKEN LIVER TERRINE WITH TRUFFLES)

Huîtres Gratinées Moscovite   £11.00
(WARM OYSTERS IN A CHAMPAGNE SAUCE)

Feuilleté de Ris de Veau   £8.50
et Homard
(CALF'S SWEETBREAD WITH LOBSTER IN
PUFF PASTRY)

Symphonie de Fruits de Mer   £9.20
"Naturelle"   C.N.
(A VARIETY OF SEAFOOD IN ITS OWN JUICE)

Potages

Goutte d'Or au Quenelles   £4.50
à la Moëlle
(BEEF CONSOMMÉ WITH MARROW DUMPLINGS)

Consommé de Gibier   £4.60
Chasseur
(A DELICATE GAME SOUP WITH A BREAST
OF QUAIL AND PEARLS OF VEGETABLES)

Soup de Moules Safranée   £4.50
aux Poireaux
(MUSSEL SOUP WITH LEEKS FLAVOURED
WITH SAFRAN)

ALL PRICES ARE INCLUSIVE OF SERVICE CHARGE & V.A.T.

Poissons et Crustaces

Filets de St. Pierre au   £14.50
Fenouil
(FILLET OF JOHN DORY WITH BRAISED
FENNEL IN A LIGHT BUTTER SAUCE)

Sole Farçie à la Brunoise   £15.50
de Légumes Gratinée
(DOVER SOLE FILLED WITH VEGETABLES
IN A WHITE WINE SAUCE)

Ragoût de Homard aux   £26.00
Nouilles Vertes
(A DELICATE LOBSTER DISH WITH GREEN NOODLES)

Loup de Mer Cuit à la Vapeur £18.80
'Orientale'   C.N.
(STEAMED SEABASS WITH STRIPS OF PORK,
DRIED CHINESE MUSHROOMS, GINGER
AND SPRING ONIONS)

Viandes et Volailles

Rosette de Boeuf Pochée Sabayon £17.50
Parfumé aux Grains de Moutarde   C.N.
(POACHED FILLET OF BEEF WITH A LIGHT
MUSTARD SAUCE)

Noisettes de Chevreuil Poelées £16.00
au Chou Rouge
(TENDER PIECES OF VENISON WITH BRAISED
RED CABBAGE)

Filets de Veau Belle Forestière   £14.00
(VEAL FILLETS WITH WILD MUSHROOM SAUCE)

Canard d'Aylesbury Rôti   £16.00
(DUCK BREAST ROASTED WITH GLAZED APPLES)

Carré d'Agneau Confit d'Echalotes £16.80
(RACK OF LAMB WITH GLAZED SHALLOTS)

FRESH VEGETABLES OF THE SEASON ARE
INCLUDED WITH ALL MAIN COURSES

Fromages

Fromages d'Ici et d'Ailleurs   £4.20
(A SELECTION OF FINE CHEESES)

Fromages de Chèvre aux Endives £3.30
(GOAT CHEESE WITH CHICORY)

Desserts

Symphonie de Sorbets   £4.60
(A SYMPHONY OF NATURAL FLAVOURED SHERBETS)   C.N.

Composition d'Agrumes et Leurs £4.60
Sorbets Sauce Orange Parfumée   C.N.
à l'Estragon
(A COMPOSITION OF CITRUS FRUITS, WITH
AN ORANGE SORBET AND SAUCE
FLAVOURED WITH TARRAGON)

Marquise au Chocolat   £4.60

Gratin de Fruits Terrace   £4.60
(A PLATE OF WARM GLAZED FRUITS)

Selection de Notre Chef Pâtissier £4.90
(VARIOUS SWEETS FROM OUR CHEF PATISSIER)

Café

Café au Choix et Délice des Dames £2.40

C.N. Cuisine Naturelle

The Menu specially created for the Terrace Restaurant by Anton Mosimann and Peter Buderath

A similar feeling of anticipation occurred on being invited by Anton to dinner in his private dining-room located in *The Dorchester* depths by the vast kitchens. The menu lived up to expectation:

Méli-mélo de homard aux pointes d'asperges
Lobster salad with asparagus

Entrecôte sauté Dorchester
Sirloin steak in cream sauce with four different peppers

Soufflé aux fruits de la passion
Passion fruit soufflé

After dinner Anton relaxed. He looked older than his years, possibly due to thinning greyish hair, but he was born at Solothurn in Switzerland in 1947, the only child of parents who moved to Nidau when he was five and opened a restaurant for bourgeois tastes. A keep-fit fanatic, Anton jogs before breakfast in Holland Park, returning to his Ennismore Gardens flat, his wife Kathrin and his two sons, Philip and Mark. The hotel

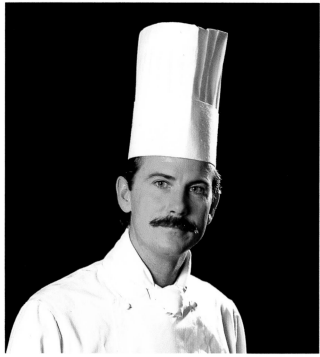

32. Executive Chef Willi Elsener

routine began at 9 am. On the wall opposite to where I sat was a large chart festooned with markers indicating staff availability. Next to it were the gold medals won in international competitions. The total then was about thirty.

Anton's flair for administration was marked by the day's programming. Menus were discussed in detail, with visits to Smithfield and Billingsgate markets. He worked closely with colleagues like Roy Raiman, sous-chef for some thirty years; chef-pâtisseur François Cachin; sous-chef John Hornby; cellar-manager Stephen Price; and the indispensable secretary, Hilary Nightingale. Smooth-running teams do not happen by chance. Routine has to be constant and flexible, to cope with the canapés for a 300-cocktail party, a Foyle's luncheon for 400, a special dinner of eight courses. Preparations for a banquet involve endless tasting, checking, testing and final inspections before service. Composing menus needs a fertile mind. Anton admitted to possessing a library of several thousand cookery books, but inspiration was just as likely to occur at unlikely moments. Whilst enjoying the challenge of *cuisine naturelle*, Anton took pleasure in traditional dishes. One speciality is bread-and-butter pudding, whilst prime foreribs of Scottish beef are always popular – up to thirty-five ribs a day are used at *The Dorchester*. Tastes are constant but habits change. The trend today, with an eye on weight and health factors, is for small selective portions.

Maybe it is just as well that Anton did not live last century; expectations then were different. When Lord Palmerston was in his eighty-first year and still Prime Minister, he had dinner with the Speaker of the House of Commons, who has left a detailed description of the occasion:

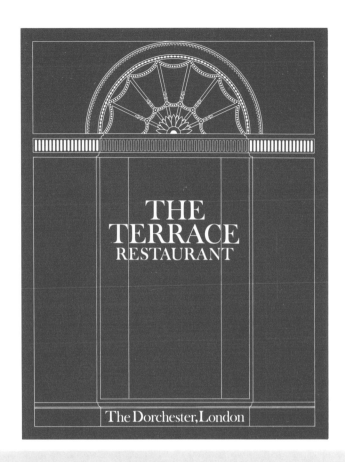

THE
TERRACE
RESTAURANT

The Dorchester, London

The Dorchester

◄ Hors d'Oeuvre ►

Hultres Natives		Prawn Cocktail	£1·70
Caviar:		Cocktail de Homard	£4·50
Iranian Imperial Beluga (1½ ozs.)	£7·30	Prosciutto di Parma	£1·85
Russian Royal Beluga (1¼ ozs.)	£7·30	Cocktail Florida	85p
Saumon d'Ecosse Fumé	£3·00	Melon Frappé	£2·50
Truite Fumée	£1·50	Potted Shrimps	£1·00
Foie Gras de Strasbourg	£4·50	Pâté Maison	£1·20
Hors d'Œuvre Varié	£1·35	Pâté de Crabe	£1·45
Dressed Crab	£2·65		

Chef's Speciality
Avocat à la Façon du Chef Avocado Pear with Crab meat and dressing £1·40

◄ Potages ►

Velouté de Homard	£2·10	Crème de Volaille	70p
Pot-au-Feu	80p	Vichyssoise (Froide)	65p
Soupe à l'Oignon Gratinée (20 mins)	75p	Crème des Petits Pois avec Croûtons	55p
Crème de Tomates au Riz	55p	Consommé Carmen	55p
Mulligatawny	70p	Gazpacho	75p

◄ Oeufs et Pates ►

Œuf Poché Florentine	65p	Omelette: Tomates, Jambon, Champignons,	
Poached egg with spinach and cheese sauce		Fines Herbes	75p
Œuf Mollet Boston	50p	Omelette with various garnishes	
Soft boiled egg with creamed sweet corn and bacon		Nouilles Eduardo	£1·10
Œuf en Gelée Yorkaise	75p	Noodles with slices of veal, mushrooms and cream sauce	
Egg in jelly with mousse of ham		Macaroni Donna Pia	£1·50
Omelette Plat à l'Ecossaise Gratinée	£1·30	Macaroni with mushrooms, sliced chicken, suprême sauce and cheese	
Flat omelette with smoked haddock and Mornay sauce			

◄ Poissons et Coquillages ►

Truite de Rivière Rochelle	£2·90	Tronçon de Turbot Normandy	£4·60
River trout fried in butter with shrimps, walnuts and grapes		Turbot on the bone with sliced egg-plant, tomato, vegetable marrow and lobster	
Truite Vivante au Bleu (2 pièces)	£3·50		
Poached blue live trout		Homard Cardinal	£5·25
Sole Grillée, Frite, Meunière	£3·90	Lobster with lobster sauce and truffle	
Sole cooked in your choice		Scampi à l'Armagnac	£4·20
Paupiette de Sole au Pernod	£4·50	Scampi cooked with spices and herbs, flamed with Armagnac and served with a spicy sauce and rice	
Rolled fillet of sole with mushrooms, prawns and Pernod sauce			
Timbale de Sole Dorchester	£4·85	Scampi Frits, Sauce Tartare	£3·40
Fillet of sole in creamed lobster sauce with mushrooms, lobster claw and rice		Deep fried scampi with tartare sauce	
Buisson de Sole Frite	£3·00	Coquilles St. Jacques au Safran	£3·25
Fried fillet of sole		Scallops with tomato, saffron, herbs and white wine sauce	
Suprême de Turbot Marie-Louise	£4·20	Quenelles de Brochet Maison	£3·60
Poached fillet of turbot with tomato, mushrooms, sherry and white wine glazed sauce		Pike dumplings with white wine sauce, Pernod and rice	

◄ Rotis ►

Poulet de Grain (2 cvts)	£4·60	Caneton d'Aylesbury à l'Anglaise (3 cvts)	£7·50
Reine de Surrey (3 cvts)	£5·75	Aile de Poulet	£2·00
Cuisse de Poulet (2 pièces)	£1·60	Poussin	£2·10
Poularde de Surrey à la Broche (4 cvts)	£7·25	Grouse Perdreau Faisan	

◄ Grillades ►

Mixed Grill	£3·25	Côtelette de Porc	£2·00
Loin Chop with Kidneys	£3·25	Minute Steak	£2·35
Lamb Chop	£2·75	Filet de Bœuf	£4·00
Rump Steak	£3·20	Châteaubriand (2 cvts)	£7·45
Côtelette de Veau	£2·85	Entrecôte	£3·10
Lamb Cutlets	£2·40	Tournedos	£3·40

◄ Entrees ►

Saprême de Volaille Czarina	£5·00	Piccata de Veau Napolitaine	£3·50
Breaded and stuffed wing of chicken with foie gras		Sliced veal with spaghetti and tomatoes	
Poussin Sauté à la Madras	£3·50	Noisette de Veau Oscar	£4·00
Shallow sauté chicken with curry sauce, saffron rice with raisins and almonds		Boned veal fried in butter with asparagus, lobster and Béarnaise sauce	
		Tournedos Sauté Landaise	£5·80
Caneton à l'Orange (3 cvts)	£9·60	Fillet of beef with foie gras, mushrooms and Madeira sauce	
Duckling with bitter orange and brandy		Langue de Bœuf Braisée Ménagère	£2·80
Foie de Veau Sauté à l'Anglaise	£3·20	Braised ox-tongue with leaf spinach and Madeira sauce	
Calf's liver fried in butter with bacon		Entrecôte Sauté Madagascar	£4·60
Côtelette d'Agneau Maréchale	£3·00	Sirloin steak fried in butter with green pepper and cream sauce	
Breaded lamb cutlets, asparagus, truffle and Parisienne potatoes		Eminceé de Rognons d'Agneau Bercy	£3·00
		Sliced lamb kidneys fried in butter with red wine sauce and herbs	

Vins en Carafe

Bordeaux Red and Burgundy
White

Large £1·90 (18 fl. ozs.)
Small £1·00 (9 fl. ozs.)

Vin Rosé

Large £1·80 (18 fl. ozs.)
Small £1·00 (9 fl. ozs.)

Alsatian

Large £2·00 (18 fl. ozs.)
Small £1·10 (9 fl. ozs.)

◄ Buffet Froid ►

Jambon de York	£2·80	Veal & Ham Pie à la Gelée	£1·95
Aile de Poulet	£2·10	Beefsteak Tartare	£2·85
Cuisse de Poulet (2 pièces)	£1·65	Dinde de Norfolk	£1·90
Contrefilet	£2·90	Langue de Bœuf	£2·20
Gammon	£1·65	Pork Pie Maison	£1·95
Virginia Ham	£1·75		

◄ Legumes ►

Haricots Verts Frais	65p	Courgettes Pochées au Beurre	65p
Chou-fleur Hollandaise	45p	Carottes Vichy	45p
Epinards en Branches ou Purée	45p	Mais à la Crème	45p
Petits Pois à la Française	45p	Lima Beans in Butter	45p
Petits Pois Bleu	45p		
Céleri Braisé à la Moelle	45p	Pommes: Nouvelles, Sautées, Mousseline,	
Bouquetière de Légumes (2 cvts)	£1·30	Persillées, Croquettes	45p
		Soufflées	55p

◄ Salades ►

Verte	45p	Viveur	45p
Tomate	45p	Panachée	45p
Cœur de Laitue	45p		

◄ Entremets ►

Ananas Fiona	90p	Profiteroles Suchard	70p
Sliced pineapple decorated with strawberries, grape ice and spun sugar		Profiteroles with chocolate sauce and cream	
Soufflé Grand Marnier, Vanille ou Chocolat	£1·60	Sorbet au Citron, Ananas, Framboises	75p
(2 cvts 20 min.)		Water Ice: Lemon, Pineapple, Raspberry	
Grand Marnier, Vanilla or Chocolate Soufflé		Glace Vanille, Chocolat, Fraises	75p
Pêche Dijonnaise	90p	Ice Cream: Vanilla, Chocolat, Strawberry	
Peach with blackcurrant ice and blackcurrant sauce		Petits Fours (10 pièces)	80p
Coupe Helvétia	£1·10	Cape Gooseberries (p. pièce)	25p
Sliced peaches with raspberries in Kirsch, lemon and raspberry ice		Marron Glacé (p. pièce)	25p
Gratin de Pêche Marjorie	95p		
Peaches with cream and caramelized brown sugar			

◄ Savouries ►

Canapé Diane	45p	Pig in Blanket	55p
Croûte Neuchâteloise	60p	Welsh Rarebit	45p
Champignons sur Toast	45p		

◄ Fromages aux Choix 65p ►

Café Dorchester	30p		
American Coffee	30p		

◄ Fruits en Saison ►

Nescafé	30p		
Café Hag (caffeine free)	30p		

Cover Charge 40p

Prices include
15% Service
and V.A.T.

10

'Dined with the Prime Minister, who was then upwards of eighty years of age.

'He ate for dinner two plates of turtle soup: he was then served very amply to a plate of cod and oyster sauce: he then took a paté, afterwards he was helped to two very greasy-looking entrees: he then despatched a plate of roast mutton: there then appeared before him the largest and to my mind the hardest slice of ham that ever figured on the table of a nobleman: yet it disappeared, just in time to answer the inquiry of his butler, "Snipe or pheasant, my lord?"

'He instantly replied, "Pheasant."

'Thus he completed his ninth dish of meat at the meal!'

This was an octogenarian's diet. Palmerston decided to drive home from Westminster in a hack at night instead of walking, and insisted that both windows were open, even though a north-easter was blowing. I fear a 'Menu Surprise' would not have appealed.

Anton Mosimann has now gone from *The Dorchester* and presides over an elegant club, Mosimann's, in West Halkin Street, London – an impressive building, tastefully equipped with kitchens that provide ample scope for one of England's greatest chefs. I am sure there must be moments when he is sad at severing his connection with *The Dorchester*, for in its rejuvenated renaissance the scope is great. The kitchens have been totally rebuilt to the designs of an American consultant, with new finishing kitchens added for banqueting and top-floor suites, a new restaurant on two floors offering oriental cuisine, and a night club with a supper area – facilities and innovations that will test the skills and imagination of the Chef des Cuisines.

That responsibility now rests on the shoulders of Willi Elsener who was appointed Executive Chef in March 1988. Born in the village of Rhazune, Switzerland, his ambition from an early age was to continue the family tradition in catering. Begining as an apprentice at the Hotel Ascot in Zurich, he had a thorough grounding in every aspect of the work in such leading Swiss hotels as the Hotel Zurich, Hotel Baur au Lac and Hotel Savoy before becoming Head Chef at the Hotel Beautus in Merligen. At the age of twenty-six his skills were recognised by the Diplôme de Cuisinier, Switzerland's highest gastronomic distinction. At the time of writing the tally stands at twenty-two Gold Medals, two Silver Medals and three Special Individual Prizes.

Willi's two years as deputy to Anton Mosimann gave him an in-depth knowledge of *The Dorchester*'s renowned kitchens, an experience that has stood him in good stead during the refurbishment of the hotel. He has supervised the complex planning of the two new kitchens, which are the most advanced in concept of any hotel of international status, also the food and beverage areas, and the recruitment of a fresh brigade of chefs. With the new Oriental Restaurant in mind, Willi attended courses in Japanese and Chinese cuisine at the Thai Cookery School at The Oriental in Bangkok and the Ecole Technique in Osaka. In many ways this temporary closure has made possible a period of exploration and experimentation. 1990 will see Willi Elsener established as one of the greatest Maître Chef des Cuisines, the international successor to Eugene Kaufeler and Anton Mosimann.

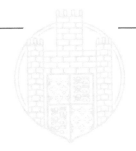

The Thirties

I T is easy to forget that, for the majority of people, the world of the Thirties now belongs to history. It was a decade of paradoxes and extremes, marking the end of an era: on one side the aftermath of a world of certainties, on the other the nuclear age. Later generations find it difficult to realise how different life was in those days or put into perspective the changes that have occurred since. Headlines can help. They pinpoint events missed, or only dimly remembered, and recall personalities forgotten.

Emancipation of women made a big impact. It meant that four million between the ages of twenty-one and thirty had been added to the Register by the Equal Franchise Act. Threat of national bankruptcy led to an All-Party Government endorsed by 554 votes against 56. Labour only won three out of twenty-eight London boroughs in the local elections. Britain was forced off the Gold Standard. The *Star Spangled Banner* became the official American anthem. *It* was the vogue word for sex-appeal. Women wore sheath dresses. Thousands joined the publicised Women's League of Health and Beauty. £3 a week was the living wage for the father of a family; £10 a week meant luxury. Butter 1/- per pound; eggs 1/- a dozen; tea 10d per pound. Thomas Cook advertised eight days on the French Riviera for less than £9. Return sea passage on the Orient Line to Australia cost £124 first-class and £57 third-class. Jim Mollison gave hope to those in a hurry with a record flight from Australia to this country in 214 hours.

Cinemas were wired for sound. Talking films had produced classics like *The Taming of the Shrew* with Mary Pickford and Douglas Fairbanks; *Disraeli* with George Arliss; *Untamed* with Joan Crawford; *Broadway Melody*; Charles Chaplin was silent in *City Lights*; Greta Garbo was still without a voice. Erich Maria Remarque's anti-war *All Quiet on the Western Front* commanded attention. Cricket purists were upset because wickets were one inch higher and wider. Golfers objected to steel-shafted clubs. President Hoover opened the world's tallest building, the Empire State Building with 86 floors, 1245 feet

33, 34, 35. LEFT TO RIGHT: *Marchioness Curzon of Kedleston; Margot, Countess of Oxford and Asquith; Dame Lilian Braithwaite*

high. Mikhail Gorbachev and Rupert Murdoch were born. George Bernard Shaw met Stalin. Wall Street collapsed with fortunes on paper disappearing. The world's first atom-smashing machine was tested in Cambridge. Unemployment topped the 2.3 million mark.

Against this background and in spite of threatening economic slump and the ominous resurgence of German militarism, the most luxurious hotel that London had known was opening with a fanfare of publicity in 1931. It was the realisation of an ambition cherished by Sir Malcolm McAlpine, after he acquired the old Dorchester House in 1929, to build on the site the finest hotel in the capital. Dreams became reality on 18 April two years later. The élite who made up the social oligarchy – aristocrats and industrialists, high finance, ambassadors and statesmen, pleasure-seekers and the Beautiful People – arrived in quick succession on a tide of colour. The social game was played for all it was worth. The trappings of wealth were paraded without apology. Later that night lights blazed in the rooms. The mood was vibrant. It had been a grand and glorious beginning of a saga of luxury that has persisted for six decades and now enters the Nineties with even greater opulence and discriminating taste.

The official guest list would have made Elsa Maxwell green with envy, yet it was naively described on the cover as a 'House Warming'. Gossip writers informed readers about the celebrities, though the treatment was bland compared with the acerbities of current diarists like Nigel Dempster, Ross Benson and Lady Olga Maitland, who would have revelled in one of the great parties of the decade. Beauty met beauty and fame was

36. CENTRE: The Dorchester *in the Thirties. Note the metal bay windows at the corners* (see page 13)

37, 38, 39. LEFT TO RIGHT: *Earl of Lonsdale; Earl of Rosebery; Sir John Simon*

taken for granted. Charismatic personalities were plentiful, like Margot, Countess of Oxford and Asquith, described by Benjamin Jowett, Master of Balliol College, Oxford, as 'the best-educated ill-educated woman I have ever met'. It is difficult today to appreciate the influence exerted on the social life of her times by this provocative friend of Gladstone, Balfour and Virginia Woolf.

Another remarkable guest was the Earl of Rosebery, who had recently inherited the famous Mentmore Stud on the death of his father. In 1932 he won the St Leger with Sandwich, a horse unlucky not to have won the Derby. Others who would have been spotted by the *paparazzi* were the Marchioness Curzon of Kedleston, widow of the states-man noted for lofty manner, grandiloquence and intransigence, qualities shared by his wife who used them to telling effect in breaking up the liaison between the Marquess and Elinor Glyn, the novelist. Equally striking was Irene, Lady Ravensdale, who inherited the beauty and charm of Curzon's first wife, Mary. There were Lilian Braithwaite, the actress who had surprised the critics with her performance opposite Noel Coward as the man-hunting society mother in *The Vortex*; Princess Bismarck; the Marquess and Marchioness of Queensberry; Sir John Simon, the Foreign Secretary. Also noticeable would have been a spruce little man with prominent nose and tight-lipped mouth, the martinet trainer, Fred Darling. Steve Donoghue, the champion jockey, almost lost his chance of winning the 1925 Derby on Manna because he was a few minutes late for the 7.30 am gallop.

Samuel Courtauld, art patron and industrialist, was present with his lovely wife Elizabeth, who tragically died shortly afterwards. In her memory Courtauld donated his

40. *'The Glorious Twelfth'. First grouse
of the season rushed from Yorkshire, 1938*

collection of French Impressionists to London University and endowed the founding of the Courtauld Institute of Art. Other guests included the Earl of Inchcape, the shipowner whose daughter had earlier died attempting to fly the Atlantic; Lady Cunliffe-Owen; the Earl of Westmorland; Gilbert Frankau; Sir Gerald du Maurier, the great actor–manager; Lord Melchet; the Marchioness of Carisbrooke; Major Beith (Ian Hay); Lord Dawson of Penn, physician-extraordinary to King George V; Viscount Castlerosse; Lord Aberdare; the Countess of Seafield; Edward Marsh, colleague of Winston Churchill, close friend and later literary executor of Rupert Brooke; Sir Jeremiah Colman; Captain Buckmaster; J.H. Thomas, Dominions Secretary, who was disgraced a few years later through leaking Budget secrets; Captain Cunningham-Reid; the Earl of Derby, massive in build, heavily moustached and immensely popular, who inherited a proud racing tradition, unlike the Astors who began one and the Primroses who married into one (Derby had twenty Classic wins to his credit); Sir Henry Curtis-Bennett; Lord Halifax, the statesman who later failed to realise that Hitler was a megalomaniac; Lord Reith of strange and complex temperament; Lord Lonsdale, easily recognisable by side-whiskers and inevitable cigar. Essentially a Regency figure, he was credited with innumerable exploits like joining an expedition to the Klondike and acting as sparring partner to John L. Sullivan, the world heavyweight champion; keen yachtsman, and, much to the annoyance of King Edward VII, a close friend of the Kaiser. Used to entertaining in princely fashion, he must have been in his element at the party.

41. *Debutantes bringing in the*
cake at Queen Charlotte's Birthday Ball in 1931

42. *One of the*
decorative glass
panels in the Vestibule

The host that evening, Sir Malcolm McAlpine, impressively supported by seventeen families of the McAlpine clan, could sit back and survey what had been achieved. Sir Malcolm, then chairman, and William McAlpine, as finance director, could take the credit for making it all possible. It was the beginning. The next decade was to be a period of challenge.

Having set a new standard for luxury and sophistication, *The Dorchester* had next to capture part of the thriving business in banquets, charity balls, dinners, receptions and other prestigious functions. Many were linked with the traditional carnival of youth and mature experience known as the London Season. Its boundaries at times are difficult to define but it begins in May with the opening of the Royal Academy and draws to a close at Goodwood in July. In between are the indolent appeal of Henley, with its gaiety against an olive-green setting; Eton on the Fourth of June, with felicitous runs on Agar's Plough and night air rent with flashing lights of fireworks by Fellows Eyot; the world of fetlocks and wisps of straw at the International Horse Show; lazy warm afternoons at Lord's; the scarlet and gold of Covent Garden with its tiers and boxes and glittering lights; Derby Day and the babel of Epsom Downs; the pageantry of Trooping the Colour; Smith's Lawns at Windsor with the clicking of polo sticks, the vivid white ball, ponies with glistening withers, the bell and the end of the first chukker; Royal Ascot, where England is shown as a monarchial country with an aristocracy. The London Season captures and retains something of the variegated brilliance of these crowded weeks when everyone tries to squeeze from life just a little more than routine, and leaves behind a touch of perfume and the blue smoke of a cigar. This brief round of enjoyment preoccupied the attention of the banqueting manager and his staff.

Results were gratifying. The bookings had wide appeal. The Speed Ball, organised by the Air League in celebration of Great Britain holding the speed records on land, sea and air, was inspired by Kathleen, Countess of Drogheda. The Duke of Sutherland consented to be President of the Ball under the patronage of the Duke and Duchess of York, the event attracting parties by Woolf Barnato, Kaye Don, Malcolm Campbell and Moore Brabazon, and over 600 other guests. The Westminster Ball, held a few weeks after the opening, was just as scintillating, with Lady Duff Cooper as chairman of the Ball Committee, the Prince of Wales consenting to be Patron. This time the financial benefits were enjoyed by the Pulford Street Site Fund whose aim was to build houses for some 900 workers. Most spectacular was the Famous Beauties Ball in aid of the Papworth Village Settlement for Tuberculosis. It lived up to its claim, with Margaret Whigham, voted Debutante of the Year in 1930, representing Mary Robinson, known as 'Perdita', the actress and mistress of the Prince Regent, whose portrait by Thomas Gainsborough hangs in the Wallace Collection. Sixty-seven other charming ladies, including Gladys Cooper, paraded in costumes, many designed by Cecil Beaton. In a capital somewhat blasé about such junkets, the Ball was memorable.

Glossy magazines kept up the tempo of interest by describing the flow of celebrities and socialites attracted by the publicity. It was like a new society bursting into full flower. The lavish Cresta Balls were 'naturals' for the international set; Eton celebrations appealed to more fastidious tastes. Hearty types were attracted by the University Rugby Balls, a blending of brawn and brains shared by Blackheath, Harlequins and St Mary's Hospital affairs. Discerning eyes turned to the Flower Ball, the Golden Ball and the Roedean Jubilee Ball. Specialised enjoyment could be found at the London Ragamuffin Ball and centenary celebrations of the RSPCA. The Lawn Tennis Association observed tradition with the Singles champions of Wimbledon being the first to take to the floor and leading the dancing. The Royal London Yacht Club centenary was an immaculate affair. Football League dinners had a distinct hint of changing-room humour. The Tailwaggers Club nailed the lie that owners acquired facial resemblance to their pets.

The banquet after the International Horse Show combined stable quips with stiff-shirted protocol. Leander Club jollifications were as spontaneous as the Stage Golfing Society. At the other end of the scale, tea parties with the RIBA were pompous affairs, unlike Lady Cambridge's exuberant Children's Parties at Christmas. The Vic–Wells Ballet Ball recalled wistful nights when stars came down to earth. Trafalgar Navy Dinners were a contrast to the Royal Academy of Music evenings. The Bugatti Drivers Club outshone the English Golf Union dinners when it came to technical know-how. Oxford University Dramatic Society functions were waiting for the inspiration that came from Nevill Coghill, the don who gave academic recognition to Richard Burton. The RSPCA remembered 100 years of its existence. Prunella Stack turned the Park Suite and Adam Room into forums for enthusiastic devotees of the League of Health and Beauty. Debenham and Freebody staged a fashion show in the ballroom. Harrods splashed out with a Ball. Even the Criminal Investigation Department showed a human face and relaxed with dreamy music.

Everyone danced the nights away to the sounds of the Big Bands, some of whose names are still famous today. The archives show how costs have changed in sixty years. Ambrose Orchestras charged 4 guineas per man; personal appearance by Bert Ambrose could be arranged for an extra charge of 25 guineas, which for the man who organised and conducted one of the world's most popular dance-bands was on the cheap side. His career began in New York at the Club de Vingts, continued in London in 1922 at the Embassy Club, May Fair Hotel, Ciro's, Café de Paris, and eventually *The Dorchester*. His elegant style of playing is recalled by the signature tune 'When Day is Done'. The rate for Harry Roy's band was slightly cheaper: £3.13.6 per man, with the personal appearance fee at the standard 25 guineas. Roy formed his band about ten years after Ambrose, attracted attention at the Leicester Square Theatre and the London Pavilion, before moving to the May Fair Hotel after a spell at *The Dorchester*. Again memories are stirred by the signature tune, 'Bugle Call Rag'. Jack Jackson was a favourite at the hotel. This English trumpeter, band-leader and disc jockey studied at the Royal Academy of Music,

43. *Bert Ambrose and his band*

worked for Ambrose, Jack Hylton and Jack Payne before forming his own band in 1933, succeeding Ambrose's Blue Lyres at *The Dorchester* where he spent six very successful years. His rates were even cheaper: 3 guineas per man, with personal appearances at 10 guineas. Afternoon sessions of 2–3 hours worked out at 35/- per man and 6 guineas for personal appearances.

These modest charges made cabaret shows viable. Felix Ferry, the New York producer, brought over a cabaret of beautiful girls to *The Dorchester* under the aegis of Clifford Whitley, who arranged the Co-optimists Concerts held on Sunday nights. Potential talent was given a chance, like the youthful Danny Kaye. The report states that he had the makings of a good parodist and vocal virtuoso with a face of absolute novelty, regarded as a woman's comedian and paid £50 per week. Henry Sherek produced a dozen highly entertaining revues at the hotel. Almost a one-man entertainment himself without rehearsal, bulky in build with features a cartoonist's dream, Sherek made a name for himself in theatrical management with a lengthy line of successes. Henry Hall was also involved in arranging cabaret turns, like an overspill from his weekly *Guest Night* programme, a BBC favourite from 1934. As an old man Hall was confined to a wheelchair, but shortly before his death he reminisced with affection about the old days in *The Dorchester*.

Whilst on the subject of charges, *The Dorchester* tariff in 1931 makes incredible reading: *Single Room with Private Bathroom from 32/6: Double Room with Private Bathroom from 45/-: Lunch 8/6: Theatre Dinner 12/6: Dîner Dansant 15/6: Souper dansant 12/6: Suite from 3½ Guineas.* Times have changed!

44. *Harry Roy with his Dance Orchestra*

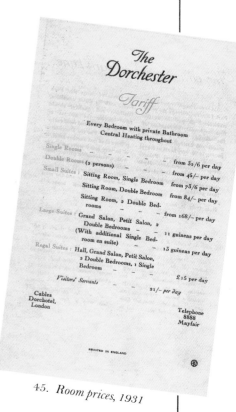

45. *Room prices, 1931*

Tributes to eminent personalities at dinners and receptions form a commentary on the decade. One such gesture was to Edith Summerskill in recognition of the role she played in the vanguard of militant feminists and her vigorous insistence on equal pay. One of the most forthright of contemporary politicians, the Doctor was a bundle of contradictions. In public she exuded confidence with an aggressive voice and astringent look, yet in private admitted to being nervous and became a likeable, vulnerable woman. Another personality fêted was Steve Donoghue. After ceasing to be champion jockey, there was no falling away in his popularity, due partly to publicity surrounding his partnership with the legendary stayer, Brown Jack. Together they won the Queen Alexandra Stakes at Royal Ascot six consecutive years between 1929 and 1934 in the colours of Sir Harold Wernher.

Just as warm was the tribute to Gracie Fields, the last great figure of the British music hall. Her pure soprano voice, with which she performed sensational loops and leaps, her overwhelming good nature and Rochdale accent exemplified the spirit of the provinces and brought a touch of it into the Park Suite. On a par with that night was the dinner marking the seventieth birthday of George Robey, the comedian known as the prime minister of mirth, with red nose, heavily blackened eyebrows, and down-at-heel respectability in long frock-coat that, in spite of irremediable tatters, had obviously known the sunshine of Piccadilly, battered hat and cane. There was nothing of listless, well-bred indifference about the way Robey used to take the red-plush benches by storm. The tributes that night in the ballroom were sincere but, as a guest said afterwards, it was difficult to associate with the figure at the top table. They were meant for the stage image

46. *Jack Jackson*

47. *Danny Kaye*

48. *Henry Sherek*

and confirmed that comedians clothed in respectability are in their wrong mind. It was recognition *in absentia*.

More sedate was the dinner given by Langley Park Golf Club to mark Henry Cotton's second victory in the Open Championship, under climatic conditions that could hardly have been worse, over Carnoustie links that rank as one of the stiffest in the championship rota, and against an entry that included the full victorious American Ryder Cup team. It was also appropriate because Cotton, for many years a resident in the hotel, had begun his career as a full professional at Langley Park. As a further gesture, a portrait painted by J.J. Berrie showing the champion in his favourite brick-red pullover was presented before the 500 guests by the veteran Sandy Herd, the 1902 Open champion.

The dinner to Tom Walls was quite an event. He was a most amusing, generous and hospitable man, remarkably versatile and energetic. Born in 1883, son of a builder, educated at Northampton County school, he served for a brief spell in the Metropolitan

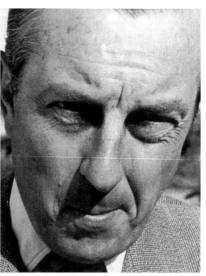

49. *Gracie Fields*   50. *Henry Cotton*

Police, found the lot was not a happy one and switched to the stage. The turning-point came with his first managerial venture, producing with Leslie Henson a farce at the Shaftesbury Theatre called *Tons of Money*. He never looked back. It was followed with a succession of farces at the Aldwych Theatre written by Ben Travers, in which he was the perfect foil to Ralph Lynn and Robertson Hare. As soon as he earned sufficient money, Walls took out a licence and started a stable at Epsom with a fair measure of success, winning about 150 races, mostly small handicaps and selling plates. His greatest moment came when April the Fifth won the 1932 Derby at 100-6 by three parts of a length from the Aga Khan's Dastur. It was the first Epsom-trained Derby winner since Amato in 1838. Tom Walls and his theatrical friends won a great deal of money, though, as he said, not quite so much as some newspapers suggested. There was one bit of luck; he only just reached the course in time to take part. The horse-box was stuck in a traffic jam and April the Fifth had to get out and walk.

There were several dinners in honour of Malcolm Campbell as periodically there were feats to celebrate. He was the first man to travel at over 150 mph, raising the record by stages to over 300 mph in 1935, then added the water-speed record of nearly 142 mph in 1939. An MCC dinner to Ronnie Aird recognised the way he had maintained the finest traditions of Lord's and in no way connected with his contribution for Cambridge in the University match. Innings of 1 and 5 left a little to be desired, but so did the Light Blues' totals of 50 and 136 against Oxford's 422.

A cocktail party for Maurice Chevalier showed how he had won the hearts of Paris and New York as an inimitable character. He was a caricature of himself, with wicked bountiful grin, fresh cheeks and eyes like diamonds. The only thing missing was the straw hat tilted into a winking position. At that time Chevalier was fast becoming the rage of musical features. A similar function for Herbert Marshall showed how he created the stereotype of the aristocratic Englishman which added a touch of upper-class fantasy

51. Maurice Chevalier with the author

52. Brigadier-General A.C. Critchley

to American films, especially after the arrival of the 'talkies'. A lunch for Sir Seymour Hicks revealed him as a personality of infinite variety with a dozen masks of comedy that he could assume at will. On another occasion, Irene Vanbrugh's vivacious style characterised her engaging qualities as an actress in a stage career that had begun as far back as 1888. Other functions were made outstanding by the charismatic personalities and antics of figures like Stanley Lupino, Jack Benny, Jimmy Durante, Eddie Cantor, a regular visitor, Ben Lyons and Bebe Daniels. Memorable was the tribute to Ivor Novello. An incurable romantic, he had used his talents as composer, actor and dramatist to launch entirely new types of English musical shows, like *Glamorous Night, Careless Rapture, The Dancing Years* and *Perchance to Dream*. His mother, Madame Clara Novello Davies, a well-known singing teacher, used to say that as a baby Ivor only cried in perfect thirds.

One of the guests at *The Dorchester* opening dinner was Brigadier-General A.C. Critchley, who became a familiar figure in the hotel over the next twenty-five years.

Those who knew him will recall his sheer zest for life. Seymour Hicks, similarly energetic, ascribed his energy to an overactive pituitary gland. Critchley was more specific: he said it began on the family ranch in Calgary where he and his brother grew up without the slightest attempt at education. They could hardly write and only just read, but could saddle ponies, ride for miles across the ranges, find their way without compasses, make their own camps and ride hard. With such a childhood, his arrival at a small Eastbourne preparatory school at the age of nine caused something of a stir. Three years in France in the First World War saw Critchley rise to command Strathcona's Horse. He was asked to take over the Initial Training Command of the Royal Flying Corps, at that time losing 50 per cent of the cadets in training accidents. A photograph of a march past shows Critchley, a Brigadier-General at twenty-seven, standing behind King George V with the future King George VI leading the column. History repeated itself. Just before the Second World War, Critchley was back in the Royal Air Force as Pilot Officer Acting Air Commodore, commanding with the same urgency the sites where this time he trained aircrews in tens of thousands to be inspected and commended by King George VI.

After the war Critchley became Director-General of BOAC, turning a loss of £2.5 million into a profit of £1.5 million. During this period he was a constant visitor to *The Dorchester* for endless meetings, business lunches and dinners. Then suddenly, and without warning, he went blind. Within a year he had adjusted his life, continued to travel all over the world, and conducted his business in London and the hotel. On the golf links Critch was a formidable player, without style or theory, and won several national championships. His courage was remarkable.

Other activities in *The Dorchester* were numerous, including popular Lieder concerts in the Ballroom. The uninitiated were told that a *lied* was simply a song with German words, but in other languages the word was used for the special type of German song associated particularly with Schumann, Brahms and Hugo Wolf. The Lieder Club members in the hotel were more selective: they looked to Schubert as the incomparable master of the art. Equally specialised were the evening sessions spent with Ely Culbertson in the Park Lounge. If there have been better bridge players than Culbertson, none have been so sharp. Vanderbilt made Contract respectable; Culbertson made it pay. His *Blue Book* acquired almost the force of a morality. In the Twenties American women suspected their husbands of adultery; in the Thirties they accused them of playing Culbertson.

The Banqueting Manager had to anticipate the requirements of international tastes; the range was global. Dinners for the Highland Light Infantry; lunches in the Oval Room for the Japanese military attaché; dinners in the Ballroom for Indian Army officers; lunches for the German Delegation; evening receptions for the Ethiopian Legation; cocktails for the Chinese naval attaché; the State of Mysore dinner in the Gold Room during Royal Ascot week; receptions for the Sultan of Muscat and Oman in the Spanish Room. The reception for the Maharaja of Baroda focused attention on a man anxious to make racing history. When the Second World War ended, he acquired Warren Place in Newmarket and invited Fred Armstrong to be his trainer. In 1945 he created a record at the Newmarket Sales by paying 28,000 guineas for a yearling bred by Sir Eric Ohlson by

53. TOP: *The Ballroom*

54. LEFT: *Floral decorations*

55. ABOVE: *Lunchtime on the Terrace in 1932*

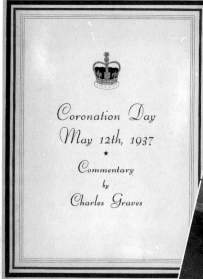

Coronation Day
May 12th, 1937
★
Commentary
by
Charles Graves

57

56

58

59

60

59. *Stanley Baldwin*

60. *Ramsay MacDonald*

61. *The British Ambassador, Sir Neville Henderson and Neville Chamberlain at the Munich meeting with Adolf Hitler*

56. *Edward VIII and Mrs Wallis Simpson*

57. *Coronation Day arrangements for guests*

58. *King George VI and Queen Elizabeth*

61

Nearco out of Rosy Legend, a full brother of Dante who had earlier won the Derby. The yearling was named Sayajirao and justified the purchase price by winning the St Leger, Irish Derby, the Warren Stakes at Goodwood, Derby Trial Stakes at Lingfield, and finished third in the 2000 Guineas and the Derby. The international political upheaval in India made it necessary for the Maharaja to trim his racing ambitions for, in 1951, the Indian government deposed him as ruler of Baroda, a decision that killed the possibility of rivalling the Aga Khan's position on the Turf. With an income of some £2 million a year the challenge had been viable. On that evening in *The Dorchester*, the shadow of such happenings did not cloud ambitions.

Four events of national and international significance affected *The Dorchester* directly and indirectly. King George V's Silver Jubilee of 1935 brought an influx of distinguished guests, many attending the Jubilee reception and ball at the Guildhall for more than 2000 guests. The Naval Conference between Britain, America, France, Italy and Japan, held at the Foreign Office, attracted many foreign diplomats. Stanley Baldwin presided, announcing that Britain was ready to prolong the principles of the existing Naval Treaties, but favoured the abolition of submarines. The marriage of Lady Alice Montagu-Douglas-Scott to the Duke of Gloucester took place in the Buckingham Palace private chapel instead of Westminster Abbey because of the death of her father, the Duke of Buccleuch; several of the bride's close friends stayed in the hotel. Royal personages and diplomatic personnel came when King George V died. Again there were guests who figured prominently at the time when King Edward VIII was proclaimed; at the events leading to the Abdication; at the moment when Edward VIII ceased to be King; at the excitement of the Coronation of King George VI and Queen Elizabeth; at the international tension leading to the moment when Neville Chamberlain announced that time had run out and Britain was at war with Germany.

62. *George VI takes the salute outside* The Dorchester

63

64

65

63, 64, 65. Preparations for war: The Dorchester *staff became air-raid wardens and fire-watchers. The front entrance was heavily sandbagged against bomb-blast within days of the first air-raid warning, later to be replaced with solid brick walls*

Events happened so quickly. Churchill joined the small War Cabinet as First Lord of the Admiralty; allied ships were sunk by German submarines; the *Graf Spee* was scuttled after being trapped in the River Plate by British warships; War Budget raised income tax to the highest ever figure of 7/6 in the pound (37.5%); the aircraft-carrier HMS *Courageous* was sunk. In October, 250,000 more conscripts were called up; the *Royal Oak* was sunk in the home base of Scapa Flow; petrol was increased by $1\frac{1}{2}$d to $1/9\frac{1}{2}$ per gallon.

Suddenly it was a different world. Overnight it looked as if the whole country had gone into uniform. *The Dorchester* readjusted to a state of war with a different role to play.

Guests of Distinction

Ingrid Bergman

Everyone is curious what the illusory figures of screen and theatre are really like. For years *The Dorchester* has housed the world's greatest artists when they have escaped the limelight of publicity. Ingrid Bergman was a rare example.

The real life of this brilliant interpretative actress outstripped in drama content the roles she played on the screen. David O. Selznick, who built up her career, described her as a genius without ostentation. Maybe he used the term too freely, but there was no doubting the rare quality of her art. At the peak she radiated health and vitality until career and marriage became soured. Roberto Rossellini provided support, but the romance that followed led to the Hollywood colony hypocritically ostracising Ingrid for being honest about her sexuality. Prestige was restored by the film *Anastasia*, but her habit of uncomplicated speaking did not appeal to the media. In retrospect I recall a woman of simple simplicity based on worldly experience, a complex personality impossible to contain in a fixed mould. Her personal integrity or courage could never be questioned.

An instance of this occurred after Ingrid made London a permanent home. Her stoical acceptance of double operations for breast cancer and the unpleasant effects of radiation treatment were an object lesson and example for all who have to cope with the dreaded scourge. Faced with the terminal disease and shortly before her death, Ingrid left her Cheyne Gardens flat and came to *The Dorchester* for lunch. She looked tired and weary. Her right arm was in a sling to give support, yet never once was there any indication of the nagging pain or discomfort. The stamina, like her acting, was inspiring.

There was another side little known to the public. For someone who had starred with Humphrey Bogart in *Casablanca*, Ernest Hemingway and Gary Cooper in *For Whom the Bell Tolls*, and was a friend of such men as Howard Hughes, David Selznick and George

66. Ingrid Bergman

Bernard Shaw, it was surprising how vulnerable she was to criticism, particularly the reaction to *Joan of Arc at the Stake*, the oratorio by Arthur Honnegger written by Paul Claudel, which was produced and directed by Rossellini at the Stoll. Some critics were fascinated if confused, others were just bitchy. I took the opposite view. At that last lunch, Ingrid told me that the wording of my phrases had meant a lot to her at the time; they epitomised what she had attempted to portray. I am glad that Ian Burgess included the lines in *Ingrid Bergman My Story*. I repeat them in memory of one of the loveliest and bravest of actresses: 'In the engulfing darkness and piercing shafts of light at the Stoll, Ingrid suggests the spiritual, statuesque calm of one who has climbed to the summit high above the gross world. She evokes the sadness of things supremely well. . . . The quality she possesses is more than beauty, it is strangeness in beauty.'

Norman Mailer

It is one of the facts of life that we are influenced by the public image, by the legend that surrounds an outstanding person, or by the living he has created. Narcissus, we are told, saw his reflection in a pool and fell in love with it. Presumably his face was the peccant part and its beauty proverbial. Since Whitman's *Song of Myself* a new figure has emerged, the whole man, not necessarily a beauty, in love with the whole of himself. In this type of man, aggression often lurks near the surface ready to be let loose on interrupters or those who in any way thwart his egomania and refuse to settle for the complete man. One such is Norman Mailer.

Everything about Mailer is sufficiently exaggerated to encourage the myth of anarchic egomania. He looks the part and has a tendency to quarrel with those who do not accept him at his own valuation. In such disputes he is always right, which tends to be an obfuscation of reality. He swamps everything in the compulsive effluvia of his own personality. His private life attracts headlines always two jumps ahead of him.

Short, wide and heavy, with a formidable physical presence, Mailer's face is Celtic rather than Jewish, deep-set blue eyes, curly hair now grizzled, endearing grin like a Cheshire Cat that gives an air of someone who has got used to charming people over the years. He would have made a perfect Regency rake. Instead he settled to be a Brooklyn whirlwind with a Massachusetts accent. Mailer writes very well when he takes trouble and quite well when he takes no trouble. *The Naked and the Dead* is one of the finest American war novels and confirmed his standing as a long-term novelist in the great tradition, though lagging behind Burroughs and Beckett. Maybe his finest writing has yet to come.

During a visit to London, we had a wager-race across town in mid-afternoon, from the Savoy Hotel to *The Dorchester*, with identical starts from the Embankment entrance. Local knowledge ensured a satisfactory result, with possibly a touch of sharp practice. It was during this stay that Mailer, in more mellow mood, revealed himself as a thwarted architect. He showed photographs of an architectural scale-model he had built of a

67. Norman Mailer

miniature town on several levels, with all modern amenities and facilities like schools, hospitals, churches, supermarkets, corner shops and thoroughfares, with no two houses the same, laid out in a comparatively small area, a mirage come true. Whether the RIBA would consider the concept acceptable is another matter, though several authorities saw its possibilities. Mailer also had strong opinions as to how a hotel of international repute should be run. Good taste should never be sacrificed. Too many labour-saving devices destroyed the illusion of elegance and comfort. If a client was prepared to pay over the odds for what he wanted, that was his concern. Wealth is not a dirty word. If you couldn't afford luxury, there were plenty of cost-effective alternatives. He had few criticisms of *The Dorchester*. A return visit will provide the answers.

Sir Gerald Kelly and Sir Charles Wheeler

The Royal Academy of Arts has had many individualistic Presidents, but few so controversial or iconoclastic as Sir Gerald Kelly. A traditional purist, he had no time for advanced cliques, half-fledged intellectuals who thought anarchy was progress. Blunt and no respecter of reputations, Kelly never minced words. Television viewers expected an apoplectic outburst and were seldom disappointed; producers were wary of live broadcasts. I sat next to him on such a TV programme. Opposite was Salvador Dali looking like an undertaker in black suit, blackened hair, black string tie, black pencilled eyebrows, black twitching moustaches, high white collar, stark white face with black button eyes. Dali set the ball rolling by saying his outrageous days were a thing of the past. He no longer slept in a black-lined open coffin; instead he had become the first atomic artist drawing inspiration from the heavens through the tips of his moustaches. It was too much for Kelly. 'Absolute balls,' he snorted, 'the fellow must be mad.' Sadly the aside was bleeped out. It was only over supper later in *The Dorchester* that he learnt the comment had been cut. Irritation killed his appetite. Dali enquired why he was so angry and an interpretation of the remark. Kelly's translation left nothing to the imagination. The effort was wasted on Dali. He gently patted the President on his head and devoted exclusive attention to a responsive female companion.

Not all RA Presidents have been so extrovert. Sir Charles Wheeler was a complete contrast to Sir Gerald Kelly. He disliked personal publicity, but accepted it with good grace as a tribute to his office. The air of reticence could be misleading: on occasions his tongue could be sharp. On one visit to *The Dorchester* he described Academicians as a prickly group of egotists who revelled in quarrelsome cliques. He was quietly proud of eliminating their controversial frittering, even making them amenable and co-operative. He was also an advocate for the recognition of women Academicians and would point out there were two founder members of the fairer sex, Mary Moser, the flower painter, and Angelica Kaufman, the decorative painter. No more were added during the nineteenth century. Not until 1922 was another woman elected. He was pleased that seven women were admitted during his Presidency, but doubted whether the trend would continue after he retired. His doubts were justified.

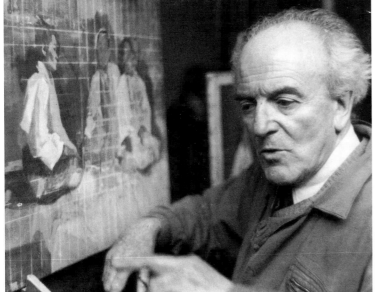

68. *Sir Gerald Kelly*   69. *Sir Charles Wheeler*

One evening he remarked how a chance happening can affect a career and recalled an incident that occurred when he was working in a small studio at the back of Chelsea Old Church, off the Fulham Road. An unexpected visitor asked if he would take a commission for a plaque in memory of his 20-year-old son who had been killed. The stranger was Rudyard Kipling, and the plaque was the beginning of a career that never looked back. Wheeler's output was considerable. I was interested to hear him say that not a single piece carries his signature. He corrected himself: there was an exception. In an inner courtyard of the Bank of England are seven stone heads of men who played a part in the building operation. The end one is Charles Wheeler, but it is there only because of the architect's insistence.

In *The Dorchester* structural alterations, it is tempting to isolate a similar number of personalities who played a significant role in its six decades existence.

Dame Edith Evans

Tireless chatterer, disarmingly outspoken, she took sophistication out of the ice-box and set it bubbling on the hob. Her stock-in-trade was nonchalance. On one occasion I sat opposite her at a luncheon in *The Dorchester* when awards were made for outstanding performances during the year in various professions. Next to her sat Freddie Mills, the boxer, nominated Sportsman of the Year for beating Gus Lesnevich to win the world light-heavyweight championship. Bubbling with enthusiasm, Mills described how he started boxing at the age of 14, recalled early days in a travelling fairground-booth when Gipsy Daniels gave him advice, went into gory details of the Lesnevich fight, sweet revenge for being knocked out in a previous title fight with the rugged American. Edith Evans listened attentively until the flow stopped, then looked at Mills with quizzical eye.

70. *Dame Edith Evans* (CENTRE) *with Henry Moore, Gladys Young, Graham Greene, Michael Wilding and Freddie Mills*

'What did you say your name was?' The pugilist obliged. 'I think you're simply sweet.' The compliment, given with a coy smile, silenced Mills as effectively as a Lesnevich chop. Talking about the incident, the actress said that in no way had she meant to put Mills down. He was just different to anyone she had met, totally natural and unaffected.

Embarrassing moments and Edith Evans were no strangers. At Cambridge she muffed her entrance at a Degree Ceremony. In her anxiety not to get out of step during the traditional ceremony, she wrongly anticipated the moment to step forward to shake hands with the Chancellor and was halted when Lord Tedder muttered, 'Wait for it, wait for it.' She said the warning had such an effect, she became rooted to the ground and had to be nudged forward when the critical time arrived.

Sir Henry Cotton

The Dorchester has welcomed many golfers who have dominated the world of golf, men like Sir Henry Cotton, an individualist in every sense of the word and lone wolf of the links. A man of few words on the course, few golfers have subjected themselves to such ice-cold, concentrated self-discipline. Henry's ambition was to become the greatest golfer. He came within sight of that peak, an experience known only by a few. We were neighbours in *The Dorchester*. It was always interesting to listen to his theories: how he justified the back-breaking, hand-blistering hours practising and experimenting when temperament refused to comply. Equally graphic were the observations of his wife, a dynamic little Argentinian affectionately known as 'Toots'. They married in 1939; it was a rewarding partnership of mutual support and understanding, with occasional disagreements as in every household. When the going became rough Henry would take a breather until the ripples settled. 'Toots' would telephone and ask if Henry was with me. I had a feeling that the answer was never believed. Once she asked if she could see for herself. I welcomed the visit but added I was in the bath. The knock never came.

Michaela Denis

It is unusual to find an elegant woman drinking gin and tonic in the bar who had lived with the Aborigines in Central Australia, journeyed to New Guinea to make friends with the Chimbu – a Stone Age people – and trekked through Africa on a journey to King Solomon's Mines. Unusual, that is, except in *The Dorchester* where anything is accepted without comment. These were some of the things that Michaela Denis had done, recording photographically remotest places in the world and capturing on camera primitive peoples and rare animals.

I asked about the likelihood of catching a tropical disease in the jungle. Apparently that happened on more than one occasion. Spending a day submerged in a swamp waiting to photograph a rare creature was tempting fortune in the blazing sun, icy-cold muddy water up to the neck and stench frightful. Hours later a feverish temperature confirmed tick fever. Three weeks of antibiotic treatment did the trick without the usual heart complications. On another safari in Central Africa, the team, including Tom Stobart of Everest fame, captured an 800-lb sealion, whilst a reptile-infested Australian pool produced a haul of 60 netted crocodiles. No animal was killed. The only shooting had been with cameras.

71. *Sir Henry Cotton on the first tee Old Course, St Andrews*

72. *Michaela Denis*

Michaela Denis was one of those unusual people who appear once or twice in a generation. Born with that most reliable prophylactic against Tedium, consuming curiosity, it took her to some of the world's strangest places. She was the only woman I have known who had a vulture for a pet. That must surely be a 'first' for *The Dorchester*.

Wilfred Harvey

In the summer of 1965 national newspapers gave extensive coverage to a major business involving the British Printing Corporation. Wilfred Harvey had been the managing director of the Purnell Group, a firm of printers and binders which in 1964 had merged with Hazell Sun Ltd to form the £20 million BPC, of which he became chairman. Early in July 1965 Sir Geoffrey Crowther, Max Rayne and other directors identified with Hazell Sun had written to the shareholders of BPC seeking the removal of Harvey and two of his colleagues (his solicitor and son-in-law) on the grounds of difficulties in reorganisation and the very large sums which it was alleged Harvey and his associates had claimed as remuneration and expenses.

The negotiations and discussions that followed are not my concern, except to say they were acrimonious. Crowther, as Cecil King described, was 'emotional, vain and speaking rather as if he were the country's conscience'. Certainly he was an acquired taste. Harvey was at the receiving end of bitter attacks. I felt his side of the case had inadequate coverage. I suggested he came with his advisers one Sunday afternoon for a private talk in the Terrace Suite with the City Editor of a London evening newspaper. He welcomed the invitation, but at the last moment sent his son and fellow director, Eric Harvey, in his place. The chance to balance the scales was wasted. In the end the sorry business was resolved. Wilfred Harvey, partly through ill-health, retired into obscurity in the West Country.

A trivial sequel occurred in the Grill. Harvey for years occupied a favourite table. Crowther arrived and with customary tactlessness informed the head waiter that Harvey would not be dining there again; from now on he would have his table. Without hesitation, the head waiter apologised and said that would not be possible; it was always booked. Crowther snapped, 'Do you know who I am?' Back came the courteous reply, 'Yes, sir, I do!' A rebuff that happened within earshot of my table.

The Forties

EACH decade of *The Dorchester* has a certain historical significance. It holds a mirror up to its time, a small mirror perhaps, but a singularly clear and revealing one. Events, personalities and aspects of that period can be drawn from the archives of memory. The Forties hold a vast reservoir of material. So much happened; everything developed so quickly. Blackout, evacuation, food rationing, the frontiers of Europe redrawn in the horrors of the Second World War. Invasion of Denmark, Norway, Holland and Belgium; Dunkirk retreat; surrender of France; German troops parading up the Champs-Elysées; the Battle of Britain; Luftwaffe raids; devastation of Coventry and London; Pearl Harbor and America at war with Japan; the atomic era beginning with Hiroshima and Nagasaki; Japan surrendering and Nazi war criminals hanged at Nuremberg. After 2000 nights of darkness we were again ablaze with light. The price of victory had left 55 million dead. We returned to near normality with the news that the pound was devalued by 30 per cent against the dollar, petrol rose to 2s 3d a gallon, a car tax was proposed at a flat rate of £10 a year, railways were nationalised, civil servants were suspended for holding Communist and Fascist views, the Derby was run at Epsom after a break of six years. The social pattern was taking shape, alternating between deep depression and high prosperity, a decade of extremes reflected obliquely in *The Dorchester* mirror.

In line with other hotels, the outbreak of war had an immediate effect on *The Dorchester*. The Manager, Georges Marin, was summoned to take up duties as an officer in the French army. Various members of the staff were required by the Territorial Army and Reserve of Officers. Emile Aymoz, the French Maître Chef, on holiday in his own country, was refused permission to return to England. Italian and German staff members were interned. Rooms emptied, functions were cancelled and all banqueting ceased, resumed later on a limited scale for bookings linked with the Services or war effort. Food

73. *Maurice Winnick*

rationing meant that guests attending lunches or dinners were restricted to a maximum of 100 couverts. Government guide-lines in this respect were observed in every detail. Five shillings was the most anyone could be charged for lunch or dinner, though luxury establishments were allowed to add an extra three shillings for lunch and six shillings for dinner, ostensibly to help with the cost of linen. Music or dancing in the Restaurant justified the levy of half-a-crown. Here there were changes. Jack Jackson, the trumpeter who succeeded Ambrose's Blue Lyres at *The Dorchester*, had moved on with his band after six very successful years. He was replaced by Maurice Winnick, whose signature tune, 'The sweetest music this side of Heaven', became familiar to diners. He too responded to the call for entertaining troops in English camps. His record was impressive, travelling some 27,000 miles and playing before a million troops in Italy, Palestine, Egypt and Syria.

In response to the demand for economies in the use of paper, hotel menus were printed on cards $4\frac{1}{2}$ inches by 6 inches deep. Jean Baptiste Virlogeux, the Maître Chef, refused any dealings in black market meat. Both residents and staff used ration books for the weekly allocations, though the 100-guest limitation did not apply to buffet functions. The Restaurant moved to the Gold Room and the Gold Foyer, where diners had the reassuring protection of eight floors of reinforced concrete instead of the glass-domed roof. The Grill Room, transferred to the Ballroom Lounge, avoided the danger of flying broken glass. Guests used the air-raid shelter, plus converted cubicles in the gymnasium, Turkish baths in the basement, sections of the kitchens and even slept in the corridors. Those more fatalistic stayed in their beds and hoped for the best. Layers of shingle on the roof were some protection from incendiary bombs. Fire watchers were recruited from the

War Economy Menu

Christmas 1941

Entertainment

Dancing to
MAURICE WINNICK
and
The Dorchester Hotel Band

At 10.30 p.m.
"ONE UP AND TWO TO PLAY"
First Part
THAT CERTAIN TRIO
Anne de Nys   John Ridley
Patrick Waddington

At Midnight
"ONE UP AND TWO TO PLAY"
Second Part
THAT CERTAIN TRIO

During the evening there will be special festivities and distribution of favours.

Menu

Les Perles grises de Sterle

Le Fumet de Tortue au vieux Sherry

Le filet de sole Riviera

Le Blanc de Volaille Perigourdine
La Timbale de Petits pois
Les Pommes Berny
La Salade des Rois Mages

Le Biscuit glace des Samaritaines
Les Frivolites

74. *The Christmas 1941 menu reproduced actual size*

staff. Often ringed by falling bombs, *The Dorchester* miraculously escaped a direct hit: its claim to be bomb-proof, fireproof and earthquake-proof was never put to the test. Such confidence undoubtedly influenced government ministers to become resident, and their number included Sir Anthony Eden, the Foreign Secretary, Oliver Lyttleton, Oliver Stanley, and Sir Charles Portal, Chief of the Air Staff.

When the United States entered the war and General Eisenhower became Supreme Commander of the American Forces in Europe, he chose Claridges as a base for it was within easy reach of his headquarters in Grosvenor Square; but whilst the situation was right, the amenities did not appeal. Kay Summersby, who acted as his chauffeur and secretary, gave a graphic description of the General's reaction in her memoirs, *Past Forgetting*. 'His sitting-room in that home away from home for potentates and multi-billionaires was decorated in black and gold like some Hollywood set, and although I always felt that Fred Astaire might come tap-tap-tapping along at any minute, the General disagreed . . . "It looks like a goddarned fancy funeral parlour to me." The bedroom made him feel even more uncomfortable. "Whorehouse pink" was his description of the colour scheme. "Makes me feel as if I'm living in sin."' Kay continued, 'He moved into *The Dorchester*, still elegant and luxurious, but somewhat noisier, somewhat shinier, somewhat, in fact, like American. He felt a bit more at home here, especially after Butch (Harry Butcher, who handled Eisenhower's Public Relations, and had formerly been a Vice-President of Columbia Broadcasting System) moved in with him.' The Suite was 104/5 on the first floor overlooking the front entrance of the hotel. The outside balcony has a wall built at Winston Churchill's suggestion; it safeguarded Eisenhower's privacy from the adjoining room. It was comfortable but did not lend itself to social gatherings, which in any case were restricted to a weekly meal with Churchill.

75. Sir Anthony Eden (RIGHT) with Lewis Douglas, the American Ambassador

76. LEFT: *General Eisenhower*

77. ABOVE: *Lord Beaverbrook and Winston Churchill*

Among those who went through the swing doors were the leading figures in the struggle against the Nazis. Many on official business, others snatching a few hours escape from reality. It was a close-knit community, cosmopolitan in character, in which anonymity was welcomed, though some guests could not hide their identity. They not only made news, they were news, as a random selection shows. Lord Beaverbrook was a frequent visitor. Summoned by Churchill to be Minister of Aircraft Production, he used his titanic energies to get the planes made. An extraordinary man, he directed the *Daily Express* personally down a battery of telephones. By the outbreak of war he had built up the largest daily net sale in the world, and used to say that the formula to raise circulation was blending politics and high life in a gin-fizz. He was a showman of genius, though his simplistic chauvinism never took root. *The Dorchester* played a significant role in his life. It was appropriate that years on it was the scene of Lord Thomson's banquet in honour of 'The Beaver's' eighty-fifth birthday.

Equally impressive though on a lower key was another visitor, Arthur Christiansen. During a dinner in his honour in the hotel in 1943 before 100 guests, he admitted that compulsive control of editorial techniques was his real strength. He structured page one around column one, the important story. Necessary for status, it was often too heavy, too lacking in human interest for the readers, so the centre columns would be a unique sugar-

78. *Lord Beaverbrook arrives with Lady Churchill for his 85th birthday party*

coated *Express* diversion, often glossy, always well written, but irrelevant to the news. Never immodest, he claimed that after a top-level briefing during the war, he would have written, subbed, headlined and displayed the news whilst other editors were still dictating the gist of the release to their secretaries. Big talk, but true. Christiansen had that touch of genius which is lacking in the paper today.

General Sikorski, Prime Minister of the exiled Polish government and Commander-in-Chief of the Polish army, was a familiar figure in the hotel. Colonel Victor Cazalet, a director of *The Dorchester*, acted as his liaison officer and was with him in the unexplained airplane crash off the coast of Gibraltar in 1943 when all passengers and crew were killed. No one could miss the arrival of Ernest Bevin, Foreign Minister from 1945 to 1951, but during the war Minister of Labour and National Service. His organisation of the labour force was a glorious achievement but, had he never entered a government, Bevin would be remembered as the architect of the Transport and General Workers Union and the most influential leader the Trade Union Movement has had. At the official dinner held in *The Dorchester* for the XIV Olympiad in 1948, his granite-like attitude surfaced when someone said of an opponent, 'He is his own worst enemy', to which Bevin replied, 'Not while I am alive, he ain't.'

79. *Arthur Christiansen*   80. *Ernest Bevin*   81. *Lord Beveridge*

The stream of visitors was like *Who's Who* come to life. One such was William Beveridge, an unusual man, a visionary and tireless worker with Teutonic respect for detail and a highly developed awareness of the value of publicity if it helped him to get his own way. Discussions in *The Dorchester* were often to that end. According to some colleagues he was conceited and unpopular. This was shown when he was relegated during the war to a side-wing committee with a brief to 'survey existing social services and make recommendations'. The limited assignment was intended to keep him in obscurity; it backfired. Beveridge crusaded passionately on a national scale, in a campaign that displeased Whitehall overlords who deplored that the chairman of a Government Enquiry should use such publicity-seeking aids. They also resented his high-handed treatment of officials. Beveridge ignored the rebuffs. He persisted until the bulk of his proposals were made law by the post-1945 Labour Government. Regarded as father of a welfare state that provides government support from cradle to the grave, Beveridge was

82. *Paul-Henri Spaak*   83. *Sir Harold Nicolson*   84. *C.B. Fry*

never a good committee man (I speak from the experience of having sat with him for several months). He was too much of a loner, both in public and private. Appearances were deceptive: this white-haired man with lean, ascetic features, gentle of voice and occasionally courteous of manner, was also a man of action. Janet, his dour Scottish wife, used to say that even Churchill was wary of her husband. Animosities and irritations were forgotten on a December day in 1942 when some 200 paid tribute to his unyielding qualities in a reception at *The Dorchester*.

Paul-Henri Spaak's status as Belgium's international statesman is largely forgotten today. Even when he entered the hotel in May 1944 few people recognised the burly socialist, but his choice as successor to Lord Ismay as Secretary-General of NATO was a predictable appointment for an energetic statesman who became known as 'Mr Europe'. A similar lack of recognition applied to Harold Nicolson, who was a courteous guest at a hotel function that same year. Primarily a thwarted diplomat, Nicolson became a politician before turning to the pen. His writing was urbane and reflected cultivated worldly insight into a varied life. He had few academic ambitions, but maintained a level of professional craftsmanship and punctiliousness. His biography of King George V was masterly. The atmosphere of *The Dorchester* appealed to his sensivity. 'Civilised and aristocratic in discrimination' was his verdict.

Sportsmen of the Forties made the hotel a favourite venue for dinners and receptions. One occasion was a select lunch given to C.B. Fry. At a time when England struggles to find fresh talent for the Nineties, it is tempting to recall what once was. Fry's total of runs in first-class games was over 30,000 and that included eighteen Tests for England against Australia and eight against South Africa. He recalled the 232 not out in 1903 for the Gentlemen against Players at Lord's. Two seasons earlier there had been eighteen centuries with an aggregate of 3146 runs including six consecutive centuries, but what gave him greatest satisfaction was 100 not out for Oxford in the University Match, not

85. *Sir Julian Huxley*

86. *Professor C.E.M. Joad*

87. *Aldous Huxley*

88. *Krishna Menon*

forgetting the six wickets claimed as a fast bowler. In other sports Fry was chosen for England at soccer and was full-back for Southampton against Sheffield United in the 1902 FA Cup Final; he played rugby for Blackheath and the Barbarians; in athletics his long jump of 23ft $6\frac{1}{2}$ inches stood as a world record for several years. In spite of all these honours and the passage of time, Fry still felt aggrieved at not being invited to serve on the MCC Committee. He thought the reason might have been an unguarded remark when he said that some of the members did not know the difference between an off-break and an off-licence. And, what was more, they were still bemused. An unguarded comment by Lord Bramall as a former President of the MCC could be illuminating.

One of the most popular wireless programmes of the Forties was the *Brains Trust*, whose members became household names. Before each session the team had lunch at *The Dorchester*, an interesting group with each man a professional in broadcasting techniques. Julian Huxley was the fictional image of an astringent professor who only came to life in a laboratory or lecture-room, yet nothing could have been farther from the truth. Brilliant in so many different ways, he was an important intellectual force in twentieth-century biology. It was sad that the public rarely saw the warmer side of his nature. He was no extrovert, yet unwittingly achieved household fame on the programme and was the only one capable of silencing the loquacious Professor Joad. Julian's brother, Aldous, was less conservative. Only on rare occasions did he visit the hotel; the last time was just before leaving for an Italian holiday with his wife. In outlook and mannerisms he had become Americanised. Failing eyesight was still a problem – he relied on a minute reading telescope – but nothing diminished his intellectual curiosity or willingness to experiment. He studied telepathy, clairvoyance and hypnosis, and concentrated on the therapeutic use of such mind-effacing drugs as LSD and mescalin. As we talked, a young man, scruffily dressed, was quietly asked to leave the Bar. During the ensuing argument, Huxley remarked it was distressing to think that his exploratory views had made him into the unwilling father of the hippies.

In 1947 there entered *The Dorchester* lounge the world's most European Oriental. Krishna Menon was a mysterious figure, with full cabinet rank but no cabinet seat. Unique in the conventional run of politics and certainly one of the most mobile figures in statesmanship, his movements covered all the chancelleries and foreign offices. I met Menon on many occasions in different parts of the world and, though circumstances altered, the impression never changed. His features were unforgettable: eyebrows, aquiline nose, voluble hands, brooding demeanour, Mephistophelean smile. He symbolised the new Asia. I reminded him of the time when he lived in a one-roomed flatlet in Camden Town. Then he wore a threadbare overcoat and shabby flannel trousers, but he was a dedicated man, dedicated to the struggle for the freedom of the people. He was an industrious member of St Pancras Borough Council and a courageous air-raid warden in blitzed North London. His friendship with Pandit Nehru was curious. Here were two men with completely dissimilar backgrounds. Nehru came from an aristocratic Brahmin family of Northern India, Harrow and Cambridge; Menon from a working-class home in Malabar and studied at the London School of Economics. Nevertheless the association gelled. A complex character, dual-faced in some of his dealings, Menon virtually nullified much that had been achieved by Menon the tireless negotiator. He had strong differences of opinion with several of his generals, whom he treated like newly commissioned subalterns. On an everyday basis, I recall several idiosyncrasies. He frowned on smoking and alcohol, and never seemed to eat. At dinner in the Grill his plate remained virtually untouched, his only weakness an endless chain of cups of tea.

The spotlight can be focused on Society figures who made valuable contributions to morale with charity functions and dinner parties at *The Dorchester*. Their numbers included such well-known hostesses as the Hon. Mrs Reginald Fellowes, the Countess of Dudley, Mrs Washington Singer, the Duchess of Rutland, the Hon. Mrs Lionel Guest, the Duchess of Marlborough, Lady Willoughby de Broke, the Duchess of Northumberland, Lady Pamela Berry (who thoughtfully gave a dinner in honour of Mrs Churchill in 1944), Emerald, Lady Cunard, Lady Sybil Colefax and Mrs Ronnie Greville. Beverley Nichols,

89. *The Duchess of Rutland*

90. *Baroness Ravensdale*

91. *The Duchess of Northumberland*

the social observer with a feline touch, referred to the last three in his book, *The Unforgiving Minute*: 'I knew all these old girls pretty well, and by an odd coincidence I was in, very nearly, at all their deaths. Emerald Cunard at the Ritz (having transferred there from *The Dorchester*) in the last days of the war, lonely, deserted by Sir Thomas, comparatively destitute but still indomitable. Maggy Greville at *The Dorchester*, equally indomitable, and still sustained by cream from the home farm at Polesden Lacey, in spite of rationing. Sybil Colefax at my own house, her body twisted with cancer, living on God knows what. Till the very last she remained a tireless hostess, but towards the end she was in straitened circumstances. And whenever one accepted an invitation to dinner, one received a few days later a little bill. It was a curious device and if it had been discovered by an unscrupulous gossip writer she could have been made to look ridiculous. But her friends were loyal and kept silent, and we always sent our fivers, which was more than adequate for three courses and a bottle of plonk.'

James Lees-Milne added his quota of snide tributes. A diary entry in *Ancestral Voices* for 8 March 1943 refers to a dinner given by Lady Cunard: 'Our hostess kept complaining how bad *The Dorchester* food was and how at this stage of the war the country should have learnt to have adequate butter and milk distribution.' He also referred to Lady Colefax's dinner parties, known as 'Ordinaries': 'because she is quite poor and inhabits a small house this is not allowed to interfere with her mode of living. She gets people just the same, and since she cannot give large parties at her own expense, she now expects people to dine with her at *The Dorchester* and pay for themselves. In other words it is interesting people she cares about, individuals and not society with a large S.' There were no complaints about the quality of her guests, including as they did such celebrities as Edith Sitwell, Cyril Connolly, Professor Joad and T.S. Eliot.

Irene, Lady Ravensdale, daughter of the Marquess of Curzon of Kedleston, inherited her father's lofty manners, grandiloquence, at times intransigence, and was of striking beauty. Resident in the hotel for several years, she was tireless in good works during the war. I recall an occasion in January 1945, after finalising arrangements for a piano recital in the Orchid Room, we returned to the hotel and to save time went up the stone steps from the garage. Irene failed to see an open window projecting over the steps, struck her head violently, suffered concussion and a nasty gash, but still sat stoically through the recital.

The film shows given by the remarkable Rosie Newman in aid of charity became very well known. Her family lived at 143 Piccadilly, adjoining the house of the Duke and Duchess of York where the Princesses lived until moving to Buckingham Palace when the Duke became King. In the blitz 145 Piccadilly was totally destroyed, and Rosie Newman's house was so damaged that she became a permanent resident at *The Dorchester*, only leaving in 1977 for an apartment off Belgrave Square. The films came about as a result of her enthusiasm as an amateur photographer. At the outset she concentrated on India and Egypt, but when the blitz started switched her attention to this country. She obtained official sanction from the War Office, filmed military operations, joined a destroyer scheduled to meet a convoy, visited Air Force stations, and took a sequence of the fire of London. Her films of Britain at War are now in the Imperial War Museum. The regular showings at the hotel were at times graced by Queen Mary.

Observers of the comings and goings in *The Dorchester* saw a remarkable cross-section of personalities. During those war years they would have noted statesmen like Lord Simon and Lord Halifax; Lord Dawson, physician-extraordinary to King George V; the Prime Ministers of Greece and Yugoslavia; the Royal Legation of Saudi Arabia; Douglas Woodruff entertaining Cardinal Griffin (the hotel was a firm favourite with the Archbishop of Westminster); Lord Reith, of strange and complex temperament; General Laycock and Viscount Wavell; Rab Butler and Sir Miles Thomas; Sir John Ellerman, who hated being photographed; Sidney Box of Gainsborough Pictures; Whitney Straight and Lady Daphne; Geoffrey Crowther, then identified with *The Economist*; Duff Cooper, the diplomat better known as the husband of Diana, one of the most beautiful women of that decade; Philip Noel-Baker when Secretary of State for Air; Edward Hulton; Brigadier Glubb Pasha and the Transjordan Delegation; Sir Arthur Elvin, the founder of Wembley Stadium; Sir Michael Balcon, producer of such films as *Whisky Galore* and *The Lavender Hill Mob*; Tom Arnold and Ben Lyon; Viscount Samuel and Sir Thomas Brocklebank; 'Raymond', presenting a sophisticated show of hair styles; Gordon Richards, honoured by a dinner given by fellow jockeys; Remembrance Day Dinners with Sir Ian Fraser; the private lunch given by the King of Greece to the King of Yugoslavia; the Golden Wedding party of Lord and Lady Baldwin; the eccentric Nubar Gulbenkian; the Empire Societies tribute to Anthony Eden in 1949 by over 500 guests; even Clarence Hatry; and the unforgettable night in 1944 when some 400 attended a ball given by the United States Fleet. These are but a fraction of the panorama against which *The Dorchester* was the setting.

When war ended, the task of recapturing *The Dorchester* banqueting business was entrusted to Max Colombi. Such confidence was not misplaced for he became the

92. *Nubar Gulbenkian*

93. *Sir John Ellerman*

outstanding banqueting manager in the hotel industry. His background was sound: trained in the hotel business; gained experience under Escoffier at the Carlton Hotel in the Haymarket; later assistant manager at Claridges where he established their banqueting reputation and introduced the famous Debutante Coming Out Balls. When the restrictions of war ruled out banqueting, Columbi decided to buy a small hotel among the mountains in North Wales. Sadly it was destroyed by fire in 1942. Rather than begin again, he returned to London and *The Dorchester*. Under his guidance the banqueting side flourished to such an extent that by the Sixties his staff included four assistants and five secretaries.

94. *Princess Elizabeth examines a cricket bat which was being auctioned at a ball held in aid of the National Playing Fields Association in 1949*

Sliding partitions meant that the Restaurant and Ballroom Lounge could be merged into the Ballroom to increase seating capacity to over 1000 guests. Adding other banqueting suites linked with closed-circuit television made it possible for 1300 guests to be seated at the Woolworth's Golden Jubilee Dinner. The hotel also became established as the ideal venue for the sporting confraternity. The traditional Ball after the Wimbledon Fortnight was headed by Yvon Petra of France and Pauline Betz of the United States who won their Singles titles in the first post-war finals. In 1947 it was Jack Kramer of the crew-cut hair style and Margaret Osborne who led the dancing in traditional fashion. On both occasions *The Dorchester* was at its glittering best. Equally outstanding was the Eve of the Derby Ball in 1949, hours before Nimbus won by a head from the French colt, Amour Drake. The Boat Race celebrations of 1948 and 1949 lived up to expectations. On a lower key but equally enjoyable were the functions for the Stage Golfing Society; the Football Association; the Bentley Drivers' Club; Victory Hunt Balls; the London Rowing Club; and, in particular, the Ball held in 1947 after the University Rugby Match in which Cambridge beat Oxford by two penalty goals. The hero that afternoon was Hugh Lloyd-Davies, whose place-kicking settled the issue. I take a morsel of credit that it was possible. Prior to the match Lloyd-Davies had been found guilty of undergraduate high-jinks that earned immediate rustication and missing the Twickenham match. I went to see Charles Raven, the Master of Christ's College and Vice-Chancellor of the University, and gained a reprieve, though not a pardon, for the fiery young Welshman, so all was well.

95, 96. *Princess Elizabeth arriving at* The Dorchester *for a charity ball* (LEFT), *and* (ABOVE) *attends her first public ball, at* The Dorchester *in May 1946*

I end the Forties recollections with two events, both memorable, each looking to the future. The first led to that eventful day in November 1947, a day that dawned in a not very friendly mood, rain and fog threatening, but neither came to mar the marriage of Their Royal Highnesses Princess Elizabeth and Prince Philip in the Abbey of Westminster. It was a week of frenzied activity at *The Dorchester* in which foreign Royalty mingled with guests of great distinction, particularly when an extraordinary variety of guests went to St James's Palace to view the wedding presents.

There was the short but impressive Palace ceremony when the King invested the bridegroom-to-be with the insignia of the Order of the Garter, followed later by the bestowal of further honours upon Lieutenant Mountbatten by which he became HRH the Duke of Edinburgh, Earl of Merioneth and Baron Greenwich of Greenwich in the County of London. After the family dinner party that evening the Royal Duke slipped away from the Palace for the bachelor party in a private suite at *The Dorchester* attended by his best man, the Marquess of Milford Haven, and ten wartime companions. The proceedings started formally enough and wound up with the Press photographers being given a taste of their own medicine. They had to pose at the other end of their cameras held by members of the Royal party. The choice of *The Dorchester* for these celebrations was appropriate, for Princess Elizabeth had attended a private dinner-party in the hotel the night before her engagement to Prince Philip was announced in the Court Circular.

97

98

99

97, 98, 99. *Guests of the newly created Duke of Edinburgh at his eve-of-wedding bachelor party at* The Dorchester *included his uncle Earl Mountbatten. The press photographers finished up at the wrong end of their cameras*

The last memory is the official dinner at *The Dorchester* in the presence of the Duke of Edinburgh and the Crown Prince of Norway to mark the end of the XIV Olympiad in London. The President, J. Sigfrid Edström, reflected that the Games had been an unqualified success, that the youth of the world had been given an opportunity to learn that all men on earth were brothers, coupled with the thought that those who had competed would one day become the leaders of their nations. Lord Burghley compared it with the Berlin Games of 1936, of being roused in the early hours of the morning by thudding drums and blare of brass bands parading the central streets of Berlin, and the Reichssportsfeld where athletes played second fiddle to arrogant figures in Storm Troop uniforms, 30,000 selected members of Nazi youth organisations, all with blond hair and blue eyes, none under 5ft 3 ins tall. Totalitarian militarism acted as host to the Olympic ideal.

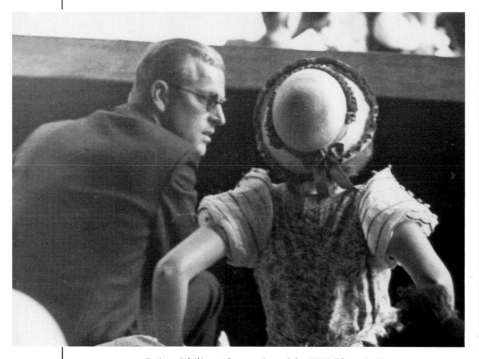

100. *Prince Philip at the opening of the XIV Olympic Games*

101. *Fanny Blankers-Koen wins her fourth gold medal in the sprint relay*

Such contrasts summarise the canvas of the Forties. Among the guests that night in the Ballroom were the cream of the athletes of fifty-nine nations. One in particular I recall, Fanny Blankers-Koen, the outstanding figure of the Games. Her vivid orange shorts, straggling flaxen hair and powerful stride had become a familiar sight. By winning four gold medals the Dutch girl had equalled the record of Jesse Owens in 1936. When the banquet ended someone remarked it was an impressive final touch. The Olympic flag had been lowered, the Olympic flame extinguished, the Games were over, the speeches had sounded the right note. At such moments the words of George Borrow seemed appropriate: 'Fame is a glorious thing, though it lasts only for a day.'

Guests of Distinction

W.H. Auden

W.H. Auden could be reticent, almost moody, but reacted quickly to the environment. If the company was on the same wavelength, discussion sparkled; otherwise he remained morose. He was surprisingly sensitive to imagined rebuffs and did not hide his disappointment at not being offered the Poet Laureateship when Cecil Day Lewis died. He was also unhappy when, after accepting the offer by Christ Church of a grace-and-favour cottage in the grounds, he discovered that the Oxford he enjoyed when Professor of Poetry had changed. He said it was a mistake to go back. It is impossible to recapture hours that have been and can never be again. 'You can never return, not in the guise you imagine. Those who do so murder their memories.' It did so in Auden's case.

Occasionally Auden would visit *The Dorchester* for a drink or dinner, usually relaxed and happy to talk. He never hid the fact that his personal life had been influenced, if not controlled, by homosexual tendencies that began as a Christ Church student in the Twenties. His very openness on the subject did much to remove any tendency to gloss over the fact. Usually the partners of homosexual writers tend to disappear from sight or are mentioned by biographers only with a certain embarrassment and reticence. Auden recalled that first the overtures were more platonic than sexual, but the urge took charge in 1939 when he met Chester Kallman, a Jewish youth from Brooklyn, at a poetry reading. The physical attraction lasted for a couple of years, after that it became a way of life, stormy at times, between two people who seemed ill-matched. Auden admitted that Kallman's waywardness and reputation for being a predacious pederast became a source of pain and jealousy to him, but the relationship survived. They became dependent on each other, an uneasy liaison tied to a pattern of spring and summer in Austria, autumn and winter in New York. Theoretically it sounded attractive, but reality was somewhat

102. *W.H. Auden
with the author at his
Cambridge home*

stark. Creature comforts exemplified by *The Dorchester* did not exist. His flat in New York's Lower East Side was shabby and badly furnished. Trotsky once lived in the basement; neighbours included dope peddlers, beat poets, Chinese hand laundries and sleazy cocktail bars. I was curious how a poet of such sensitivity could live in such a neighbourhood. The answer was that a misplaced sense of loyalty had made him purblind to Kallman, who admittedly could be a bitch.

Auden's sense of judgement at times was suspect. Possibly the relaxing effects of a good dinner in the Grill made him recall a remarkable incident involving Christopher Isherwood and his friend, Erika, daughter of Thomas Mann. The young lady found to her horror that she was on the Nazi list of wanted enemies. To escape detention she asked Isherwood to marry her so she could become a British subject. Isherwood ungallantly declined, but suggested that Auden might help. For reasons that Auden could not recall, he consented to marry the girl he had never seen. The ceremony took place at Ledbury in June 1935, and she was still legally married to him at the time of her death in 1970.

In the autumn of 1973 Wystan Auden died suddenly in Vienna. He was buried at Kirchstretten. We in this country commemorate him by a memorial stone in Westminster Abbey. He was one of the most celebrated poets to have passed through the hotel's swing-doors. I like to remember him by the graceful tribute by Geoffrey Grigson in his poem 'To Wystan Auden':

> *... there was a Time
> I recall — when you were not. Once more
> you are not. But time, after you, by you
> Is different by your defiance ...*

Prince Paul von Metternich

Prince Paul von Metternich, President of the Fédération de l'Automobile and the Automobileclub von Deutschland, colleague for many years, bears a proud family name. His relative presided over the Congress of Vienna, created the diplomatic system that controlled inter-European relations for thirty years, became Foreign Minister, and later

103. *Prince Paul von Metternich*

Chancellor, of Austria. Prince Paul, married to Princess Tatiana, daughter of a Russian nobleman, Prince Wassiliahikoff, presides over one of Germany's great traditional estates, the imposing Johannisberg Castle overlooking the Rhine, founded by Benedictines who established a monastery and cellars here in 1100. The link with *The Dorchester* is the Johann-

isberg wine, full and rich with spicy fruitiness from the vineyards that slope in unending terraces to the river. They featured in an elegant gastronomic dinner held in the Terrace Restaurant in 1984. Afterwards Paul asked who was the man who sat near him and never stopped talking. I identified him as Alan Whicker. 'What does the fellow do?' 'A television personality who specialises in verbal description.' 'Not surprised. Never heard of him!' The bespectacled commentator, like Mrs Thatcher, has yet to conquer Europe.

Robert Frost

Octogenarians are usually frail. Robert Frost was an exception. This rough-hewn man with a slab granite face and abundant white hair displayed amazing energy that belied his eighty-three years when he came through the swing doors. During his stay in England, he took the opportunity of giving a few lectures. On this particular day it was in the hall of the University of London, where he received spontaneous acclaim. His conversation in a rich baritone voice ranged widely, unaffected and spiced with ironic humour. Few if any of those sitting nearby could have guessed that here was not only a great American poet who had influenced the work of young American poets and critics, but was also a great American institution. This was what puzzled him. As a poet he despised fashion, yet he had become fashionable. He wrote poems and about poetry in the plainest terms, yet critics discussed his works in terms of the greatest complexity. Looking down at his big black boots, he said that maybe recognition had come from craftsmanship and integrity – at least he hoped so.

His work earned four Pulitzer Prizes, a unique citation from the United States Senate in honour of his poetry, and he was the only American poet to receive honorary degrees from both Oxford and Cambridge. On this last point, Frost remarked drily that, whilst James Russell Lowell had been similarly honoured in 1873, it was in part recognition of

104. *Robert Frost*

diplomatic service, whilst Longfellow in 1868 received similar degrees but not at the same time.

Whilst Frost's writing was simplicity with a colloquial touch, it was never twee. He showed no preference for sardines rather than caviare and did not regard heaven as a bed-sitting-room. That sort of attitude was like free love, a contradiction in terms. He recalled once receiving a card from Ezra Pound bearing his name, a number in Church Walk and, scrawled across, the words 'at home sometimes'! In self-deprecating mood, he regretted that he had never been a real anything, not much of a farmer, not much of a poet, and reckoned his output had been about ten pages a year over a period of sixty years. Liqueurs put an end to such indulgent pessimism.

Frank Leavis

More controversial was Frank Leavis, the enigmatic figure of Cambridge University who split the English faculty into two camps and became the talking-point of every Combination Room. It was virtually civil war in the world of literary criticism. Some academics regarded him as an irritating nuisance, whilst members of the faculty looked on him as the finest critic since Matthew Arnold. His abrasive attack on C.P. Snow resulted in the most significant upheaval in English literature since the nineteenth century. Leavis the private man was unlike the don who blossomed in the glare of publicity. As a near neighbour in Cambridge he would arrive unexpectedly, invariably dishevelled. Ties were out of favour, open-necked shirt, frayed khaki shorts, sandals never shoes, books and papers crammed into a knapsack, and the inevitable tired-looking bicycle. Eccentric in habits, it was no mean feat to get him suitably attired for London. It had to be midday, for he never ate after lunch; at dinner he would look at an empty plate. Other guests became self-conscious if not guilty about enjoying their food. Incidents in Leavis' academic career left him embittered. Real disappointment was failure to be elected to the Chair of Poetry at Oxford. On the other hand, Oxford was spared many a shock.

105.
Frank Leavis

106.
John Sturges

John Sturges

John Sturges is an individualist. Gritty and abrasive, with a distinctive brand of humour, his films, such as *The Magnificent Seven,* bear an unmistakable hallmark of his skill as a director. He has a way of short-circuiting trouble that on one occasion did not work. It began when *Grand Prix* was being evaluated as a film. John Frankenheimer was made director; MGM backed the project; proposed stars were Steve McQueen and Yves Montand. Trouble began over the financial terms. McQueen stalked off in a huff and went straight to Warner Brothers, persuaded them to do a similar film, and signed a contract. Both companies were committed to filming similar stories. MGM were more clever: exclusive rights were secured for filming on all circuits in the World Championship, failing only to finalise an agreement with the Germans on the use of the Nürburgring circuit. It went to Warners. Grand Prix sequences were shot in various countries without knowing how the rival film was taking shape. Eventually John Sturges had lunch in the Grill and asked how the timetable was shaping. I was able to say the project was well ahead of deadline. Sturges admitted they had experienced problems and were behind schedule. Although the exercise had cost Warner Bros several million dollars, the decision was taken to cut the loss.

Ben Nicholson

Ben Nicholson was self-consciously anonymous. On rare visits to London he would relax in *The Dorchester* and appreciate the lack of recognition. In many ways he found the architectural style too formal. He thought the influences of Piet Mondrian, the Dutch pioneer of geometric painting, would have introduced the effect of neo-plasticism, the pure abstraction suggesting three-dimensional space by curves and lines that exercised such significant influence in Nicholson's early development. There was no doubt about Mondrian theories affecting his work, but given full rein for expression in hotel design and décor would surely have had bizarre results. Certainly many illusions would have been shattered.

Sir Martin Ryle and Sir James Chadwick

Sir Martin Ryle's achievements in science and his pioneer work in radio astronomy were rewarded by the Establishment with all the honours in its gift. The list made impressive reading: Fellow of the Royal Society; first Chair of Radio Astronomy at Cambridge; Gold Medal of the Royal Astronomical Society; knighted. When Sir Richard Woolley retired, Martin became Astronomer Royal, the first time in the 300-year existence of this office that the honour had gone to someone not previously the Director of the Royal Greenwich Observatory. Finally he was awarded the Nobel Prize for Physics jointly with Antony Hewish. It was a dream come true, yet at that point everything went sour. Disillusionment set in. The reasons were personal and were discussed during visits to *The Dorchester*. We had a mutual interest in design techniques, particularly the complicated engineering exercises of racing engines, occasionally going to Silverstone to see the finished product in action. Sailing was another of Martin's relaxations, and an opportunity for his designing skills that produced a 16-foot catamaran that he built and exhibited at the International Boat Show.

Such diversions were forgotten in the phase when doubts and fears of his scientific work became uppermost. Some of his achievements were brilliant in the development of radio astronomy and the discovery of quasars. He put forward the theory that radio astronomy could decide between the evolving universe and the continuous creation theories of cosmology. Martin favoured the former and became involved in heated controversy with Fred Hoyle, the argument going in favour of the Ryle theory. Over dinner he voiced doubts about the energy programme based on fast-breeder nuclear reactors. He believed time to be very short and that either through error or a first-strike decision a nuclear holocaust was likely within years rather than decades. He began to rethink his priorities. The reasons for such a change of heart were quite specific; they were not just a personal cry of despair. He felt his scientific researches had been misdirected. Failing health made necessary an operation for lung cancer. In 1984 he died. A sentence scribbled among his papers said it all. 'Our world is one – yet evolution has now reached the stage where as a species we may soon die. We as scientists should be able to see this more clearly than most and must use our influence to change the too limited aspirations of governments.' Over coffee Martin summarised his doubts: 'Our cleverness has grown prodigiously, but not our wisdom.' No one would dispute that opinion, just as the solution seems hopeless.

Martin Ryle's predicament was similar to that of Sir James Chadwick, physicist and Master of Gonville and Caius College, Cambridge, who made a rare visit to *The Dorchester*. Social niceties did not interest him. As a scientist he achieved a personal triumph in the discovery of the neutron and was involved in mastering the problem of nuclear fission. He led the British team of scientists who co-operated with the Americans on the Manhattan Project, finally determining the operational application of the bomb. Chadwick was by nature introspective, but after Nagasaki he became even more aloof and inaccessible. Like Martin, he discovered a social conscience. The nightmare memory of what atomic

107. *Sir Martin Ryle*   108. *Sir James Chadwick*

power can do in war became a heavy mental burden. He envied a luxury enjoyed by Lord Leverhulme. When he shared a platform the noble lord not only had hearing problems, but the subject under discussion was too technical to understand. To overcome his physical disability and maintain contact with the outer world, he had a box-like contraption that acted as a microphone, regulating loudness by a dial and listening ear-plug. The struggle to comprehend was too much. He switched off and enjoyed the silence with an expression of relief. Chadwick recalled the incident, a placebo denied when most wanted.

Raymond Mays

The eclipse of reputation that commonly befalls great drivers as soon as they die has not happened to Raymond Mays. He takes his place among the élite of the old school of 'greats', remembered as a hill-climb exponent with innumerable successes at Shelsley Walsh, holding the record for the Mountain Course and the Campbell Circuit at Brooklands as well as Crystal Palace. He was always a welcome guest at lunch along with vintage drivers like his rival Prince Bira of the famous ERA's – *Romulus* and *Remus*; Kaye Don, the first man to lap Brooklands Outer Circuit at over 130 mph; Jack Dunfee, one of the 'Bentley Boys' with Woolf Barnato; and Earl Howe, one of the best-loved figures in motor-racing whose victories included the Le Mans 24-hour Race in 1931 in an Alfa-Romeo.

In a rash of reminiscences Mays' comments were unending. He enjoyed life in his own

109. *Raymond Mays*

distinctive way, courteous and responsive to detail. One of his achievements was that he lived on his nerves for so long without getting on ours. He was not selfish, but life was whittled to his dimensions with discriminating taste. An incessant smoker of other people's cigarettes, he was known as the chain-smoker who only bought matches. A few days before he died I visited him in Stamford Hospital. Enquiring if there was anything he wanted, the answer was simple. Could I locate any watercress soup like his favourite in the Grill. *The Dorchester* kitchens, in conjunction with Fortnum and Mason, came to the rescue. It was one of Raymond's last pleasures.

Henry Moore

The quietly spoken Yorkshireman, seventh son of a coal-miner, was not the type to attract attention. No arty pose or need of it, for his influence was responsible for the emergence of British sculpture in the international arena of Modern Art. Henry Moore was a national monument in his lifetime; yet, in spite of honours showered upon him, culminating with the Order of Merit, he retained the informality of earlier, more carefree days – reflected in the domestic routine of his country home in Perry Green. I was fortunate in that friendship meant Henry and his wife would periodically dine with us in Cambridge with fellow guests drawn from academic and sporting circles, occasions when he took immense interest in the activities of other professions. As a guest in *The Dorchester,* Moore was more inclined to talk about sculptural tastes and expression.

He was conscious that his work did not appeal to everyone, inevitably for it was meant to be a challenge. If the viewer was unsympathetic, his figures would seem incongruous, large-busted, big-bellied, cavernous, tub-thighed tortoise-headed women lolling about on pedestals with pin-headed men. If that was the verdict, so be it. Moore never attempted to imitate flesh form of features. When I asked why he persisted in certain particular groups, he replied that the formal relationship between mother and child had a continuous appeal, likewise his vision of the archetypal men and women, kings and queens, groups evolved from the days when he read stories to his daughter in which kings and queens featured that somehow opened his mind to wider possibilities. In his time Moore took a lot of stick from biased critics, but it never upset him. When Munnings dismissed the *Reclining Figure* as 'an outrage, fit for the dumping-ground and nothing else,' he declined to comment, contenting himself with the aside, 'After all, you don't ask T.S. Eliot what he thinks of Ethel M. Dell'!

110. *Henry Moore*

The Fifties

I n the Fifties our lifestyle changed more drastically than in any other decade this century. At the time we did not recognise or realise the fact, partly because the changes were so gradual, often against a background of political upheaval. The General Election of 23 February 1950 saw Clement Attlee's Labour Party retain power, but with its majority cut to six. Twenty months later the Conservatives became the Government with Winston Churchill again Prime Minister. It was the time of the Korean war, with British and Commonwealth forces involved, and anti-British rioting in Egypt, factors that underlined the need for a rearmament programme. The first test-explosion of a British atom bomb took place off the coast of Australia. In July 1953 the Korean war ended. On 7 April 1955 Churchill resigned as Premier and was replaced by Anthony Eden, an appointment confirmed a month later by a General Election with an increased majority. Escalation of the EOKA terrorist campaign in Cyprus and Egyptian seizure of the Suez Canal in July 1956 led to political pressure from other countries. British forces were withdrawn. Eden resigned in 1957 and was replaced by Harold Macmillan whose majority was increased to 100 seats at the next election.

111. *Clement Attlee*

Whilst the political merry-go-round held the headlines of world affairs, everyday life in the country was slowly assuming a familiar pattern. Petrol was three shillings a gallon and we still complained. Tea rationing ended. 1951 had the wettest February since 1870. Television licences were raised to £3. Parking meters were introduced in London. Radar speed checks came into use. Unemployment was in the region of 620,000. In their wisdom British Rail closed 230 stations. The Berlin Airlift ended. Liberals lost a record 314 election deposits. Identity cards were

112. *The Royal Coach following King George VI's funeral procession*

abolished. The Queen made her first Christmas broadcast. Hillary and Tensing conquered Mount Everest. Gordon Richards won his first Derby. The Boat Race was called off after the Oxford boat sank. To take our minds off earthly distractions, we had the first-ever pictures of the dark side of the moon from a Soviet spacecraft.

Two events had special significance. On 6 February 1952 King George VI died at the age of fifty-six and was succeeded by his daughter Princess Elizabeth, then on a visit to East Africa with her husband, the Duke of Edinburgh. The Coronation of Queen Elizabeth II was a glittering occasion, further evidence of the relaxing of post-war austerity. *The Dorchester* celebrated by extending the centre wing of the hotel on the Deanery Street side to provide an extra thirty bedrooms and bathrooms, reaching to the sixth floor. The seventh and eighth floors had residential and entertainment suites added. Oliver Messel, the theatrical designer, was briefed to design and create luxury apartments. The Oliver Messel Suite, now world famous, was completed in time for the Coronation. The entertainment Penthouse Suite above it became so popular that an additional room, the Pavilion Room, was opened in 1956, whilst another floor of suites was built on the hotel roof.

113. *Bedroom in Oliver Messel's Suite*

114. *Statue of Bacchus in the Penthouse Suite*

115. LEFT: The Dorchester, *specially decorated for the Coronation by Oliver Messel*

116. ABOVE: *Queen Elizabeth II leaves Westminster Abbey after her coronation*

After the shabbiness of the war years in a besieged island where a drab and bombed existence became a way of life, Harold Macmillan welcomed the change by assuring us we had never had it so good, and proved the point by reducing income tax. When the decade ended the Fifties had come of age against a kaleidoscopic background. *The Dorchester* reassumed its role as arbiter of fashion and luxury. The swinging affluent Sixties were round the corner.

To recall *The Dorchester* of the Fifties in more detail is a nostalgic exercise. It is strange that what is so close in time should now have so remote a feeling. Unlike today, when media personalities are infected with the disease of terminal trendiness, it was a period of personages who had no need to submit themselves to inquisitive questioning by television interviewers. Larger-than-life figures do not need a build-up. For many it would have been counter-productive; illusions would have been destroyed. They were years of imitation: vagaries of fashion created by the Fifties image. Girls modelled themselves on the bony, exquisite clothes-hanger Barbara Goalen, the 'golden girl' of the day. They all seemed alike, with innocent, deodorised good looks, tight sheath dresses and stiletto-toed shoes, mirror personalities identifying themselves with the mould of fashion. Many who came through the swing-doors of *The Dorchester* were laws unto themselves, international figures of literature, moguls of the film industry, churchmen, film and theatre celebrities, politicians, statesmen and royalty. Such eminence was not made of common clay.

One such was Somerset Maugham, a frequent visitor once described as one vast shrug of the shoulders in human shape, an unfair description though he was a rag-bag of contradictions. Even closest friends knew him so well and no further. Many never found themselves wholly at ease in his presence. Like many men of wealth, Maugham insisted on getting value for money. At that time the hotel had introduced roof-garden suites claimed as the ultimate in luxury, creature comforts that cost thirty guineas a night. Maugham considered the charge extortionate. Over dinner one night he got Alan Searle, secretary and companion for many years, to break down the cost. It worked out at 26s 3d an hour or 6d a minute; Maugham felt indignation had been justified. The trouble was he thought in terms of the past. He recalled that when he entered St Thomas's Hospital, a couple of furnished rooms in Vincent Square cost 18s per week. His landlady produced a good breakfast, high tea when he returned at 6.30 pm, both meals costing 12s per week. For lunch he ate at the hospital on a buttered scone and a glass of milk for 4d. I pointed out that the hotel could provide such simple fare, but probably not match the prices.

117. *Somerset Maugham celebrates his 80th birthday at* The Dorchester *in 1954*

John Siddeley, designer of the Harlequin Suite, said he planned it for glamour and romance, with specific personalities in mind. He imagined Marlene Dietrich in it one week, Rita Hayworth the next, and Elizabeth Taylor the week after. Fantasy became reality and applied equally to the Terrace, Audley and Oliver Messel Suites. Dietrich was one of the first. As an actress her magnetism personified unconventional morality in films portraying the women who are shadowy figures in the twilight areas of whoredom. In real life Marlene was surprisingly modest about the success that was to make her a glamorous legend of longevity with famous legs. Danny Kaye, equally unassuming, always asked for the Harlequin suite. He radiated gaiety with a personality that made an immediate appeal and a sense of humour as liberal as an Italian's use of garlic. He once told me that a hotel stenographer found difficulty in keeping pace with his dictation, hardly surprising for his volubility could reach a speed of 250 words a minute. Elizabeth Taylor, a frequent visitor, stayed in the luxury suites with several of her husbands; Richard Burton, not always famed for delicate phrasing, expressed surprise in later years that each conquest had not been notched on a bed-post. The retort is not recorded, but her remarks could be equally earthy: Elizabeth Taylor was and is the ultimate movie star, a curious blending of legend and unreality, the epitome of Hollywood glamour.

Other recalled vignettes include Joan Greenwood, the diminutive blonde whose intriguing voice was like a champagne gargle; James Stewart, who whittled life to his dimensions with discriminating taste, though at times he seemed almost work-bound. Gary Cooper, the lead archetypal American who preferred understatements, was always a popular visitor. Unforgettable was the delicate beauty of Vivien Leigh, the first lady of the London theatre, whose appearance could be deceptive. She had what the Lunts described as 'a whim of iron'. Her movements were as graceful as a ballet dancer, on a par with Merle Oberon, whose transcendent beauty and ever-widening eyes seemed to absorb everything. Another attractive guest was Greer Garson; discovered by Louis B. Meyer, she made a comeback playing Eleanor Roosevelt in *Sunrise at Campobello*. During one stay she described how President Roosevelt, on seeing *Mrs Miniver*, had urged the producers to get it before the public as a morale booster.

One personality who attracted attention was Brigitte Bardot, the teenage sex symbol and tonic for a war-weary generation. Roger Vadim, her first lover and first husband, recognised her unique quality. She was a 'natural' for the *paparazzi*. I recall how she swept into *The Dorchester* lounge with piled-up hair, tumbling pony-tail, gingham and jeans with an escort of pretty young men. Maybe her forty or so films were not memorable but there was no doubting her star quality. Peter Sellers, a regular visitor, lacked the inner conviction to remain serious for very long. Alert, moody, highly nervous, chameleon in habits, his lips would pucker with amusement as he enjoyed his own stories. Intrigued by motor-racing, I remember him plying Joakim Bonnier, the Swedish champion, with countless semi-technical questions over lunch. Eventually he became converted to the convenience of helicopter travel, just like a magic carpet, and hoped *The Dorchester* would install a helipad on the roof.

I recall Alfred Hitchcock, maturely rotund with a body like an inflated embryo,

118. *Greer Garson*

119. *Alfred Hitchcock*

120. *Peter Sellers*

121. *Marlene Dietrich*

122. *Sir Laurence Olivier and Vivien Leigh with Noel Coward*

123. *Brigitte Bardot*

124. *Mr and Mrs Gary Cooper*

125. *Elizabeth Taylor*

126. *Danny Kaye*

looking out of the window and remarking that a film featuring *The Dorchester* would be ideal for a murder with so much turf available in Hyde Park to bury bodies under. It had to be that way; his public insisted on gory incidents. Even if he made a film about Cinderella there would have to be a corpse. Otto Preminger was a complete contrast, so unemotional with a sad anonymous face. Not so Harold Lloyd. Of his contemporaries he was the only one to quit the screen when sound came in; he said it enabled him to spend premature retirement in pleasant places like London and the hotel, an ambition easily realisable when his films had grossed over $30 million.

A cross-section of personalities with the Grill Room as background yields an extra-ordinary mixture. Thumb-nail portraits show the range. Miles Thomas, a regular diner, was a man's man: if you didn't like him, you knew what you could do about it. Sir Ralph Richardson was unpredictable: he parked a powerful motor-cycle in the forecourt, then brought a crash helmet into lunch. Sir Alfred Munnings was refreshing: he was like an ambulant cigar in which the memory of old port and gamy pheasant still lingered. Naturally inquisitive, he would analyse fellow diners with a salty sort of humour. Alan Sillitoe I found was an average sort of man with the average man's lack of equipment for coping with sudden success. C. Day Lewis, most scholarly of poets, least complex and uncomplicated, shunned publicity.

Billy Graham was quite different. This good-looking, square-jawed evangelist from

127

128

129

130

131

North Carolina dined before leaving on the night-train for Glasgow at the beginning of his Scottish Mission. I asked why he had booked in at The Ritz; it seemed a strange choice. I imagined that Christ would have picked a Salvation Army hostel rather than five-star luxury (I trust I have not been too generous with the star-rating). Graham agreed his choice might seem rather over the top, but he found it easier to work in comfortable surroundings. *The Dorchester* might be the next. So far there has been no sign; maybe it is a hostel's turn. Malcolm Muggeridge had no qualms about the luxury angle, but equated it with a tiresome habit of self-accusation amounting almost to self-flagellation. Lord Soper, then Donald Soper, showed no such inhibitions: he enjoyed the meal without mentioning the deprivations of Hyde Park Corner. Soper's confidence in spiritual matters was total; he could talk his way out of any heckling and reminded me of a poker player who holds a pair of knaves, expanded by bluff into a full house. The Almighty has in Soper a sturdy henchman.

James Mason made his name on the screen as a master of sadism. Many recall him as the inebriated husband of Judy Garland in *A Star is Born* and the self-torturing paedophile in *Lolita*. He used to agree with Kubrick and Nabokov that the actress should have been younger. In real life Mason was a dedicated conserver of wild life and a pacifist. In the Fifties it was a common sight to see a uniformed nannie emerge from the lift pushing a pram holding his precocious infant daughter, Portland, dressed in a mink coat, mink hat

133

134

132

135

127, 128, 129, 130, 131. OPPOSITE:
Otto Preminger; Mr and Mrs Harold Lloyd with their son Harold Lloyd Jr; Sir Alfred Munnings; Alan Sillitoe; Sir Ralph Richardson

132, 133, 134, 135. THIS PAGE:
Cecil Day-Lewis; James and Pamela Mason with their son and daughter Portland; Donald Soper; Billy Graham

and mink muff, cultivating an expensive taste at an early age. On the screen the creased face of Humphrey Bogart typified the sardonic loneliness of unshaven seediness. After his death, Bogart was to become a cult figure. Tough guy maybe, but in private he could be gentle and essentially natural. I recall one early evening when he had difficulty in getting the hotel florist to understand the flowers he wanted for Lauren Bacall. My sympathies were with the girl: Latin names are bad enough without American pronunciation. One of *The Dorchester* managers, who shall be nameless, confided that a guest who had arrived was the supreme symbol of feminine sexuality. As he had reached the time of life when appetite is often mistaken for ability I was sceptical, until learning that the lady was Sophia Loren. Vittorio De Sica's description was not so blunt: 'In spite of having the usual womanly defects, Sophia Loren is the only really spiritually honest woman I have ever known.' After seeing her, I believed them both.

Three more Fifties recollections. No celebrity who stayed at *The Dorchester* had such a wicked, bountiful grin as the Frenchman who was Mistinguett's partner in the Folies-Bergère. Maurice Chevalier had the gaiety of a youth who had just discovered the facts of life. His carefully fragmented English accent was unmistakable. In complete contrast, Gloria Swanson could be caustic and was an accomplished hand in the acerbity business.

136

137

138

136. *Jayne Mansfield with a* Dorchester *page-boy*

137. *Gloria Swanson with the author*

138. *Lauren Bacall and Humphrey Bogart*

139. *Sophia Loren*

140. *Maurice Chevalier*

141. *Cecil B. de Mille*

No one was spared: Mary Pickford was a screwball, Greta Garbo anaemic, Bette Davis insecure. Even *The Dorchester* did not escape. The Harlequin Suite was nothing like her home in Hollywood where a hundred guests could sit down to dinner. The comparison was hardly apt. In her career spanning the entire history of the twentieth-century cinema, six Paramount films directed by Cecil B. de Mille established Swanson's fame as an international star. It happened that de Mille was staying at the hotel. He was appreciative of the amenities and approved the Oliver Messel Suite, particularly the bathroom, smilingly admitting that he was something of a connoisseur. He invented the screen bathroom; in his fertile imagination, people loved, dined and died in baths and showers. He thought the titillating delights of soaks, suds and semi-submerged sex were more than possible in the Messel tub.

A more personal footnote. About 3 am I was wakened by a commotion in the corridor, raised voices, muffled scream, then someone banging on my door. I telephoned the desk and reported the disturbance. Next morning the duty manager described what had happened. A domestic row had ended with an irate husband shoving his young wife into the corridor, pulling her nightdress over her head, and then tying it tight. His description was almost photographic – overexposed but not underdeveloped. My resolve to respond to any future nocturnal call for assistance has never been tested.

A Pride of Prelates

Arthur Michael Ramsey, the 100th Primate of All England, was something of a contradiction. He was a true man of God rather than an instinctive leader. His instincts were more to prayer, meditation and retreats, but he had some infuriating mannerisms. Questions would be twisted into an academic exercise on polemics. He continually finished your sentence before you had. After a time it was pointless to correct the emphasis. Indulged in excruciating facial contortions when stressing a point with twitching eyebrows, wobbling mouth and cheeks puffed out. Professional in argument, Dr Ramsey was a formidable apologist, but on financial matters tended to be impractical. A meeting in Lambeth Palace ran late: a stubborn financial problem seemed insoluble. As we had to be at a luncheon in *The Dorchester* the session was adjourned. When we left, the Primate soothed three eminent but baffled committee-members with the bland assurance that all would be well. He was confident they would find the money by the next meeting, only forgot to say how.

After the luncheon I asked Dr Ramsey why a large signed photograph of Pope John XXIII occupied pride of place on his study mantelpiece. He replied that this Pope was more loved and respected by more non-Catholics than any previous occupant of the throne of Peter. He envied his simple charismatic approach, a role that never came naturally to him. One of the speakers complimented Dr Ramsey on his remarkable stamina for someone of his years. That was a fallacy the Archbishop encouraged. His patriarchal appearance made him look old. On one occasion I was invited to tea by the Archbishop's aunt in her almshouse home in Castle Hill, Cambridge. The Primate was late as the London train had been delayed. Duly apologetic, Dr Ramsey remarked that he was often mistaken for her father, adding that she was his senior by more than twenty years.

142. *Archbishop Michael Ramsey*

143. *Dean Hewlett Johnson*

Dr Hewlett Johnson, Dean of Canterbury, was an ecclesiastic with a flair for self-advertising and a liking for the relaxed luxury of *The Dorchester*. Appointed by the first Labour Prime Minister to the deanery of the industrial diocese of Manchester, Ramsay MacDonald next moved him to the Mother Church of the Anglican community. As a keen ritualist, Canterbury made a wonderful backcloth. He was an extraordinary mixture, and said he only became dogmatic when discussing politics. The term 'discussing' was academic, on a par with Denis Healey. Over dinner Johnson would never stop talking about his beliefs. He was convinced that God intended him to be the interpreter of the inherent goodness of Communism, like a Gorbachev in gaiters. Stalin was rated a great leader whose policy made it possible for Russians to enjoy a true life-style. Saw what he wanted and no more. The Chinese Revolution was progress, though the Peking student massacre would have taxed his purblind dogmatism.

The Dean was a vain man. At the enthronement of Geoffrey Fisher as Primate of All England, he made a striking figure in blue vestments, domed balding head with white hair, sun-tanned features, wearing a magnificent pectoral cross. In the blaze of television lights, Dr Fisher, in white vestments, was made to look insignificant, which perhaps was not too difficult. One final vanity. Over coffee the Dean told me that in the Soviet encyclopedia he had seventy-five lines against the nine devoted to Christ . . . the inference was obvious.

Martin Sullivan, who succeeded Dean Matthews at St Paul's Cathedral in 1967, was a complete contrast. His appointment came as a surprise and upset traditionalists. He was a New Zealander and the first cleric in this post for many years who had no claim to scholarship. A bundle of contradictions, he was a fluent speaker, agile wit, popular in the City, especially with children, but could not handle the Press. Liberal in doctrinal matters, very Protestant in churchmanship, he disliked ceremonial gatherings, which made life difficult in St Paul's. He welcomed experimental worship in the cathedral but refused to tamper with the Prayer Book. His great successes were with youth. We met in *The Dorchester* on several occasions to discuss plans for a youth festival in the cathedral that was labelled 'Pop in St Paul's'; purists were upset and surprised when the attendance reached capacity proportions. Another occasion that had immense teenage support was a service of Holy Communion attended by the cast of *Hair,* the American rock musical. As a preacher Sullivan commanded attention, but he admitted one evening after dinner that unorthodox success had widened the gap between the cathedral and the diocese. He was not popular with the clergy, but made his mark with a younger generation on the fringe. One final recollection was the Service of Thanksgiving and Blessing which he conducted on the steps of the cathedral before our mobile hospital left for the Grand Prix circuits of Europe.

Joost de Blank I knew when, as Bishop of Stepney, he lived in a Georgian house at Highbury Common. He was no meek-and-mild church bazaar cleric, but a tough prelate who looked bull-shouldered in a purple cassock. It was always stimulating to listen to his views when he came to *The Dorchester.* His interests were so wide, embracing foreign films, American musicals, modern paintings, literary items from American thrillers to Shakespeare; he once edited an avant-garde review, was something of a gourmet, and an addict to fast driving. There was never a shortage of topics. They acted as a safety-valve after the frustrations of seeking answers to the social problems of the dockland parishes of his diocese. He was also an opponent of the death penalty. I recall his comments about a visit to Ruth Ellis in the death cell. He did not go on his own accord but by the invitation of the prison chaplain. It was ten days before she was hanged, but he found her calm and composed. She would not appeal and gave the bishop her reasons. Grief-stricken at what she had done, she told him that such was her love for the man she could not explain her act. It was an inexplicable tragedy and she was ready to take the consequences. The bishop said he had visited several condemned men and had confirmed five. Each man had been reconciled to the thought of sudden death.

Joost de Blank's appointment as Archbishop of Cape Town was an imaginative stroke. Some felt that his Dutch stock would be less offensive to the anglophobic government.

144. *Archbishop Joost de Blank*

It was a daunting challenge that failed. His spirit could not cope with the vicious intensity of South African opposition. I saw him once more before he died disillusioned.

Professor Donald MacKinnon was never shy of making provocative judgements. 'The historians of the Church of England may yet recognise that the worst misfortune to befall its leadership at the end of the war was less the premature death of William Temple than his succession by Fisher of London and not by Bell of Chichester.' It was, of course, a MacKinnon value-judgement, but many agreed that *George Bell* would have been a better Archbishop of Canterbury than Geoffrey Fisher.

The reasons were convincing. George Bell was one of the most significant Christian figures of this century, a world churchman and pioneer of the Ecumenical Movement. He worked closely with Archbishop Davidson, was knowledgeable of Lambeth routine, demonstrated his powers of leadership in the churches of Europe and had seniority as a diocesan bishop. His credentials for the Primacy of All England were outstanding. What then went wrong? The answer in part was Bell himself. He was an unusual mixture. Having served with him on committee work, often returning afterwards to *The Dorchester* for tea or dinner, usually with Lady Irene Ravensdale, for long a resident in the hotel, certain individualistic characteristics stood out. He lacked charisma, eloquence in speech was absent and, incredibly dull at times, he made no claim to be scholarly or academic, yet he possessed immense natural dignity. The German theologian, Dietrich Bonhoeffer, regarded Bell as one of the most influential Christians of his time. Bonhoeffer was hanged at Flossenburg just before the war ended on Hitler's personal orders and it was to Bell that his last message was sent as he was led away to execution.

Another contributory factor was discussed several times over dinner. It was caused by Bell's over-pertinacious insistence in his pleadings for humanity in war and controversial speeches against obliteration bombing. In his opinion indiscriminate use of atomic bombs made a mockery of the distinction between a just and unjust war. When Temple died, Bell's name was put forward to Churchill by Halifax as a possible successor, but it seemed that a Christian who took an unpopular stand had committed an unpardonable offence. Bell expressed surprise that the Crown advisor could be so vindictive when he had acted as his conscience dictated. The Church was denied an Archbishop who might have succeeded where many succeeding primates have failed.

Durham has had a chequered career in its choice of prelates. The present maverick bishop has outraged both clergy and laity by flaunting his intellectual limitations. A previous choice, Dr Hensley Henson, liked to hit the headlines without adding to the chaotic state of doctrinal and moral theology in the Established Church. He was an entertaining speaker though hardly a persuasive advocate. More often than not members flocked into the Upper House of Convocation when he rose, listened to him with delighted cheers and laughter, then voted solidly on the other side. This never ruffled him; in fact, he expected it. He decried false modesty and quoted as an example his classic autobiography *Memoirs of an Unimportant Life*, in two substantial volumes. In contrast to the turbulent bishops

145. Archbishop and Mrs William Temple

this See attracts, *Cyril Alington,* Dean of Durham, was a gentle relief. He told me, again over tea, that he had at last achieved real fame. Every morning he tackled *The Times* crossword. That particular day one clue had been elusive until he realised it was his own name. Such was the seal of recognition.

Some years ago my guest was a somewhat rotund man wearing plain-rimmed glasses. He looked a good trencherman. There was no doubting his ability to enjoy himself, occasionally unleashing a body-shaking laugh that was infectious. The head waiter tactfully whispered to me that perhaps the robust mirth might be modified if only for the sake of other diners. On leaving after the meal I introduced my guest to the restaurant manager – he was *William Temple,* Archbishop of Canterbury, who said he felt duly rebuked!

The Sixties

THERE was about the Swinging Sixties a sense of freshness. London had become the swinging capital of material affluence, a new aristocracy emerging which required as credentials a classless life-style and unfettered youth in which flower power, free love, long hair and waif-like appearance became the trademark. Status symbols were the name of the game. It was a milieu foreign to Park Lane, more at home in King's Road, Chelsea, yet segments of the mood invaded *The Dorchester*. The deafening beat of the Beatles invaded the ballroom with its frenetic harmonic singing, the irreverent influence of George Harrison, Paul McCartney, John Lennon and Ringo Starr. Temperamentally they were rangy and individualistic with possibly McCartney the most talented; Lennon, who visited the hotel with Yoko Ono, decidedly eccentric; Starr likeable but unpredictable, as I found to my cost. Accompanied by his then wife, Maureen, they were

146. *Harold Wilson and the Beatles at a Variety Club lunch at* The Dorchester

guests at an official luncheon, not in *The Dorchester* but the Hotel de Paris, Monte Carlo. The menu would have done justice to the imagination of Mosimann, but did not appeal. Ringo wanted chips and peas and a strong cup of tea. The request was translated into *pommes frites, petits pois à la français* and mint tea. Convention was preserved.

Personalities of the Sixties were thick on the ground. Virtually all were seen at one time or another at *The Dorchester*. Twiggy was perhaps the image of the decade. Wide-eyed, pale, orphan-boy alertness, the starved child-woman, Cockney accent, unsophisticated and vulnerable, half-innocent, half-wanton, she cornered the market. Jean Shrimpton was another. A fashion model at the top of a highly competitive tree, chameleon expressions, blown-back hair and endless legs made her a valuable property. Mark McCormack came into the sitting-room, picked up a glossy magazine, looked at the beauty on the cover,

147. *George Harrison, Cynthia and John Lennon, Ringo and Maureen Starr*   148. *Françoise Hardy*

and identified Jean as one of his girls – such is the clientèle of promotion entrepreneurs. Appearances were all-important. In France the norm of the Sixties was typified by Françoise Hardy. Like Twiggy, she was tall, thin, with thick black hair framing a beautiful face, vibrant green-grey eyes. She wrote all her own songs, played a guitar as she sang the ballads with winsome simplicity. The MGM film *Grand Prix* confirmed the quality of her acting, but the effect was always low-beat. Conversation over meals was usually quiet but invariably thoughtful. She seemed to light up in front of the camera.

It was with such girls in mind that a thousand imitations were launched and Mary Quant came into her own. Skinny clothes for skinny girls, a generation of youth that needed to express itself on its own terms. Mary Quant was ideal for the role. She too was skinny, leggy, with pale lipstick, upper and lower lashes emphasised with a heavy black liner, soup-bang bowl, cut heavy, shiny and dead straight. She lunched in the Grill with her tall husband, Alexander Plunket Greene, and talked of future projects. One fact emerged: women depend upon women for their dress appeal. Fashionably dressed women are not interested in the appraisal of men. With microscopic carefulness their eyes are for ever upon other women. In theory, women dress for men. In reality, women dress for women and undress for men. I was tempted to ask whether the rumour was true that she shaved her pubic hair into a heart shape, but somehow over coffee it seemed somewhat indelicate, if not bad taste. The opportunity never occurred again.

Satirists were much to the fore. When *Beyond the Fringe* was tried out in Cambridge, it was hardly considered satirical but mainly May Week undergraduate humour. Surprisingly the iconoclastic, anti-social jokes of Jonathan Miller, Peter Cook, Dudley Moore and Alan Bennett appealed to Edinburgh Festival audiences. It was a success as a cabaret-

149. LEFT: *Mary Quant*

150. CENTRE: *Twiggy*

151. ABOVE: *Jean Shrimpton*

revue. David Frost and Ned Sherrin gave a fresh meaning to entertainment in *That Was The Week That Was*, lampoon efforts that found expression every fortnight in *Private Eye*, an undergraduate publication that printed fifty copies at the outset. The social structure was subjected to shock tactics to make audiences discover their social conscience.

Leading figures in this trend frequented and stayed at *The Dorchester*. The Establishment was fascinated by the Profumo scandal, some censorious, but from the hotel point of view several of the leading figures were always welcome guests. Harold Pinter introduced a note of menace in *The Caretaker*; Peter Shaffer's *Five Finger Exercise* turned bickering into an art-form; Arnold Wesker confirmed his reputation as an anti-Establishment play-

152. *Lady Docker*   153. *Jane Asher*   154. *Liza Minnelli*

wright. Nancy Mitford published an entertaining novel, *Don't Tell Alfred*, in which the heroine was thinly identified with Lady Diana Cooper. Jessica Mitford was more outrageous in her scorn for some undertakers in *The American Way of Death*. James Baldwin continued to dip his pen in vitriol whilst attacking the white community in hysterical outbursts. Desmond Morris added his contribution in *The Naked Ape: A Zoologist's Study of the Human Animal*, a line of reasoning that claimed the terrifying rate of population increase would lead to an explosion of uncontrollable aggressiveness. Less controversial, but just as explosive, was the appointment of Georg Solti as musical director at Covent Garden, on a par with the arrival at the Garden of Rudolf Nureyev after defecting from the Leningrad Kirov Ballet Company at Paris airport.

The visit of Andy Warhol created interest. His antics and serious work earned him a well-deserved reputation for tomfoolery and genuine artistic ability. He mixed a playful brand of lunacy with an underlying serious purpose. Even then, silk-screen Campbell soup tins and Marilyn Monroe cut-outs were not everybody's taste. An attempt was made to introduce the new Brazilian beat, the *bossa nova*, to *The Dorchester*, led by Lady Docker whose interpretation was somewhat free-style. More edifying was the appearance of the folksong trio, Peter, Paul and Mary; outgoing was the barefoot singer, Sandie Shaw; the vocal urgency of Bob Dylan; the doleful, twittering high-pitched voice of the ill-named Tiny Tim. More serious tastes were anticipated by the dead-pan approach to espionage from the chilling pen of John Le Carré. *The Spy Who Came in from the Cold* hit the jackpot, figuring in the American best-seller list for fifty-six weeks.

It was a decade of theatrical brilliance that saw Paul Scofield and Peter Brook blend talents in the production of *King Lear*; Maggie Smith delighting us with perfect sense of timing in Jean Kerr's comedy, *Mary, Mary*; Rita Tushingham unforgettable in *A Taste of Honey*; the distinctive voice of Michael Caine in *The Ipcress File*; Marlon Brando, brilliant but sullen, uncouth, at times a mumbler; John Ford, who could make a dull man seem interesting; Danny Kaye, a woman's comedian; Noel Coward, talented but vain with

155. *Peter Sellers*

156. *Danny Kaye meets old friend Jack Jackson*

predictable habits; Robert Bolt's dramatic *A Man for All Seasons*; the simple buffoonery of Tony Hancock; Peter Sellers, frequent visitor to *The Dorchester*, successor to Charlie Chaplin as the most brilliant comedian, who shared the film *After the Fox* with his wife Britt Ekland; Vanessa Redgrave starring in the English film *Morgan* with that underrated Mancunian, David Warner; Clint Eastwood, tall, cool, very much his own man provided he is a cowboy; Warren Beatty, for some the pin-up of the decade; others preferred Sean Connery as the hero in the James Bond films. *The Night of the Iguana* by Tennessee Williams had tension as gripping as Albert Finney's portrayal of Martin Luther.

Talented youngsters included many who visited *The Dorchester* in semi-anonymous fashion. Their faces were familiar but the name escaped. Jane Asher of freckled countenance; Liza Minnelli, who won a Tony Award at nineteen; Tom Courtenay, who received recognition for the lead in *The Loneliness of the Long Distance Runner*; Geraldine Chaplin's emotional touch of tenderness in *Doctor Zhivago*, when romance meant something with meaning; Mireille Mathieu, who at nineteen expressed the same conviction in Piaf-like songs; Charlotte Rampling and Julie Christie joined Jacqueline Bisset in piercing audience awareness of their talents; Joan Rivers of the abrasive voice and winsome smile also hit the headlines. Richard Branson gave a foretaste of things to come: at seventeen his *Student* magazine printed and sold out its first issue of 55,000 copies.

Another youngster who commanded attention was Fiaimina Ferragamo, who at eighteen assumed the management of the Florentine Company founded by her father, Salvatore Ferragamo. At his death in 1960 he had designed over 20,000 models and held 350 patents. Fiaimina held a luncheon for 200 at the Savoy, and, though legally too young to be an officer of the Company, gave the assurance that the business would continue as before. When asked if she was staying at the Savoy or Claridges, her reply was that, in deference to her mother's anxiety about her staying in London alone, she chose the Convent of the Sisters of the Resurrection. Had the choice been hers it would probably have been *The Dorchester*. It is reassuring to note that the hotel ranks second to the Almighty.

During the Sixties *The Dorchester* played host to a long line of eminent stage and film directors. One such was Jean-Louis Barrault, whose brilliant and physical presence made him the artistic director of the Théâtre de France. His whole life was absorbed by total devotion to the theatre of his country of which he is the doyen. He is an artistic patriot. It is common knowledge that, of God's four archangels, one at least was black. Jean-Louis' manner implied that another might have been French, and that the end of the world, when it arrives, will surely be announced in French from the Théâtre de France. Federico Fellini is like a whirlwind, using Concorde as a commuter's bus. He passionately believes that what lives in the imagination is real. His power to do just that was eloquently demonstrated in such films as *La Dolce Vita* and $8\frac{1}{2}$, but at the beginning of the decade he was passing through a period of melancholy. Ingmar Bergman had many successes, but the movie that stood out was *Winter Light*. Another outstanding one was *Knife in the Water* directed by the controversial Roman Polanski. The urbane, slow-sounding voice of John Huston was deceptive. He knew what he wanted; woe betide anyone who tried to fob him off with second-best. The same could be said of John Schlesinger, more animated in expression than Joseph Losey, who prefers to be enigmatic in his highly selective films. Of those mentioned so far, John Huston's name lingers more as a legend. His tall figure dominated everybody. As a director he had a touch of genius; as a man, an enthusiasm for the married state with a tally of six wives. A glutton for punishment, a story records how at a party a pretty young girl sat on his lap. Huston's wife came across and introduced herself. 'I'm his wife and that woman over there is his mistress. I don't think there's any room for you, honey.' I am not surprised he suffered from emphysema. Such traumas must have required frequent use of the canister of pure oxygen which he inhaled through a mouthpiece linked to it by a plastic tube.

Vittorio De Sica's film, *Two Women*, captured the rage and wit of Alberto Moravia's book of the experiences of a mother and daughter in the turmoil of World War II in Italy. The secret lay in the smouldering passion of Sophia Loren. In 1960 the Old Vic invited Franco Zeffirelli to direct *Romeo and Juliet*. It was a gamble. Influenced by his conception of life in fifteenth-century Italy, the interpretation was acclaimed by the critics. Conventional-minded students of Shakespeare were upset when Zeffirelli turned the lovers into a pair of wild teenagers living it up in a Verona swarming with Capulet and Montague Teddy boys. His retort pointed out that emotionally the Renaissance had a great deal in common with our own time. He then became absorbed by the problems of the middle class during the Renaissance, a subject he believed to be admirably suited for a film. His script became *The Taming of the Shrew*, his stars Elizabeth Taylor and Richard Burton, the venue Rome. After the Royal Command World Première attended by Princess Margaret, the Burtons gave a Supper Dance in *The Dorchester*'s Terrace Restaurant, an occasion that coincided with the eve of Elizabeth's birthday. Guests included all Richard's brothers and sisters with their respective families and friends. At midnight the birthday cake was wheeled in. The singing of Happy Birthday was in Welsh. This was but one of many personal functions enjoyed by the Burtons at *The Dorchester*. When in London it was their base. To Elizabeth it was like home; to Richard his 'local'. So much

157. *Jean-Louis Barrault*

160. *Ingmar Bergman*

158. *Federico Fellini*

159. *John Huston*

161. *Roman Polanski*

happened to them in the hotel it formed a cross-section of their turbulent lives. Richard Burton was a man of real power, unafraid of the big gesture, and endowed with rare charm that tended to become over-flamboyant when he was drunk. Women loved him and were not discouraged. He was married five times. Some of the weddings were bizarre, but the brides always looked lovely. Suzy, former wife of James Hunt, I knew from motor-racing days. She succeeded in bringing him back to self-respecting health after a wearisome spell of trying to solve a drink problem. It was never fully cured. His last wife, Sally Hay, whom he met on the set of *Wagner* in Austria and married in Las Vegas, was twenty-two years younger, but the age-gap seemed not to matter; the marriage worked. A week before he died we met in *The Dorchester*. I found him leaner, fitter and alert. Some years earlier Richard had accepted my invitation to act as a patron on the Jim Clark Foundation and always wanted to know of the Foundation research projects. It became a routine discussion whenever he was in this country.

His last marriage was different, for Sally was unlike his usual type. Clearly they were happy. She was good for him. His sudden death was a terrible shock, but she responded to

162. *Elizabeth Taylor and Richard Burton at* The Dorchester

163. *Elizabeth dancing with Rudolf Nureyev*

his whimsical humour up to the very end. He won a bet made with his old friends, Peter O'Toole and Stanley Baker (who predeceased him), that no one would see him without at least one item of clothing that was red. Sally chose a jacket, polo-necked sweater and trousers all red, so in death he had the last laugh.

Without in any way detracting from his obvious love for Sally, there was never anyone like Elizabeth Taylor, the Cleopatra to his Antony. They had differences and violent rows, the relationship was volatile, almost volcanic, anything could happen and often did. At times his repartee was lusty, particularly on the size of Elizabeth's 'rump'. Once over drinks with a group that included Alistair MacLean, someone recalled how the artist who painted Helen of Troy used five young women as models to produce a synthetic ideal of beauty by taking the arms of one model, the shoulders of another, the breasts of a third, and so on. Richard applied a similar synthetic model of his wife with relevant parts recalled from memory, but ended by saying he preferred the statue of Venus Kallipyges, better known as the Venus of the Beautiful Buttocks.

A long-standing friend was Nevill Coghill, Merton Professor of English Literature at Oxford University. He called Burton a genius on the strength of a University production of Shakespeare. It was a spontaneous evaluation not far from the truth. Once over dinner he summarised the assessment: '. . . a natural extrovert with great gifts that needed the theatre as an auditorium: complex, impressive presence, strong personality, controlled energy, brilliant technique in theatrical effect, matchless voice, penetrating candour, infectious humour. Such qualities should have moulded the genius he had perceived, but promise fell short through gnawing flaws like domestic traumas and a drinking problem. Heroic and tragic roles came natural on the stage. In private life self-destructive forces were just as intense.'

164. *Elizabeth Taylor leaves the hotel*   165. *Elizabeth Taylor with the author*

It has been said that Elizabeth Taylor might have saved him, but the intensity of their combined emotional natures proved too much. Two such turbulent creatures could never blend for long. When they were together in *The Dorchester* I felt on many occasions the atmospheric tension. It quivered in the air like an exposed live wire. Human electronics defy control. In the case of Richard, its lacerating effect cut short a man of real power endowed with the gift of the gods.

Elizabeth Taylor's career has followed a course-pattern of several marriages, divorces and tragedies, a compound of legend and unreality in keeping with the fantasy world of a movie star, except that in Elizabeth's case most of it is true. Her way of life has meant never being off stage. She neither refuses nor insists on showing off; it just happens. She has no private personality, everything is public and open daily. Her imagination, free from the shackles of ordinary people, moves in a different world. Thoroughly spoilt, Elizabeth has collected husbands, diamonds and success as a matter of course. Only illness and death have denied her whims. Against this turbulent background, Elizabeth is a megastar who since eight years of age has only had an identity as an actress, or, more accurately, a public personality. For better or worse, her entire life has been devoted to living a dream peculiar to her time and place, a compound of legend and unreality, an inextricable tangle of the real and the unreal which she, least of all, seems capable of sorting out. She is a survivor. The tally of near-disaster reads like a black catalogue: slipped disc, tachyxardites, pneumonia, tracheotomy scar on her neck, plus more than twenty operations. Every time Elizabeth came through in regal fashion. The Burton–Taylor saga had many rare peaks, flamboyant gestures like his present of a twin-jet Hawker Siddeley executive aircraft christened *The Elizabeth* at a cost of one million dollars, and fabulous diamonds that included the 33.19-carat Krupp diamond as a birthday present.

Not to be outdone, Elizabeth reciprocated with a present of a helicopter valued at more than £200,000.

This emphasis on wealth underlined a luncheon party to which Jean and I were invited by Walter and Elizabeth Hayes. Walter was Vice-President of Ford in Europe; it was therefore appropriate that Cristina, wife of Henry Ford, should be at the table. Next to me sat Elizabeth Taylor. The two women faced each other with thoughts they almost kept to themselves. Elizabeth was then proof that a woman can be big and still be sexy, a point that Richard Burton never tired of making, which invariably brought a cutting retort of being contentedly enslaved by what Ben Jonson called 'the fury of gullet and groin'. Trivialities were discussed with earnest insincerity. When the meal ended, honours were even.

It would be misleading to suggest that *The Dorchester* was preoccupied with cosseting the rich and famous. Everyday routine had its quota of idiosyncratic behaviour. Sir Malcolm Sargent enjoying a drink with a budgerigar, Hughie III, sitting on his shoulder patiently waiting for a sip of sherry, completely indifferent to waiters or the public.

166. *The author with Sir Malcolm Sargent*

167. *Glenda Jackson*

Sargent used to say that the bird was sufficiently intelligent to imitate a stock phrase whenever the telephone rang, 'Of course I remember you!' I never heard the utterance, but at least it was apt. Princess Radziwill, formerly Lee Bouvier, the attractive raven-haired American sister-in-law of John Kennedy, used to bring her pug called Thomas to tea and then declared she preferred the Ritz. The indignation-reaction to the news that the first day of parking tickets and traffic wardens in Central London had resulted in 344 offenders. The near panic when the worst financial crisis for nearly twenty years ended with another devaluation of sterling. Regret at the unimaginable when the Windmill closed its doors. Sexist delight that the first British-made oral contraceptive pill could be available on prescription. Anger that beer went up one penny a pint to 1/7d. Agreement with Enoch Powell's warning that immigrants could change the character of England. The fact that Neil Armstrong had become the first man to set foot on the moon.

With strong personalites you tend to see the world through their eyes. Sir Malcolm Campbell was of their number. Passionately keen on motor-racing, he won over 400 trophies and became the first man to travel over 150 mph. He was a regular *Dorchester* visitor like his son Donald, also fascinated by speed. As a family we were responsible for the design of both Bluebird I and II, as well as contributing to the financing of the land-speed record. Donald was superstitious and believed he was in contact with his late father. Nothing shook that conviction. Reaching agreement with Donald over financial matters could be troublesome. Protracted disagreement was amicably resolved over lunch, papers were about to be signed, when Donald announced he had been in touch with his father who advised against settlement. The impasse was cleared when I suggested it must have been a wrong number.

No survey of the impact of the Sixties on *The Dorchester* would be complete without recalling some of the beautiful young women who came through the swing-doors. Claudia Cardinale, who rivalled Brigitte Bardot, had a unique quality that disarmed all criticism; Audrey Hepburn haunted by Eliza Doolittle; Geraldine Chaplin with a melting, moon-like candour of speech, yet tender and romantic. Entirely different was the capricious sophistication of Barbra Streisand, even more pronounced against the gentleness of Mia Farrow. One final name, an actress neither young nor beautiful, but quite outstanding. Glenda Jackson is a contradiction, with a puritanical streak but who takes nudity in her stride. Looking at her in the lounge, she was a thinking man's Marilyn Monroe without the latter's looks, shape, make-up or social graces. Glenda Jackson has been outstanding

168. *Donald Campbell and Bluebird*

in roles unglamorous or deranged, like the nympho wife in Ken Russell's *The Music Lovers*. Box-office appeal is due to her refusal to be satisfied with anything less than first-class in standards. Given the right part, Glenda is in a class of her own, gaining two Oscars in four years with *Women in Love* and *Touch of Class*. A role in socialist politics now beckons.

To celebrate winning the Formula One World Championship in 1962, we held a Victory party in the Penthouse and Pavilion as a tribute to Graham Hill. Guests were a cross-section of industry, sport and the arts. At that time Graham was universally popular and enjoyed every moment of adulation with a saucy wink. Television highlighted his understated humour, yet, in spite of this extrovert image, few really knew him. In that sense I count myself fortunate for he was seven years with BRM, the formative years of his career as most of his Formula One victories were at the wheel of a BRM, including ten of his fourteen World Championship wins. The man who joined us was not sophisticated;

169. ABOVE: *Duke Ellington in his suite at* The Dorchester

170. LEFT: *Graham Hill*

instead he looked a clipped, well-scrubbed conformist with short-back-and-sides haircut and a no-nonsense moustache. His tactlessness at times was so authoritative that I remarked he didn't know the difference between tongue-in-cheek and foot-in-mouth, but any offence was minimised by an open-eyed manner. As a driver Graham was not a 'natural', like Clark, Stewart or Senna, but with experience he became more polished and mature.

One guest of particular interest to Graham was Duke Ellington. Neither composer nor musician nor a leader in the usual sense, he was a combination of all three, had the finest jazz ensemble in the world, and was acclaimed as the most accomplished composer of Negro folk music. He spoke of the satisfaction gained by achievement. Topping the list in his case were receiving America's highest civil award, the Presidential Medal of Freedom, from President Nixon and the memory of a hit recorded under the title 'Take the A Train'. He asked what was Graham's most satisfying memory. It was not a championship race, but the last lap of the 1962 International Trophy at Silverstone. With a couple of

171. *Sir Winston Churchill lying in state in Westminster Hall*

laps to go the BRM was 9 seconds behind Jim Clark. The last lap began with a deficit of 5.5 seconds, which on a rain-soaked track and against a driver of Clark's calibre seemed hopeless. Graham made a ferocious charge, drove to the limit up to Woodcote Corner, and took the flag inches ahead of the astonished Lotus driver. The passage of time has not brought reassessment. Graham Hill was Britain's finest ambassador for sport.

For three bitterly cold and very grey days in January 1965, Sir Winston Churchill lay in state in Westminster Hall in the heart of the Houses of Parliament. Thousands filed past the coffin by day and all through the night. *The Dorchester* arranged for chosen guests to enter the Hall and watch quietly in the wings. The silence was audible. The service chiefs of staff as their own mark of respect had taken over the watch at the catafalque. It was the most poignant moment of the decade.

Guests of Distinction

Joan Collins

In unwavering pursuit of success, Joan Collins, like Marlene Dietrich, has become an ageless wonder. She is the original with immense dark eyes that widen as they absorb everything, scarlet claws, high lip gloss, the lot. For a woman approaching sixty, her face and figure must give hope to thousands of women. The only image she recognises is the reflection in the looking-glass, in other people's eyes, and she knows exactly what that reflection looks like. Success returned at a time when her long film career was drawing to an uneventful close. Then the unexpected happened. Her sister Jackie wrote two novels, *The Stud* and *The Bitch*, that were turned into films. Joan's comeback was the springboard for *Dynasty* and Hollywood once more.

During her marriage to Ron Kass, who laboured tirelessly in her interests and played no small part in the revival of her fortunes, their London home reflected joint interests. Ron specialised in music; Joan was an avid collector of Art Nouveau pieces that in style matched her tastes. Other items had special significance and recalled her friendship with John and Robert Kennedy. Choice pieces from Christie's and Sotheby's were scattered around. The bedroom was worthy of Alexis, with silk wallpaper, pleated-silk circular ceiling, ornate mirrors, alluring photographs of Joan, an enormous waterbed with exquisite covering, and sauna in an adjoining room. Critics maintain that Joan's face is as hard as a porcelain doll; if she decided to become blonde, her hair would be electroplated, not dyed. Such a cynical dossier does not tally with the private image. At home Joan is relaxed, casually dressed, often in a leotard or tracksuit with minimum make-up. She still looks lovely. Both in private and public her image ignores the toll of time. She remains professional and assured. Once, as our guest in Monte Carlo, I watched her strategy with others. It was revealing. She had the panache of someone dealing herself a fifth ace in a card game with children.

172. Joan Collins

Living in close proximity to *The Dorchester*, both Ron and Joan were frequent visitors to the hotel, particularly when Michael Caine and his wife patronised the Grill for lunch. Her two children by Anthony Newley were motor-racing fans. In the basement was garaged a BRM go-cart that was over-polished daily. At Silverstone the high spot was to sit in the BRM cockpit. Both are now in their teens. Ron's child, Katy, narrowly escaped death in a car crash and was lovingly coaxed back to life by the devotion of both parents. Unfortunately the high-pressure artificiality of Hollywood and the publicity disadvantage of having a settled domestic background proved too much and contributed to the break-up of the marriage.

The Dorchester played a part in a sequence that had a tragic ending. After the divorce Ron picked up the threads in Los Angeles. Things were going well when, unexpectedly, he telephoned in the early hours of the morning, clearly deeply distressed. A routine medical check-up had ended with the doctor diagnosing terminal cancer of the liver, with probably only a few days to live. The first liver transplant had been successfully carried out at Cambridge. I contacted a specialist and made the necessary arrangements. Within 48 hours Ron flew from California with medical report and X-rays and came straight to *The Dorchester*. Examination at Cambridge sadly showed the disease was too advanced for surgery, but the treatment recommended would maintain the quality of life for about a year. The report was grave, but relief of the predicted extension of time made the hotel stay seem light-hearted. The specialist's diagnosis was accurate. Joan's compassion was spontaneous. She helped enormously in the final weeks and assisted with the high cost of medical care and treatment. From the sideline it was sad that the marriage failed when in private it had so much going for it.

Gilbert Murray, OM

Gilbert Murray, scholar, teacher, poet, dramatist and peace crusader, was Regius Professor of Greek at Oxford University for twenty-eight years. A delicate figure but a potent force in international politics, principal initiator of the League of Nations at the end of the First World War, President of that forerunner of Unesco, the International Committee of Intellectual Co-operation, and Chairman of the League of Nations Union for fifteen years, he was a realist and an idealist at the same time. Outstanding of his generation, he was a member of the Order of Merit. Working with Murray over a period of months in a House of Commons committee-room, we would periodically enjoy lunch in *The Dorchester.* In a relaxed mood, he recalled meetings with Presidents Wilson and Theodore Roosevelt; the friendliness of Einstein; of breakfasts with Mme Curie, the discoverer of radium; Edison and Smuts; friendship with Bertrand Russell, George Macaulay Trevelyan, and the young poet Rupert Brooke; of a rehearsal of Milton's *Comus* in which Brooke was a most spirit-like spirit; how George Bernard Shaw told him he was writing a play called 'Murray's Mother-in-Law' that eventually became *Major Barbara,* in which Gilbert Murray and his tireless wife Lady Mary were accurately caricatured. In such a flood of reminiscences food was of secondary importance.

173. Dr Gilbert Murray

Lord Brabazon of Tara

Lord Brabazon of Tara was another man who achieved so much in so many different fields. It is hard to describe his influence to anyone who did not feel the impact of his personality. He was the personification of thoroughness. Much of what he achieved has vanished through the sieve of memory, but he is remembered as holding the Aviator's Certificate No.1 of the Fédération Aéronautique Internationale, dated 8 March 1910. Some thirty years later he marked that occasion by securing a personal car number, FLY 1. He won the £1000 prize offered by the *Daily Mail* for a circular flight of one mile by flying a hotch-potch of a flying machine at an average height of 40 feet. He won the Circuit des Ardennes in 1907 in a Minerva, and was not only one of the earliest riders on the Cresta toboggan run but the oldest when in his seventies. During the war he was Minister of Transport, then in charge of Aircraft Production. One of his contacts with *The Dorchester* was the English Golf Union which often used the hotel facilities. At an Executive Meeting the routine became almost standard. He offered me a cigar, then a cigarette, followed by tobacco, and finally snuff, before accepting the fact I was a non-smoker. His fund of stories was constant, a favourite his reference to the Opposition in the Commons as 'a lot of inverted Micawbers waiting for something to turn up'.

Lord Moran

Lord Moran of Manton, President of the Royal College of Physicians, was outstanding in the medical world. Winston Churchill called him 'a devoted and personal friend to whose unfailing care I probably owe my life'. In the professional field Moran was austere and demanding; in private he relaxed completely. Among students he was affectionately known as 'Corkscrew Charlie', a nickname that amused him but irritated his wife. I recall an incident during a golf tournament at Walton Heath. Without warning the weather changed; torrential rain swept across the fairways. We fled to the car drenched and bedraggled. Shirley took command as was her wont. John Bolitho, Dean of Middlesex Hospital, was standing in an ever-widening pool of water dripping from his clothes. She advised discarding jacket and shirt; his nakedness was covered with a travelling rug secured with a safety-pin. Moran rolled up soaking trousers to the knee and sat in the rear seat. Shirley stopped rainwater running down her neck

174. *Lord Moran*

by donning an old-fashioned bathing cap kept for some reason in a handbag. My plight was beyond aid: taking off a sodden jacket, I sat next to Bolitho. In this damp state we set off for *The Dorchester*. Unfortunately we were stopped by a young policeman and asked to produce driving papers. Bolitho accidentally snapped the safety-pin and left himself somewhat exposed. Moran, anxious to help, got out of the car but forgot to roll down his trousers. Shirley added to the confusion by calling to the officer who looked through the car window to see a sodden female wearing a rubber hat. The Law reacted as if such sights were commonplace. Once inside the security of *The Dorchester*, a change of clothes and a bath restored professional dignity. Lord Moran was again the professional physician, an acute observer as sensitive to human weakness and strength as a barometer to the changes of pressure, but ill-prepared for sudden climatic changes.

Ted Dexter

After leaving Cambridge, Ted Dexter came to see me in *The Dorchester* and asked if I could recommend a job that would allow him to play cricket in the summer and possibly tour during the winter. I remarked there would not be such time left for work; back came the modest answer that they could use his name. This naive flair for self-publicity has never left him. Only once have I seen his ego pricked. At a dinner-party I placed next to him an eminent academic figure. Asked what he was reading, Dexter named Italian plus a discourse on his prowess. Reaction was sceptical: 'Strange I have never seen you at any of my lectures,' mused the Professor of Italian.

175. *Ted Dexter*

Gloria Swanson

Reminiscing in *The Dorchester*, Gloria Swanson recalled *Male and Female*, in which her charms were discreetly shown in a bath without upsetting the censor. She reckoned the gimmick reached its peak in *The Sign of the Cross* when Poppaea, in the person of Claudette Colbert, surrounded by flimsily clad handmaidens, was shown in a remarkable sunken bath filled with asses' milk. Theoretically it was meant to show depraved decadence. Unfortunately the heat of arc lamps caused a cheesy crust to settle on the surface. An unfortunate visitor, mistaking it for a marble floor, stepped on it and disappeared into the unpleasant liquid. By comparison Elizabeth Taylor's compulsory bath-scene was tame alongside Colbert's dip thirty years earlier.

176. *Gloria Swanson*

Louis Armstrong

Drinks with Louis Armstrong always had special significance. He had many imitators but none could match the piercing flare of his trumpet. He made jazz an international language, but fame never robbed the man from the New Orleans honkey-tonk of his unspoilt honesty. He never forgot the early difficulties of his stay in a State Home for Delinquent Children, or the money earned as milk roundsman, rag-and-bone merchant and coalman, and how he made a four-string guitar out of a cigar-box and copper wire. He was always the same, bubbling over with high spirits. His voice was in a category of its own. It sounded like a hoarse shout for beer, yet had a melodious and rhythmic touch. He said that one of his most enjoyable experiences was his role in the film *High Society*, in which he sang with Bing Crosby 'Now You Has Jazz', specially written by Cole Porter.

He was interested in a Mobile Hospital I had designed, equipped and sent to Ghana where it was received by the President as the prototype unit inaugurating the Ghanaian National Health Service. Armstrong said that he felt instinctively drawn to Africa as if his roots were in the Third World. This feeling was shared by his wife, Lucille, who had been with him in Ghana. He said that when he retired and before reaching the Pearly Gates and blowing a kiss to Gabriel, they planned to strengthen this sense of kinship by

177. *Louis Armstrong in his suite at* The Dorchester

Some thirty years with friends. Sadly that wish was not to be realised. He said that musicians often asked what was the secret of his trumpet playing. The answer was simple. All you had to do was harden jaw muscles and develop air pressure to the point where you could strike and hold high C longer than any other swing trumpeter. It sounded easy but Louis was the ony one to make such a grade.

James Bridie

Few people outside the medical profession have heard of Osborne Henry Mavor. He was Consulting Physician of the Victoria Infirmary and Professor of Medicine in Anderson College, Glasgow. His status was high and respected, but it was as a playwright under the name of James Bridie that he was best known. Forty plays appeared under the pseudonym. The list included *The Switchback*, presented by Sir Barry Jackson in Birmingham; Henry Ainley in the leading part of the London production of *The Anatomist*; Alastair Sim starring in *Mr Bolfry*. Dame Edith Evans led in *Daphne Laureola*, whilst memorable biblical plays were *Tobias and the Angel*, *Jonah and the Whale*, *Susannah and the Elders*. No mean record for the secondary career of a Scottish medic. In private he would talk about almost anything except his medical activities, but admitted, like Somerset Maugham, that his work had taught him pretty well all he knew about human nature, for in hospital you saw it in the raw. Only once did this formal professional approach falter. I shared with him a public discussion on the subject of euthanasia. He took a practical and compassionate line, arguing that a terminal illness involving great pain required a humane approach. Provided it was established without reasonable doubt that the case was medically hopeless, it was right to end such fruitless suffering. On four occasions he had acted on that decision. The following morning at breakfast in the Grill, he showed me a newspaper carrying the headline 'James Bridie Commits Four Murders'. It required the tact of Bridie to get Mavor out of an embarrassing situation.

Stephen Potter

Stephen Potter was a specialist of light relief who had to endure the backlash that shadows every humorist. He built up such a reputation for gamesmanship that the most innocent action became suspect. Ploys were expected and usually happened. *The Dorchester* was a favourite watering-hole. Without warning he would invite himself to lunch, but an irritating habit was typing personal letters without spacing. Deciphering was a tiresome business. A warm man, a genial man, he created an ambience in which ludicrous anomalies were believed. He tried to convince you he was a simpleton, whereas he was as sharp as a tack.

178. *Stephen Potter*

Dame Edith Sitwell

Lunch with Dame Edith Sitwell was somewhat unreal. It was like looking across a dining-table at a Holbein study. All the ingredients were there: the dignity of a magnificent Gothic head and features; grey-green eyes peering out of thumbed eye sockets; long shapely hands heavily loaded with numerous rings of semi-precious stones and two large gold Urin and Thurins; incredible hat seen nowhere else; unconventional clothes that defied description. Her appearance was accepted as poetic exhibitionism, and the same might be said of her varying moods: when bored, witheringly cold; in relaxed mood, extremely convincing. Psychiatrists said it was reaction to memories of an unhappy childhood. Her father, Sir George, resented her sex, whilst her mother, idle and bored, wanted a pretty debutante at Renishaw Hall instead of an ugly duckling preoccupied with books and music. Any inhibitions did not affect her appetite.

179. *Dame Edith Sitwell*

The Seventies

EVERY decade has its fingerprints of style. In retrospect the Sixties possessed a certain enchantment, a spontaneity of gaiety that somehow evaporated in the confused and moribund years of the Seventies. It was a decade of moods. The search for self-awareness became a near-narcissistic cult with encounter sessions, group therapy and sexual liberation. Health foods, disco boom and jogging became crazes. The discovery of being a woman, a gay, a lesbian or a black man assumed almost dramatic importance. Fashions changed. Simplicity was the essence of a trend led by Calvin Klein. Yves St Laurent used the loose freedom to launch the peasant look. The tendency for nostalgic revivals overlapped to the point of confusion. Punk became funny rather than fearsome. Split-sided skirts provided glimpses of thighs. Elton John showed off his new hair. Britt Ekland told all. The Wilson years ended. The Thatcher reign began. Ted Heath found solace aboard *Morning Cloud*. George Gale became editor of *The Spectator* in succession to Nigel Lawson. A Middle East crisis became an oil crisis, then an economic crisis. All these happenings affected the social pattern of everyday living. Although recent in point of time, many were quickly forgotten. Test your memory.

In the Seventies Labour voted two to one to leave the EEC. The Government abandoned the Channel Tunnel. The North Sea gushed up its black treasure. OPEC sent the price of petrol sky-high. Decimal currency was introduced. The first wide-bodied Boeing 747 Jumbo Jet landed at Heathrow. The first baby was born from a test-tube. Unemployment rose above a million. It was a decade of kidnappers and terrorists, the mugger and the raper, Despots toppled. There were three American Presidents, including the first to resign. The Queen's daughter married, her sister was divorced. Earl Mountbatten was murdered by the IRA. Men of power died, like de Gaulle, Mao, Stravinsky and Picasso. The triumphant Silver Jubilee of the Queen reflected the warmth of her subjects' affection.

The Dorchester was affected by these events in many ways. There was a marked increase in visitors to London from the Middle East. It became commonplace to glimpse Gucci shoes and Rolex watches beneath flowing robes, accompanied by black-masked womenfolk. Gambling, which the Koran forbids, was the attraction in London, just as Marks and Spencer wares were snapped up even though it had been outlawed by Arab boycott. Lip service can be hypocritical. The Yuppy and Filofax era had not begun, but a new type appeared on the scene. Apart from the financial rewards, it had become culturally and socially respectable to be an art dealer. For the Brobdingnagians of the art world, selling art to a rich, gullible public had become a profitable way of making money. It was a belt-and-braces exercise. If the market collapsed, they could do almost as well selling other commodities. In Bond Street, for instance, one dealer used to run a garage for vintage cars as well as a discothèque in Spain. Another had been a tailor, whilst a third owned a clothing factory. *The Dorchester* attracted its share of gallery owners who considered themselves the impresarios of the art world, though few were art historians or great collectors. There were also the arty poseurs, fringe irritations, who like the importunate widow seem always to be with us.

180. *Maria Callas' fans include Aristotle Onassis after the dinner he organised in her honour*

The Seventies saw the usual round of dinners, balls, receptions, cocktail parties and conferences, yet few had the touch of escapism that prompted the impulse of Aristotle Onassis to celebrate the début of Maria Callas at the Royal Opera House. On the opening night of *Medea*, the Greek shipowner took over the Restaurant, flooded it with cascades of red roses, and invited guests to arrive for dinner at 11 pm. The stream of socialites arrived on time. Unfortunately the guest of honour was missing. After more than an hour of waiting, it seemed that the Greek had been stood up. Tension eased when Callas arrived after midnight with her husband, Giovanni Battista Meneghini. The party lasted until the early hours of the morning, a stuttered start of whirlwind infatuation. Three weeks later the opera singer joined Onassis on board his yacht, *Christina*, along with such guests as Winston Churchill and Giovanni Agnelli. Shortly afterwards Onassis and his wife divorced. The traumatic involvement always had the seeds of potential tragedy. Jackie Kennedy came into the Greek's life after the President's assassination. Callas has left her version of the events leading to his marriage with Kennedy's widow. It was an operatic tragedy that never reached the last Act. That came in a Paris flat where Maria Callas died of a heart attack at the age of fifty-three.

On a par with the Onassis gesture was the surprise party given by Elizabeth Taylor to celebrate not only Richard Burton's fiftieth birthday, but the fact that they had just remarried in Botswana. The actress telephoned *The Dorchester* from Johannesburg and asked that doyen of public relations, Marjorie Lee, to make arrangements, send out invitations, and make suggestions about the menu. With characteristic efficiency, Marjorie

181, 182. *Elizabeth Taylor and Richard Burton arriving at* The Dorchester *for his 50th birthday party*

excelled and asked Oliver Ford, the hotel's consultant designer, to prepare the Orchid Room. It was transformed with gold as the dominant motif. The buffet had Burton's favourite dishes. Arranged on costermongers' barrows were bangers and mash, fish and chips, tripe and onions, York ham and roast pork. It was a homely night remembered by 150 guests. Sadly the marital bliss was not to last.

Few functions had such flamboyant touches. The majority followed conservative lines like the exclusive Garden Society dinners held twice a year, usually about Chelsea Flower time and again in the autumn. This is a private, all-male club whose members own gardens of exceptional beauty. It is customary for each member to arrange in vases specimens of his flowers of special interest, often of exotic appearance, and set them out for inspection on an oval table, King George VI was a keen member. After he died, the all-male rule was waived. An invitation was extended to the Queen Mother, which she graciously accepted and afterwards regularly attended the private dinners, observing the club tradition by leaving behind her lady-in-waiting and her secretary.

Service functions were numerous. They included the dinners of the Royal Hussars and the Welsh Guards; RAF Battle of Britain Ball, usually attended by some 600 guests; luncheons of the Association of Naval Attachés; 68 Squadron Revival dinners; the exuberant dinner-dance given by the United States Navy just before Christmas. The annual reunion dinner of The First Guards Club, a tradition only broken at the first gathering after the Second World War when it took the form of a Reception graced by Princess Elizabeth as Colonel-in-Chief of the Grenadier Guards; 300 officers attended, the Princess and her lady-in-waiting, Lady Mary Strachey, being the only ladies present. Since that evening she has attended many such receptions and dinners as Princess Elizabeth and later as Queen. Another military club of distinction is the Nulli Secundus Club whose history dates from its inauguration in the reign of George III in 1793. The tercentenary of the raising of the Coldstream Regiment of Foot Guards was marked by the annual dinner at which King George VI was present as Colonel-in-Chief of the Coldstream Guards, the first reigning Sovereign to dine with the Club since William IV in 1836.

183. HM Queen Elizabeth The Queen Mother arriving for a charity function

184. LEFT: *Mohammed Ali (Cassius Clay) arriving at The Dorchester*

185. ABOVE: *Bjorn Borg and Mariana Simionescu celebrate their engagement with Paul Grunder and Malcolm Watson*

Sporting functions were frequent. Leander Rowing Club joined forces with the Universities of Oxford and Cambridge for the Boat Race Ball with a ratio-success of 2 to 1 in favour of the Light Blues. Rugby did not feature so prominently, quality being preferred to quantity, although the centenary of the Saracens Rugby Club was attended by 547 guests. Football had dinners given by Arsenal Football Club, the Old Carthusians Club and Fulham Football Club. The AAA Olympic Ball attracted top-liners and also-rans. The Lawn Tennis Association held the Wightman Cup Dinner, which, in the light of our dismal record, might have been called a 'wake'. The World Series Cricket function held in the Penthouse and Pavilion confirmed that controversial topics can be discussed in civilised fashion without affecting appetites. More traditional was the I Zingari dinner attended by seventy-two members. To the uninitiated the name suggests a Masonic or eccentrics gathering; 'exclusive' is the correct description. I Zingari is the name of the most famous of all wandering cricket clubs and was founded in 1845 by the Ponsonby brothers, Lord Bessborough and Sir Spencer Ponsonby-Fane, along with J.L. Baldwin and R.P. Long. To strike the right note, the first match should have been played at Lord's. Reality is more mundane: Newport Pagnell provided the opposition on 25 August 1845. In contrast the Club's finest victory was at Lord's in 1904 when they beat the Gentlemen of England who included in their team such giants as J.E. Raphael, C.J. Kortright, K.J. Key and H.T. Hesketh-Prichard. I Zingari can also claim to have established the Canterbury Week and made possible the Scarborough Festival, both highlights in today's fixture list. The name is unusual – Italian for 'the gypsies'. The colours – black, red and gold – signify 'out of darkness, through fire, into light'. Membership is by invitation only. The Rules are explicit: 'the entrance fee be nothing and the annual subscription do not exceed the entrance'. The next time I Zingari hold their dinner in *The Dorchester*, members should be treated with respect as upholders of an old tradition.

Motor-racing figured prominently. The awards for each season are presented at the annual dinner of the British Racing Drivers Club, the World Champion honoured, and the general public survives the shock of seeing the gladiators of this potentially lethal sport cut down to size in dinner-jackets. Racing helmets should be worn if only to bolster up the illusion of macho-figures. The Ferodo Trophy Award is given for the outstanding achievement in the World Championship, an honour we were proud to have won. Coventry-Climax Engineering Company had luncheons in the hotel for the racing confraternity. It was a great shock when Leonard Lee, their Managing Director, announced that his firm was withdrawing from the sport. Teams like Lotus, Cooper, Brabham and Bowmaker-Lola were dependent on these V-8 engines that had won no fewer than twenty-two Grands Prix and two World Championships. The reason for the withdrawal was economic. In spite of establishing British supremacy in Grand Prix racing, the cost of design and development has meant heavy financial loss. No one could expect this small firm to subsidise motor-racing. It had been a remarkable exercise of engineering ingenuity, praise being shared by chief engineer, Walter Hassan. It began as far back as 1946 when John Cooper built a 500-cc car using a JAP motorcycle engine and motorcycle gearbox in the rear of a chassis built from two front halves of Topolino Fiats welded back to back, incorporating the two fundamental principles of Cooper cars, rear-engined and all-independent suspension.

Champion Sparking Plug was another Company involved in motor-racing that came to *The Dorchester* for dinners and receptions. Their President's son, Frank Stranahan, had another keen interest: for years he was the biggest threat in the British Amateur Golf Championship, on a par with Jack Nicklaus' domination of the Open Championship. It is difficult to contain in a word-picture this player whose skill was incredible even on an off-day. His ambition was to equal Bobby Jones' feat of winning the four major titles in the same year. Frank came close to doing so. I admired his single-mindedness, though I could not understand it. His secret was a unique ability to cencentrate to the exclusion of everything else. *The Dorchester* was not his favourite London hotel. The reason had nothing to do with creature comforts; it was due to the carpets. He found them impossible for putting practice. Claridge's was better: the pile was not so thick. He demonstrated by putting for a couple of hours to an upturned cup on the floor of this suite.

Golfers tend to gravitate to *The Dorchester*. Sir Peter Allen, when Director and later Chairman of Imperial Chemical Industries, registered more than a million miles in his travels. Quite by chance golf clubs formed an important part of his luggage. The spin-off was a delightful book, *Famous Fairways*, written from the viewpoint of a single-figure handicap player rather than the angle of a long-hitting, verbose professional. Charles Sweeney, one-time husband of the Duchess of Argyll and frequent visitor to the hotel, was an aggressive golfer who won a Blue at Oxford University but lacked the graceful style of his brother, Bobby, who became British Amateur Champion at Sandwich. Ronald Alexander, another familiar guest with his wife and family, was a former Cambridge

University captain, Chairman for three years of the Professional Golfers Association and former Captain of the Royal and Ancient Golf Club. Harry Bentley, tireless with business meetings and dinners, never looked championship material, but appearances were deceptive. Playing against him at Hesketh and Southport, his shot making showed why he won the English Amateur Championship, collected the French and German titles, and had a significant role in winning the Walker Cup for Britain against the United States for the first time. The annual dinners of golf clubs are always convivial affairs. Coombe Hill is no exception; it has a tradition of Open champions like Sandy Herd, Arthur Havers, Henry Cotton and Richard Burton as its club professionals. It also has a membership with immense capacity for enjoying the annual sit-down. None had any doubts about *The Dorchester* dinner.

186. ABOVE: *The British Racing Drivers Club annual dinner*

187. RIGHT: *Jack Nicklaus*

The importance of diplomatic gatherings in the hotel cannot be exaggerated. Protocol is strict. At times relationships are fragile. Frontiers are ignored. The gift of tongues is almost obligatory. The list includes: the Arab League; Cyprus High Commissioner; Ivory Coast Republic; Greek Orthodox Community; Jordanian Embassy; Malaysian High Commissioner; Hong Kong Trade Council; Vietnamese Ambassador; Sudan Embassy; Chilean Foreign Minister; East African Conference; Shaikh Ahmed Al-Thani of Qatar; South African Ambassador; Embassy of the Sultanate of Oman; Greek Independence Ball; Embassy of Korea; Emir of Bahrain; Embassy of El Salvador; India–Pakistan–Bangladesh Conference; Japanese Embassy; Iraqi Embassy; Costa Rican Embassy; Israeli Ambassador; Egyptian Embassy; Russian Trade Delegation; Embassy of Somali Democratic Republic; Anglo–Argentinian Society; Embassy of Burma; Venezuelan Naval Attaché; Italian Embassy; Government of Ontario; Embassy of Saudi Arabia.

Although security is paramount, there have been a few embarrassing moments, The heads of two warring states stayed in the hotel at the same time; accidental meetings had to be avoided. Security, internal and external, agreed on a warning system so that when either VIP left or returned to the hotel, confrontation of any sort would be avoided. Unfortunately fate can be devious. Mechanical failure left only one lift working at the front of the hotel. Both men arrived back at the same time. There was no way of giving precedence. The lift is small; both ascended together with token security. Pleasantries were exchanged; red faces elsewhere were noticeable.

Security precautions were stepped up for the visit of Mrs Golda Meir, the Russian-born Prime Minister of Israel who grew up in America before settling in Palestine. From that moment she was identified with the Jewish Community, became a founder member of the Mapai (Labour) Party, played a significant role in the struggle to establish a Jewish State, served as Minister of Labour for seven years and Foreign Minister for ten. During her stay in the hotel, Golda Meir had to cope with Arab–Israeli tension. She looked tired, weary of trying to find a peaceful solution. Not long afterwards, public criticism of the lack of preparedness when war finally flared up caused her to resign disillusioned. At a press conference in the hotel, she had outlined her hopes and fears. She was statesmanlike in approach and moderate in rhetoric, but the situation was too volatile. As King Faisal once said, 'Public speaking is like the sand of the desert: it blows constantly without doing any good.'

Prince Fahad of Saudi Arabia stayed in *The Dorchester* on several occasions. During these visits he set aside an hour in the afternoon to receive and listen to pleas of fellow-

188. ABOVE: *Golda Meir*

189. RIGHT: *Dr Hastings Banda*

countrymen who by custom could claim an audience. The suppliants came by special jumbo jets and were so numerous that congestion in the foyer and lounge created a problem. It came to a head when pilgrims insisted on squatting on the hotel steps, even leaving half-emptied bottles of camel milk with the doormen. The solution was simple. Entrance was restricted to the Deanery Street doors. Waiting-rooms became a clearing ground for the 'empties'.

On another occasion Dr Hastings Banda entered the lift wearing his European hat like an official headdress. Two American ladies dressed for the theatre took exception and suggested that Western etiquette and good manners ought to see the offending object removed. As tranquil as Buddha and about as inscrutable, the Doctor took it off with a flourish, but insisted on leaving the lift first. Not so peaceful was the visit of a VIP that was arranged secretly by the Foreign Office. The identity of the guest was not disclosed until the day before arrival. It was Archbishop Makarios, the Cypriot Orthodox cleric who, after becoming Archbishop in Cyprus, became involved in the conflict for union with Greece and was exiled by the British government to the Seychelles. The Conference lasted for several days at the Foreign Office and throughout his stay the hotel was beseiged by pressmen and photographers, many guests were hostile, and there were protest marches in Park Lane and effigies burnt. Everything was done according to *The Dorchester*'s highest standards but there was relief when the Archbishop finally left. He attended later Commonwealth Conferences in London, but Government Hospitality was tactfully requested not to consider the hotel.

It is only when the list of hotel functions is seen in total that the wide range of

190. LEFT: *Prince Fahad of Saudi Arabia*

191. ABOVE: *Part of the crowd greeting Archbishop Makarios*

interests are appreciated. This is best seen by the juxtaposition of a dozen picked at random. The Bookmaker's Protection Association; The Metropolitan Police Fraud Squad; coffee-meeting of the Church of Scientology; the Guild of Catholic Doctors dancing the night away; Friends of Bacchus Conference, with 900 enjoying the dinner; the Siamese Cat Association that had a hundred members drinking afternoon tea; the Shop Stewards meeting in the Orchid Room; lunch for the Playboy Club, and a similar repast for Miss World; the Lifeboat and Mermaid Ball; the Dickens Fellowship dinner when Dickensian characters came to life; the National Union of Teachers enjoying themselves without Trade Union restrictions.

Other memorable dates were the General Election night dinners, when political fortunes affected appetites; the Golden Wedding anniversary of Lord and Lady Thomas, followed three months later by the Silver Wedding anniversary of Earl Lloyd George; the Society of British Aerospace Conference during the Farnborough Air Show; the correctness of the Roedean Ball; the naivety of the Cygnets Ball. The list is endless, but ones that have a special appeal to the masculine eye are the fashion shows always presented with such professional panache. At these displays men can be made to feel like strangers on a butterfly farm. We make the mistake of looking upon models as human. No ordinary person could face such an ordeal in languorous, sophisticated grace. A model glided into a pool of light, a luxury fashion plate with the inprimatur of a well-known designer. She was the complete gamine. The rhythmic body, tilted neck, provocative eyes, slow caressing smile proclaimed her as the artiste consummate in coquetry. Her face was a magnet, her eyes an invitation. Here was the real Maupassant gamine, the personification of what the medievalists portrayed in stained glass and wood-carving as luxury. Then I thought of those for whom she was deploying her blandishments. I looked round and studied three rows of potential customers. Beside the model they were dowdy. Some might be wheedled into buying, but few would fit, let alone look right in, the creations we had seen. In the West End fashionably-dressed women cast roving eyes, not on men, but at other women. They value approbation of their equals. Bond Street and *The Dorchester* are their parading-grounds, cosmopolitan, self-assured and well-bred. These Shows stand out as the glass of fashion and the mould of form on the platform of salesmanship.

I find as an observer that hotel functions become more interesting if they are personalised, to identify the occasions with individuals. The host or guest of honour is usually a figure known by the media and recognised by the general public, yet often the image you see and possibly know is quite different to their private ego: a duality that can impress, sometimes disillusions, occasionally surprises. I think of a birthday party in the Pavilion for Bernard Levin, the best polemic columnist of our generation. Wicked in wit and easy to read, he always looks like his own caricature. His views prompt a reaction, though he at times suffers from a kind of inverted snobbery; he invariably looks sad. One host was and still is a familiar figure in the hotel: Graham Dowson, who presided over many Rank Organisation gatherings. He is always good value; conversationally without peer, as he demonstrates on *Question Time* appearances; wry wit, erudite, caustic, confidential, ideas at times garbled, but always dogmatic. Only kept in place by his attractive, patient wife.

192. ABOVE:
Graham Dowson

193. RIGHT: *John Paul Getty with Margaret, Duchess of Argyll (right)*

Lord Crowther was quite different. A one-time Director of *The Dorchester*, he was seen about the hotel projecting the image of a remote man, perhaps understandable, for his company could be as stimulating as a glass of cold water. Margaret, Duchess of Argyll, could be seen at many functions, a gracious aristocrat of incredible elegance, with the mannerisms of one who had done it all before. Time has mellowed the shock of originality in behaviour, permutations can be monotonous. Today, defying the years, she is still as attractive as ever, with the rare ability to preserve the fleeting moment like a fly in amber.

Other thumb-nail impressions recall Sir Ronald Howe, a tireless host; always impressed by his vitality, physical fitness and optimism when it came to women. Harry Seltzman was several people in one; ambitious, determined with steel elbows, lightning-quick brain and retentive memory, he seemed anti-sentimental but had nostalgia for the golden years. Richard Marsh is recalled by his habit of articulating every word to perfection. The inevitable presence of Betty Kenward was like turning back the clock. This social diarist occupies a world unto herself; it holds memories of someone who has known the antics of the Beautiful People for six decades. Little is now original. It is just a matter of comparison. Duncan Sandys used to reflect talent as sure and strong as a natural phenomenon. Edward du Cann, emerging from a Penthouse dinner, had the bland manner of a well-travelled oyster. Sir Charles Clore mirrored the ferocity of a success-driven businessman. Lord Shawcross was an unobtrusive visitor. In politics he was in a difficult situation: legal training is something of a disadvantage because it becomes necessary to see both sides of a question. A politician only sees one side and believes passionately in it; Shawcross never managed quite to do that. He matured like a good vintage wine; it remained the same vintage almost as bottled. Lord Franks was interesting: behind the austere manner was a curious intensity. Derek Nimmo at a supper party in the Pavilion displayed a charm of personality that made you forget his appearance. Not so long ago he had a serious heart operation. During a live broadcast called *Start the Week*, he expressed concern about a pending Far East tour in case electronics in the hotels might upset his heart machine. I was able to reassure him by quoting a Cambridge don who had experienced the same operation and his house had every electronic gadget imaginable. The only problem was highly personal: every time he made love, the garage doors opened. Richard Baker flustered. Sir Roy Strong murmured the situation was hardly likely to arise.

One of the most interesting figures was Sir Iain Stewart, for several years a Director of *The Dorchester*, and an industrialist with wide-reaching interests including BEA, Eagle Star Insurance, Royal Bank of Scotland, Beaverbrook Press and the PR company, Industrial Connections. A keen golfer, he was a one-time Captain of the Royal and Ancient Golf Club. He enjoyed a rich life of action. Unassuming, with a ripe Scottish accent, Stewart presided over innumerable meetings, business lunches and dinners, but few knew him well. It was only after playing golf with him on the Old Course at St Andrews that I realised how in Scotland he was regarded as a revolutionary industrialist through his vigorous campaign to reduce unemployment and rejuvenate Clydeside. It was linked with his Fairfields Shipyard Plan, a five-year project that envisaged a labour-saving experiment to cut through crippling Trade Union regulations and encourage a worker's voice in management. The scheme had been tried in England without success. Iain's aim was to bridge the gulf between the bosses and the workers, break down the petty suspicions between Unions. He had carpenters doing painters' work when necessary and Union men sitting in the boardroom. The experiment won the approval of George Brown at the DEA, Jim Callaghan at the Treasury and Ray Gunter at the Ministry of Labour. Unfortunately the plan was never put to a full test. Stewart admitted that a mistake was made by allowing Fairfields to enter the disastrous Upper Clyde Shipbuilders merger. He agreed to serve as Deputy Chairman, given the assurance that the methods successfully used at Fairfields would be adopted, plus the recommendations of the industry's working party. This did not happen. Stewart resigned after two months, predicting failure. The scheme ended in bankruptcy fifteen months later.

It was an imaginative experiment that commanded considerable support, particularly from Sean Connery who was so taken by Stewart's vision that he visited Glasgow to see for himself how it worked. He decided to make a documentary about Clydeside problems, producing *The Bowler and the Bunnet*. For the benefit of Sassenachs, a bunnet is the Lowland Scots equivalent of the flat cap. It was written and directed by Connery in a matter of weeks, but he failed to sell it to Regional Independent Television or the BBC. The documentary was good of its kind and highlighted the progress made by Stewart at Fairfields. Both Stewart and Connery next became involved in other interests with a Scottish flavour, like the establishment of a Merchant Bank, Dunbar and Company, in Pall Mall. In March 1971, after talking with Cubby Broccoli, Connery agreed to do another James Bond film for a fee of $1.2 million plus a percentage. Every cent earned would go to the newly-formed Scottish International Educational Trust, which had Sir Samuel Curran, Vice-Chancellor of Strathclyde University, as Chairman, and Iain Stewart and Jackie Stewart, the racing driver, among its trustees.

Such were some of the Scottish activities of Sir Iain Stewart, the unassuming industrialist and loyal friend of *The Dorchester*. Only once, over a drink in the hotel with Sean Connery and the Earl of Westmorland, then a *Dorchester* Director, did Iain light-heartedly remark how nice it was to own a bank. His tragic death was a real loss.

Lord Rank, who was a long-term resident in the hotel, was a mixture of extremes. It was difficult to reconcile this middle-aged tycoon with the man who bought projectors for Methodist churches and dabbled in religious films. He challenged the Hollywood grip

194. LEFT: *Sean Connery and Diane Cilento*

195. ABOVE: *Lord Rank being presented with a scroll by Sir John Davis at* The Dorchester

on the British film industry, controlled a £50 million empire that included 539 Odeon and Gaumont cinemas, General Film Distributors, and Pinewood and Denham Studios. He financed directors like David Lean and Carol Reed, and films like *Henry V* and the Ealing comedies. It would be true to say that he saved the film industry from collapsing in the Second World War and prevented America taking over British cinemas and temporarily British productions. Circumstances brought about its downfall. The causes were indulgence of spendthrift producers, ill-timed assaults on the American market, entertainment tax, over-production, an £18 million overdraft, and the decimation of its circuits through television. Lord Rank was many men. Without being an idealist, he wished to be one. He believed he had a direct line to the Almighty, to say nothing of divine inspiration. In so many ways he was brilliant, a self-created genius.

196. *Charlton Heston returns to* The Dorchester *after jogging in Hyde Park*

Another long-standing guest from the United States is Charlton Heston. In appearance and mind he has been the natural choice for roles requiring authoritative bearing for such spectaculars as *The Greatest Show on Earth, The Ten Commandments* and *Ben Hur*. In these films his superb manner of underplaying, through voice and a minimum of gestures, have become recognisable mannerisms. It is not often that guests put into writing their observations about *The Dorchester*. Charlton Heston is the exception. In his book *The Actor's Life – Journals 1956–1976* his comments spanned twenty years and make interesting reading. He is still a regular guest. Just before the hotel closed for renovations, he dined in the Grill, but had an interrupted meal having to cope from John Curry's desk with a fragmented long-distance telephone call. Relaxed in manner, casually dressed in a tweed jacket that had known better days and creased slacks, he looked comfortable, no different, with the same physical stature and presence. Charlton Heston is the Francis X. Bushman of the Nineties with certain differences. Heston can act, is sincere, intelligent and immensely likeable.

The decade ended for *The Dorchester* in traditional fashion with the New Year's Eve Gala Ball when 600 guests welcomed the New Year in extrovert fashion. It is always a marvellous night, with resolutions made and broken almost immediately. Not that it mattered. Everyone had. It is an interesting custom, in many ways contradictory. Cynics with a Socratic turn of mind argue that it is impossible to determine the precise moment when a thing ceases to be new and becomes old. Even the heartiest of New Year celebrants in the Ballroom would have found it difficult to pinpoint how 12.05 am on 1 January was essentially different from 11.55 pm of the day before. Nor was it. The astronomers can inform us to the tick when year merges into year and century into century, but time-division is a creation of our own devising. A New Year has no boundary outside our imagination, but nobody that night was convinced. 1979 was on the way out. *The Dorchester* had entered the Eighties, a decade that promised to be eventful in many ways.

Guests of Distinction

Sir Alfred Munnings and Sir Stanley Spencer

Sir Alfred Munnings was always a lively companion, volatile and unpredictable. Indignation would cause him to vent spleen on individuals or schools of thought not in accord with his rigid guide-lines. In-house assessments are rarely flattering, certainly not those that surfaced during a meal in the Grill. A chance mention of Stanley Spencer lit the fuse. Reaction was immediate. Taking a wallet out of his pocket, Munnings scattered several photographs on the table. 'Look at these. The charlatan who calls himself the ecclesiastical painter of the decade, turns out controversial daubs like *Resurrection* and *Christ Preaching at Cookham* in between painting pornographic filth like this!' The prints were undoubtedly explicit. Erotic self-portraits showed Spencer naked, clearly sexually aroused to a degree that flattered his virility, an ego-trip in self-indulgence worthy of Freud. When the plates were cleared, an intrigued waiter raised an eyebrow and moved on.

Munnings' distaste for Spencer was deep-rooted. He dismissed him off-hand as a nasty piece of work, which of course was true, but then Munnings in turn was not everybody's taste. His work was more the expression of personality than the result of intellectual absorption. Either way, Munnings was not bothered. Critics knew what they could do with their opinions. The ebullient artist had a flair for enjoying himself, with an ever appreciative eye for a graceful filly, particularly *The Dorchester* florists who have always been winsome girls.

I never succeeded in persuading Sir Stanley Spencer to have a meal in the hotel. He was suspicious of 'ostentatious service – it doubles the cost and makes me feel uneasy'. The nearest was a drink after a barman had found him a tie. Formality was not Spencer's forte. He was a troubled man. Inner worries and fears affected his work, but he found inspiration in the community of Cookham that provided the material for everyday life.

197. *Sir Alfred Munnings*

198. *Sir Stanley Spencer*

The effect was hardly flattering. The village figures portrayed were nasty earthy creatures, goblinesque, almost ghoulish, not unlike the artist who assumed several guises – village idiot, rebel, recluse, and egotist, invariably obsessed by religion and eroticism, emotionally involved with women, caught up with sexual problems, and infected with a chatterbox complex.

Such is the anonymity of hotel life that those in the bar had no idea of Spencer's identity. He was just a dwarf-sized, bespectacled man, innocuously pallid, quietly sipping tomato juice. Yet in fact he was arguing that all problems could be solved through sexual indulgence; that nothing the Church had to offer, be it prayer or meditation, could match the spiritual renewal induced by the physical act of love. He believed that erotic paintings conveyed something of the purpose of living. His ambition was to hang a series of thirteen canvases called *The Beatitudes of Love* in a building named the Church House, a meeting-place of the sacred and the profane.

In a flash of whimsical nonsense, Spencer posed the question why not hang them in *The Dorchester*, which was a temple of luxury and temptation. The titles suggested something of the overall theme. *Adoration of Girls* formed Spencer's harem. He saw himself married to each of the village wenches. *Sunflower* and *Dog Worship* epitomised sexual activity. *Adoration of Old Men* showed a group of girls in rapture before ten stupid old men. *Village in Heaven* and *Promenade of Women* featured Cookham Village. Others included *Desire, Contemplation, Nearness* and *Worship*. Spencer always denied they were studies of self-identification. Evidence suggested otherwise. The man was small and masochistically dominated by grotesque women.

On reflection Spencer thought *The Dorchester* might be too conventional. Guests might miss the underlying significance and hidden meanings, a thought that was complimentary. Gulping down the tomato juice, he left for Cookham and took the tie with him.

Grand Prix Racing Drivers

For several years the Grand Prix Drivers Association met in *The Dorchester*, always in my suite. About thirty leading drivers would attend. At that time there was anxiety about safety standards, with every cause for concern. Appalling accidents usually resulted in serious injuries or death. The GPDA was the drivers' official body, working closely with the Commission Sportive Internationale and the Constructors' Association. A driver had died when his car burst into flames. The need for specialised protective clothing had become urgent. It was a complex problem. The garment had to perform well under a rigorous set of conditions and protect the driver from the intensive convective heat from flames of burning petrol. The outer fabric must not burn, melt, or become excessively weak or brittle. The garment system had to retain a very high degree of thermal insulation properties for a limited period of time, an absolute minimum of 30 seconds, but more desirably for between one and two minutes. Not all manufacturers were fussy about such niceties. One driver badly burnt had complications through the protective material melting into the flesh. The garment had to be comfortable in a very warm environment for trackside temperatures are well over 100°F (37°C), plus engine and radiator heat. It had to allow full mobility, not contribute to driver fatigue or loss of concentration, with adequate fit without chaffing or skin irritation.

These last two points were put to a mild test. Some twenty drivers spent the afternoon in the Messel Suite on a scorching summer afternoon. Graham Hill, Jochen Rindt and Bruce McLaren sat encased in protective garments of several inner layers of material. During the break for tea one of the floor waiters asked if he might quietly obtain some autographs and finished with a full grid. From such beginnings the sport has been made safer. Concentrating on basic requirements for pilot and machine, horrendous crashes that would in the past have been fatal now end with the driver walking away unharmed. The difference is that, of those who sat in the Messel Suite, thirteen died in crashes. They lived their lives wholly in the sport and died through it. Today that would not happen.

Sir Compton Mackenzie

An evening with Sir Compton Mackenzie was a tonic. He was a prismatic personality, a romantic throwback to the aesthetic days of the First World War, typical of the generation at Oxford that loved the poetical phrase and a romanticised decadence, poses responsible for his early ambition to be a poet. Reality turned him into a versatile writer. As an individual, Mackenzie had a strong awareness of himself, due, he claimed, to being related to half the theatrical families in England, a sweeping but typical assertion. War experiences only heightened this belief in himself, attached to the staff of Ian Hamilton, then Director of Intelligence in Greece. Secret Service work appealed to his temperament. When hostilities ceased, he returned to writing, bought an island in the Hebrides and became involved in Scottish Nationalism. His literary output was prolific and successful, particularly books that became films like the hilarious *Whisky Galore*.

Conversation over a meal was never dull. It couldn't be with so many interests. Listing just a few, he was Life President of the Siamese Cat Club; President of the Croquet Association; the Song-Writers' Guild; the Poetry Society; the Dickens Fellowship; not forgetting the period as Rector of Glasgow University. Life was never without variety. A raconteur and improviser with a wilful fancy, he described the latest novelty. In the basement of his Edinburgh house, he had established an exclusive Ladies Hairdressing and Beauty Salon, managed by two young ladies described as 'exquisite'. Greeting them was an invigorating way to start the day. The second was an old-fashioned dentist's chair dramatically altered. Richly upholstered in red velvet, it was established in the centre of his study; the adjustable swing-table had become a writing-desk; on either side mobile book-rests had writing materials; crowning glory was a mini-bar. After a good meal, Mackenzie confessed to becoming drowsy. When that happened, a lever at the side converted the chair into a horizontal couch, a luxury that might have halved output, but was a sheer joy.

With advancing years Mackenzie's imagination worked overtime. That evening he asked what were my earliest recollections. A somewhat strained memory-shift relived an incident at three years old. Mackenzie suggested I was not trying. By concentrating he could recall quite clearly happenings from eight months onward. He remembered sitting on the knee of an old soldier who had fought at Waterloo. As the battle was in 1815, I suggested he must have been a precocious baby. When he left that night he said hopefully such pleasures would continue in a future existence, though possibly on a less earthly note.

Orson Welles

Orson Welles had a physical presence that was overwhelming, with brows contracted above tawed jowels and eyes bulging reproachfully, but the effect was softened by a voice of superb quality. Orson's career, marred by frustration, was not dissimilar to that of Gordon Craig. Both were viewed with suspicion because of their many skills. Critics welcome a genius who excels in one thing. A legend who stays within that orbit can be reassuring. Orson's talents were too spread and innovative, a huge potential was wasted. Over lunch this Hollywood *éminence grise*, aided by wine, unburdened the woes that followed after *Citizen Kane*. It began when RKO gave him a carte blanche contract as producer, director, writer and actor to do his own thing. *Citizen Kane* was the result, according to many critics the best film ever made, and Orson was only twenty-six. That freedom was never repeated. Everything afterwards was anti-climax, apart from isolated successes sandwiched between cameo parts in indifferent films and voice-overs. He never hid the disappointment, though as raconteur he sweetened bitterness with anecdote. That afternoon an introspective catalogue of gloom was interrupted by Korda's wife asking how he would like to be remembered. Not unexpected, he named the role in *Citizen Kane*. Several years later he answered the same question in more imaginative fashion. He settled for the line in *The Third Man*: '500 years of Swiss democracy had produced only the cuckoo clock.'

199. *Sir Compton Mackenzie*

200. *Orson Welles*

Elizabeth Arden

It is disconcerting when a lady sitting next to you at a dinner suddenly asks whether you use toiletries and, if so, what brand, particularly as immediately before the conversation had been about racehorses, the intoxicating smell of early morning meadows in the Blue Grass country and the satisfaction of winning the Kentucky Derby with a horse called Jet Pilot. The petite little lady had been quite forthcoming about her background. Daughter of a Scottish–Cornish marriage; christened Florence Nightingale Graham; not surprisingly destined for a nursing career; changed her mind; took a dislike to her names; decided on a fresh identity. At that time she was reading *Elizabeth and her German Garden* and also liked Tennyson's Enoch Arden. Doodling with permutations she settled for Elizabeth Arden. The mystery was solved.

Next morning a selection of masculine Arden toiletries arrived at *The Dorchester*, followed by a visit from a charming Arden executive from the Bond Street shop who enquired whether I had received any photographs taken at the dinner. If so, could she have any prints of Elizabeth Arden. As a souvenir of the occasion would I accept a studio portrait of the lady. Curious about the request, I was told it was contrary to Company policy for photographs to be in circulation showing their founder with signs of age or facial wrinkles. The studio portrait had been taken years earlier. There were no wrinkles or blemishes, and as much character as a billiard ball. I preferred to keep the untouched likeness of a gracious lady without the aid of a pot of cream.

Noel Odell and Frank Debenham

Coffee-time in Cambridge is something of a ritual. A popular centre used to be a small upstairs café opposite Emmanuel College, noted for excellent coffee, crisp rolls and comfortable wicker chairs. Cliques formed, most popular being a table presided over by Frank Debenham, the first Professor of Geography at Cambridge and founder of the Scott Polar Research Institute: others included Gordon Manley, President of the Royal Meteorological Society and expert on polar climatology, Noel Odell, and occasionally Edward Welbourne, Master of Emmanuel, an instinctive devil's advocate whatever the topic. In due course these interludes became a memory of the past, but two maintained contact with periodical meals in *The Dorchester*. Both were outstanding in their respective fields, men of immense courage and vision.

Noel Odell was not known to the general public, but this tall geologist and Fellow-Commoner of Clare College was unusual in that many of his achievements were beyond the range of ordinary folk. One of his soap-boxes concerned the fate of Mallory and Irvine. To appreciate the significance of these two men it is necessary to recall an episode in Odell's career. In 1924, under the leadership of General G.C. Bruce, a possible route up Mount Everest was discovered on the North Col at an altitude of 23,000 ft. Dr Somervell and Lt-Col. Norton reached a height of 28,000 ft. During this attempt Mallory and Irvine were going strong for the summit when a blizzard broke. Odell was at Camp V (25,000 ft) and last saw them climbing steadily at a height shown by the theodolite as 28,227 ft, less than 1000 ft from the summit, at that time the highest ever reached by man. Darkness fell. They never returned. Odell believed they died on the summit and that their bodies might have been preserved in ice and snow, like Maurice Wilson, the man who tried to climb Everest alone. Dr Charles Warren discovered Wilson's body and buried it where it lay in 1935. Twenty-five years later the body re-emerged from the ice and was found by a Chinese climber. The Mallory and Irvine mystery remains unsolved. Odell believed they were the first to conquer the mountain.

Frank Debenham was no stranger to such hardships. A survivor of the Scott Expedition, the recollection of those days remained fresh. He used to say that the average man could not imagine the hazards; the fact that Antarctica is a continent larger than Europe, with an area of 5,450,000 square miles or sixty times the size of Britain. The expedition had set off on 2 November 1911 on a round journey of more than 1700 miles without radio links and largely without maps. Beyond the Beardmore Glacier supply caches had to be set up en route. The men were on foot because the dog parties had been sent back. Then came the terrible disappointment when they arrived at the Pole on 17 January 1912 at seeing the fluttering Norwegian flag planted by Amundsen a month earlier. They retraced steps in worsening weather with the necessity to reduce rations, suffering appallingly in the blizzards that never lessened. Then followed the accident to Evans that led to his death through injuries, the gangrene and frostbite that caused Oates to leave his tent during a blizzard to certain death, the weakness that sapped the strength of Scott, Wilson and Bowers when only eleven miles from the One Ton Camp, and the blizzard that never abated for ten days during which the three men perished.

There was an unfailing way of making Debenham angry. Any mention of the Fuchs Expedition invited the criticism of feather-bedding. He would point out that all they had to do was take equipment and provisions for the journey to the Pole where shelter was waiting at an American research station. Fuchs had at his disposal mechanical snow-cats, tracked vehicles, radio links, even plane surveillance. As regards the return journey, once the polar plateau and the formidable Beardmore Glacier had been cleared, everything was plain sailing. Debenham plotting the route on the dining table was so detailed, it was like outlining the M6 from Liverpool, coping with Spaghetti Junction, on to the M1 and home.

Sir Robert Helpmann

Sir Robert Helpmann was unpredictable, with sparkling wit, highly developed ego, and pernickety about food. Anything suggestive of a fixed menu was out of the question; taste buds had to be wooed. Regretted not being taller; superstitious, he added an 'n' to his surname to avoid having nineteen letters in the name; conscious that, as a son of Aries, he was affiliated to the pioneer sign; admired the memory of Anna Pavlova; fond recollections

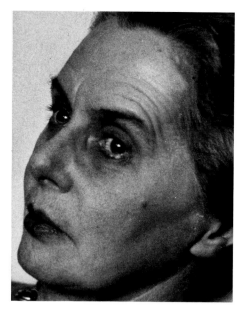

201. RIGHT:
Dame Ninette de Valois

202. BELOW: *Sir Robert Helpmann with the author*

of playing Oberon to Vivien Leigh's Titania in Tyrone Guthrie's production of *A Midsummer Night's Dream*; enthused about Moira Shearer's colouring in *The Red Shoes*, for which he did the choreography; had some odd habits that caused Dame Ninette de Valois' eyebrows to be raised but 'Madam' said nothing. He swore never to retire; there was still so much to do. One ambition was never realised. He had returned from a Middle East tour and described how a visit to Jerusalem and the traditional sites reawakened the choreographic dream of a ballet presenting the life of Christ. Some years later he said it was probably just as well that nothing had come of the idea. Casting would have been a problem. He might have been chosen as Judas Iscariot . . . and people do talk!

The Eighties

WHAT kind of years were the Eighties? 1984 failed to produce the fantasies predicted by George Orwell in the Forties. Thought Police dictatorship did not happen, though television has become all-pervasive: psychologists inform us that the average child of this decade will have spent some 5000 hours watching the television screen by his or her fifth birthday. The luxury of retrospect applied to the Eighties is marred by violence, fanaticism and barbarism. Dreams melted in the cauldron of politics. Failed assassinations were President Ronald Reagan and Pope John Paul II; less fortunate were President Anwar Sadat and Prime Minister Indira Gandhi. Terrorism ran riot from Beirut to Brighton. Thousands of civilians were murdered by Chinese troops in Tiananmen Square. Malevolent IRA bombers failed to kill Mrs Thatcher. Benazir Bhutto became Pakistan's Prime Minister, the first woman to lead a Moslem state. After-effects are still felt from the melting-down of the Soviet nuclear reactor at Chernobyl. Victims of drought in Northern Ethiopia recalled toddlers, bloated and matchstick thin. The earthquake in Mexico City; the death of Emperor Hirohito at eighty-seven, ending sixty-two years reign over Japan; the unexpected parting and destruction of the Iron Curtain. It was a decade that spawned far-reaching upheavals.

At home there was the polarisation of Britain in the bitterest industrial dispute since the war. The greatest bear market since 1920 wiped a third off the entire value of British industry. The scourge of Acquired Immune Deficiency or Aids assumed plague significance. The West Indies savaged England by five Tests to none, but England trounced Australia 3–1 in the Test series. Lord Shinwell made his century, but Ian Botham was not so lucky. Jayne Torvill and Christopher Dean took ice dancing to new heights. Britain's Olympic team returned home from Los Angeles with five gold medals, eleven silver and twenty-one bronze. The Cambridge cox sank the Light Blue boat before the University Boat Race had started. Boris Becker, at seventeen, became the youngest to win the Wimbledon Singles title. We had the coldest January since 1940 and the worst storm since 1703. Those who missed Halley's Comet will now have to wait until 2061.

Throughout the Eighties, *The Dorchester* has been a lively indicator of the social scene, with the authentic flavour of those traumatic years. In an alerted historical memory, events and personalities provide continuity linking the past to the present. An occasion of special significance was the Masked Ball celebrating the hotel's Fiftieth Anniversary. Graced by Princess Margaret, Countess of Snowdon, other guests included Sir John Tooley, General Administrator of Covent Garden, Christopher and Jennifer Druce, Lady Lichfield, Lady Anne Tennant, Merle Park and many stars of ballet and opera. Anniversaries were also remembered: Charlton Heston and his wife stayed at *The Dorchester* for their thirtieth wedding anniversary milestone, and Richard Burton went to town with Elizabeth Taylor on her fiftieth birthday.

203. ABOVE: *Sir Claus Moser welcomes Princess Margaret to the Masked Ball. Mouaffik Al Midani, then owner of* The Dorchester, *is on the right*

204. RIGHT: *Colin Tennant and Anouska Hempel dancing at* The Dorchester

More restrained was the dinner in honour of Björn Borg and his fiancée, Mariana Simionescu. It coincided with the Swede's visit to London for the 'love-doubles' tournament played before Princess Anne in aid of charity. Tributes were paid to the player who had won the Wimbledon Singles title five years in succession. When John McEnroe beat him in the 1981 final, it broke a sequence of 41 match wins in a row. One guest afterwards compared the styles of Jimmy Connors and John McEnroe with Borg, three players who ruled for a decade. Connors was usually in arrears and frequently had problems handling Borg's top spin. McEnroe was the only single-handed player of the three. Whilst Borg looped his shots, lured his opponent to the net and then passed him, Connors was the hustler, punching his shots flat and straining to follow in. McEnroe, supreme master of his racket, had a shot for every occasion. Each had astonishing mobility. Borg was brisk about the court and in his serving, unlike Connors who bounced the ball nineteen times before his grunting service. In retrospect Björn Borg's reign was extraordinary, his nerve outstanding. For six years he showed no sign of emotion. He played all men and all points alike. The bigger the better. But the pressure took its toll. He went, as he had played, without fuss. At that dinner he was as taciturn as ever, but the tension had gone.

The Dorchester hosted the usual diplomatic functions, as well as a full diary of Embassy dinners and receptions. Mrs Indira Gandhi attended the Indo–Britain Association Dinner marking the beginning of the India Festival. After lunching at Buckingham Palace with the Queen and the Duke of Edinburgh, President Mitterrand came to the hotel for the

205. LEFT: *Indira Gandhi is met at London Airport by Margaret Thatcher*

206. ABOVE: *President Mitterrand is welcomed to* The Dorchester *by Udo Schlentrich, then General Manager*

reception given by the French Chamber of Commerce. The Summit Conference in London saw Prime Minister Craxi of Italy and his wife as guests. Entirely different was the extrovert party celebrating Britain's longest-running television series, the 25-year continuity of Granada's *Coronation Street.* The doors of the *Rover's Return* opened in December 1960 and has continued to do so twice a week ever since until the autumn of 1989 when the number increased to three, plus repeats. Several of the original characters had retired or died, but at the Silver Jubilee everyone looked larger than life, maybe a trifle overdressed, but still recognisable, with no sign of the wooden acting of the 1989 Royal Variety performance from the London Palladium. Also joining the party was Alex Bernstein, chairman of the Granada Group, the oldest independent television company

207. *The cast of* Coronation Street *with the iced cake for the 25th anniversary celebration*

and the only one of the original four companies of 1950 still on the air. Unrecognised by the public but responsible for the storyline was Tony Warren, creator of the series; Harry Kershaw, the first script writer; Bill Podmore, John Temple and Adèle Ross, who injected reality into the character roles. The most authentic touch came from the mammoth 4-foot, 1½cwt iced cake – a scale replica of Coronation Street itself.

We are apt in our indolent English manner to take Derby Day for granted. It is a mistake because the race is unique, even though the ingredients remain the same. The race takes about 2 minutes 30-plus seconds. It is remarkable that such a brief span of time assumes such importance to so many people. Isolating a single Derby for special mention is difficult. Maybe 1840 should be nominated for it was in that year Queen Victoria attended the race for the first time with the Prince Consort, a gesture that acted as a tonic for the sport was languishing. From that moment racing became fashionable. Disraeli referred to it as 'the Blue Riband of the Turf'; Parliament adjourned to watch it. During the Crimean War the winner was inserted in General Orders. The Derby has had imitators, but none with the same appeal. Luigi Miglietti and his wife Maria would agree. After winning the 1984 Derby with Secreto, their celebrations began with a delightful touch. They came downstairs and set the Cup on a table in the Bar. The following morning the jubilant Italians sat a few tables away from Robert Sangster and trainer Vincent O'Brien, philosophically accepting that their fancied entry had been beaten.

When Sangster had enjoyed Derby victory with Golden Fleece, their party was held in the Terrace Restaurant. The Derby Day Ball of 1983 was special through Lester Piggott recording his ninth Derby on Tenosa, whilst earlier that year the 1981 winner was again in the news, Shergar being held to ransom for £2 million. Sadly there was no happy ending; it is still an unsolved mystery.

It is claimed, and rightly so, that sooner or later every celebrity of note visits *The Dorchester*. The Eighties confirmed that reputation. The choice was bewildering. No one expected to see Mohammed Ali sparring with kitchen staff when he was undisputed world champion. Sylvester Stallone created a stir among those impressed by brawn. George Scott stayed in the hotel whilst filming *Oliver Twist* at Pinewood Studios. Shirley Bassey was once again in residence as she planned her nationwide tour. Richard Burton returned to complete the filming of *Wagner* for a television series. Howard Keel arrived for a personal appearance on the Val Doonican Show. Charlton Heston was happy in his favourite Suite for the launch of *Once upon a Murder*. Aaron Spelling, producer of *Dynasty*, became a resident and entertained a bevy of beauty. Cubby Broccoli, creator of the Bond 007 films, left for the première of *A View to a Kill* accompanied by other stars in the production. He had been a guest for the première of *Octopussy* at the Odeon, Leicester Square, also for *For Your Eyes Only*, with Roger Moore and Lynn-Holly Johnson.

208. *Ava Gardner and Shirley Bassey*

209. *Sylvester Stallone*

210. ABOVE: *Charlton Heston and Anton Mosimann in the hotel kitchens*
211. RIGHT: *Cubby Broccoli*

Somewhat different was a Breakfast Radio item on the LBC *AM* programme hosted by Michael van Straten. His guests included Marion Hales, Patrick Moore, Mark Hales and Edwina Currie. Topics for conversation ranged from mid-life crisis to healthy breakfasts, subjects ideal for Currie prognostications. Michael Caine on another occasion, in confidential mood with Udo Schlentrich, General Manager of *The Dorchester*, in Anton Mosimann's dining-room, recalled how as an out-of-work actor he once earned money washing dishes in the hotel kitchens, a spectacle as difficult to visualise as Doug Sanders taking a lesson from Anton in the mysteries of *Cuisine Naturelle* by getting down to basics in a graphic and simple way. This happened when the tall golf professional from Georgia and his attractive wife were shown over the kitchens by one of England's greatest chefs. It is possible that those present were unaware that Sanders was the man who saw golfing fame and fortune disappear because of a mistake brought about by tension. It happened in the 1970 Open Championship at St Andrews. The final round had become a duel between Jack Nicklaus and Sanders. Everything turned on a last putt of several inches. If the ball dropped, Sanders would have become Open Champion, a title that guaranteed commercial contracts in excess of at least a million dollars. He took far too long on what should have been a 'gimme'. You could sense tension building up. Inches from a dream and he blew it. The ball trickled past, a cruel end to a wonderful fight.

Still on the subject of golf, there was the occasion when Zenya Hamada entertained Jack Nicklaus, Severiano Ballesteros, Bill Rogers and Isao Aoki in the Oliver Messel Suite on the eve of the First Invitation match at his club, the Old Thorne Hotel and Country Club at Liphook, Hampshire, for prize-money of $100,000, an agreeable interlude before competing in the Open Championship at Turnberry. Hamada's choice of professionals was excellent. Jack Nicklaus was a man who had won almost everything, a catalogue of success almost folklore. He does not age, he matures, with a genius more easily recognised

212. ABOVE: *Aaron Spelling with* (LEFT TO RIGHT) *Candy Spelling, Susan George, Stephanie Powers and Brenda Vaccaro*

than defined, and shared with Ben Hogan the recognition of being the best golfer in the world. Severiano Ballesteros has a cavalier style of play that captures the imagination through immense powers of recovery. Bill Rogers was 1981 Open Champion, immensely popular with the galleries; the gangling young Texan had rare charisma. Isao Aoki is a man apart, with distinctive style and technique. Just to watch him swing convinces onlookers that here is a wayward amateur, yet shot after shot is well-nigh perfect. Criticism is silenced when classical swings are beaten. Aoki's short game resembles a combination of digs and stabs, but the ball emerges with regularity dead on target. Putting is a game on its own. Aoki heels and does not sole the blade of the putter and strikes the ball from the toe of the club rather like driving a car on two wheels. Again results are magic. Udo Schlentrich never hides his enthusiasm for the game. It could be that in a golfing sense he mistakes appetite for ability. What he hits is history, what he misses is mystery. Aoki's style might suit his temperament.

One May afternoon the Promenade had a celebrity atmosphere, with Jane Asher, Willie Rushton, David Jacobs, Stephanie Lawrence, Graham Stark, Derek Nimmo and William Franklyn sitting around waiting to savour tea. It was the brainwave of Sam Twining of the speciality tea company. He organised a Tea Tasting competition with six different Twining teas. The winner was William Franklyn; the reward a Wedgwood teapot. Twining was able to send a cheque to the Multiple Sclerosis Society, as everybody enjoyed the traditional afternoon tea for which the hotel is noted.

An interesting and quite beautiful occasion took place in the Orchid Room where, in a traditional Indian marriage ceremony, Bhagwan Mahtari and Rikha Dalmal took their vows under a flower-draped canopy, observing all the traditional ritual details. Later, guests were received in the Ballroom, flower-decked with an impressive gazebo. More down to earth was the Beatles reunion when Paul McCartney and his wife Linda, Barbara

Bach and husband Ringo Starr joined Yoko Ono for discussions about the Apple Company which handled the Beatles' business affairs. Yoko's trip from America also also included a visit to John Lennon's birthplace in Liverpool and the famous Cavern where it all began. After business matters had been settled, mother and son Sean spent a week sightseeing in London with the hotel as base.

Another favourite guest at *The Dorchester* was David Daniel Kominski, at least that was his real name, but better known as Danny Kaye. This gentle jester, son of a Ukrainian tailor, was immensely popular with the staff. On one visit he was met at the airport by Mosimann and several assistant chefs all resplendent in working kit, a return gesture for his customary visits to the kitchens. Kaye's interest in the well-being of others was demonstrated in his tireless work as roving ambassador for UNICEF, performing for needy children and enthralling them without the help of languages. In more serious vein, he gave a dinner party in the Penthouse in honour of Luciano Pavarotti, the opera singer, and among the guests was Zubin Mehta, the Los Angeles Orchestra conductor, who took the baton for Pavarotti's *Aida* in the Opera House.

213. *Danny Kaye is met at London Airport by Anton Mosimann and a bevy of assistants*

Julie Andrews looked every inch a star at a Press Reception in the hotel when her film *Duet for One* was discussed. Made at the Elstree EMI Studios, her performance as Stephanie Anderson, a concert violinist stricken by a wasting disease, received rave notices. *The Dorchester* hosted a cocktail party in the Penthouse for the publication of the biography of Oliver Messel. Delightfully written, it did justice to this talented man so meticulous in his creative work, as seen by the many examples of his skill in the hotel. With his friend, Rex Whistler, the standard of theatre design was raised to a very high level. His collection of designs, masks and costumes were lent by his nephew, Lord Snowdon, to the Victoria and Albert Museum for display in 1982, four years after his death.

Of interest to cricketers was the Benefit Dinner for John Emburey on the eve of the Australian tour; racing enthusiasts enjoyed the annual dinner-dance held by the British Racing Drivers Club. Engineers were quick to note the juxtaposition of two luncheons on the same day: Rolls-Royce welcomed sixteen guests in the Penthouse; next door in the Pavilion, Fords of Europe entertained twenty-one. Whether any guest found himself by mistake in the wrong camp we shall never know. The 20th Century-Fox reception marking the première of *Chariots of Fire* saw over 300 guests drink champagne to its success which exceeded all expectations. There was also in the Eighties a rebuilding and redecorating programme that meant parts of the hotel being closed for two years. Guests who stayed at times had to endure considerable noise and inconvenience, but in the end it

215. *Michael Flatter, Banqueting Manager, and Willi Elsener, Executive Chef, being introduced to HRH The Prince of Wales at Windsor*

214. *Mrs Louis Stanley at The Guards Polo Club*

216. *Susan George and Clarissa Mason at Windsor*

was worth it. The reopening of the Terrace Restaurant and the new Promenade justified a champagne reception and a *Menu Surprise* dinner concocted by Anton Mosimann and enjoyed by such guests as the Earl and Countess of Westmorland, Lord and Lady McAlpine, Earl and Countess Spencer, Sir Robin and Lady McAlpine, and Margaret, Duchess of Argyll and her son Brian Sweeney.

217. ABOVE: *Lord McAlpine of Moffat with Paul Grunder, Deputy General Manager*

218. RIGHT: *Earl and Countess Spencer*

For six decades the elegant women who graced *The Dorchester* have worn creations of fashion's greatest innovators. Cristobal Balenciaga shaped the silhouettes of the Thirties women and was rightly regarded as the designer's designer. Something of a mystery man, he made no pronouncements, gave no interviews and disliked being photographed. Many top designers worked under him, notably Cardin, Courrèges and Ungaro. The creations of Courrèges made a lasting impact. He launched the mini-skirt and played an essential part in the changes which overtook fashion in the Sixties, an influence as revolutionary as Christian Dior. When Dior opened his luxurious couture house on the Avenue Montaigne in Paris, he changed the face of Western fashion. His 'Corolle' line, which Americans dubbed the 'New Look', was instantly bought, copied and publicised all over the Western world. The success of the 'Corolle' line – best described as a tight bodice shaped into a tiny waist below which a long skirt burst into fullness like a flower – was due to its extreme femininity. Women had become weary of the mannish clothes of the war period and Dior was exactly the man for the hour. His talent never stood still. After the New Look, he created the Umbrella, Scissor, Horseshoe and H & A lines, all influential and commercially successful. He brought back elegance, colour, fine workmanship and a sense of quality to a scene that had been forgotten.

The range of designers is wide. They include names like Yves Saint Laurent, the Emanuels, Bruce Oldfield, Gino Fratini, Jean Muir, Janice Wainwright, Roland Klein, Karl Lagerfeld and Victor Edelstein. The Caroline Charles Collection shown in *The Dorchester* was unquestionably addictive, in total sympathy with the upstyle and needs of her customers. One of the most impressive was the 1988 Winter Collection displayed by

Yuki in the ballroom. Superbly staged, the clothes showed why the Princess of Wales commissioned him to design part of her wardrobe when she went to Japan. She paid him the compliment of wearing his dress on the most important occasion, the banquet at the Emperor's Palace. It was sapphire blue, the colour of the Japanese Royal Family. The Princess added a further touch with a sapphire on her forehead.

Critical appreciation at times is complicated by the Freudian discovery that public characteristics can be a defence against private tendencies. The gossip of the popular Press had made us want to know more about the private lives and habits of our public heroes and heroines. For sixty years Foyles Literary Luncheons have helped to make prominent figures far more familiar. Every month we have been introduced without oversolemnity to outstanding personalities. Some have been more friendly than others, some more politically biased, in keeping with the *persona* that everyone in public life gathers round him, a public image which may or may not be the sort of person he or she is. That is one of the attractions of the Foyles Luncheons. The element of surprise is always there and they have become a familiar happening in *The Dorchester* year. All the guests of honour have their own fingerprints of style. Like most people who experience it they have acquired a taste for fame, and though it may sometimes be irritating to be recognised wherever you go, it is even more irritating, as any actor or politician knows, to feel that you may not be recognised at all. There is nothing wrong in liking fame. The Foyles list is a personal one. It is not meant to be definitive, nor to represent every aspect of contemporary life. It is simply, in vintners' parlance, a first growth from a vineyard of six decades. Every one has enlivened the times in which we live.

The Dorchester has always valued the patronage of Royalty. The Eighties had many such moments. Some were less ceremonial, sometimes private but usually linked with official appearances. Before the war protocol could be very flexible. The Prince of Wales, later the Duke of Windsor, and his brother, the Duke of Kent, set the tone and often dined and danced in the Restaurant. Many of the functions are linked with good works. Princess Anne, indefatigable in her engagements, was guest of honour at a luncheon given by a woman's magazine to raise money for a bone-marrow transplant wing at Westminster Hospital. The present Duke of Kent, equally conscientious in his official duties, attended the British Computer Society's silver jubilee in the Ballroom. Prince and Princess Michael of Kent gave their support to the White Dove Ball in aid of the Royal Marsden Cancer Fund. The Duke of Gloucester accepted an invitation to the Evian Health Awards Society luncheon in aid of Birthright. The Duchess of York launched a Charity Campaign for war on Cancer with a target of £75 million within a year. Princess Margaret visited Harry Winstone's exhibition of jewellery. Princess Alexandra made a tour of flag sellers for Rose Day and visited the stall in the Front Hall. The Duke of Edinburgh, as Colonel of the Grenadier Guards, attended a dinner of the First Guards Club. These are but some of the Royal engagements at *The Dorchester* in the Eighties.

Foreign Royalty were frequent guests at the hotel, usually private. King Constantine of Greece dined in the Grill Room. Prince Paul von Metternich enjoyed one of Anton Mosimann's gastronomic dinners in the Terrace Restaurant. The King and Queen of

219. *Lady Diana Cooper and Joyce Grenfell*

220. *Lord Boothby and Sir Compton Mackenzie* (STANDING)

221. *James Callaghan and Harold Wilson*

222. *Douglas Fairbanks Jr*

223. *Earl of Snowdon*

224. *Earl Mountbatten of Burma*

225. *Lionel Bart, John Lennon and Sir Osbert Lancaster*

226. *The Prince and Princess of Wales with their children at a day of polo sponsored by* The Dorchester

227. *The Princess Royal is welcomed by Deputy General Manager Paul Grunder*

228. *Her Majesty The Queen with Banqueting Manager John Brooks*

229. *Princess Alice, Duchess of Gloucester, the Duke of Gloucester and Christina Foyle*

230. *Princess Alexandra with Mrs Shilling*

231. LEFT: *Prince and Princess Michael of Kent with Mrs Ruth Isaacs*

Sweden stayed in the hotel so they could attend a dinner given by the Swedish Chamber of Commerce. The atmosphere at many of these functions is relaxed, and never more so when Prince Philip ma___ remarks that are often piquant, as when he commented that 'the trouble with senio___ ___agement to an outsider is that there are too many one-ulcer men holding down two-ulcer jobs'!

Every year of ___ decade brought its tally of highly talented people who made their exit leaving us the poorer. We said goodbye to many who were regular visitors to *The Dorchester*. It was difficult to realise that David Niven was no more; that Ingrid Bergman had lost a long and ___ful fight. Professor Glyn Daniel's death came as a shock, a creator as well as a chronicler, enthusiastic about everything, even trying to convince the chef of the delights of his 'Les Poires Salagos', a dish of pears in spun sugar. Alfred Hitchcock, who was planning a new film when he died in Los Angeles; J.B. Priestley, last of the great literary all-rounders; Roy Plomley, who was host to 1790 castaways in *Desert Island Discs*; the high talent of John Huston; the ubiquitous Welsh voice of Wynford Vaughan-Thomas; Cary Grant, who had a deep love for fame – success was his fairy wand; Richard Burton, an adopted resident of *The Dorchester*, a star in a world where stars are a dying breed.

Another frequent visitor with many associations was Peter Sellers. It was while

232. ABOVE: *Richard Burton with Marjorie Lee, then Public Relations Manager of* The Dorchester

233. RIGHT: *Peter Sellers and his wife Lynne Frederick*

staying in the Oliver Messel Suite that he first met Britt Ekland. She was staying at the hotel at the same time; an introduction was arranged. Sellers invited her to see *The Pink Panther* and ended the evening with a champagne supper. Shortly afterwards they married; five years later it was dissolved. His next marriage was with Miranda Quarry, daughter of Lady Mancroft, who worked as a florist in the hotel, then acted as a publicity assistant on Sellers' film *The Magic Christian*. That partnership lasted four years. Three years later he married Lynne Frederick. In July 1980 he made an unscheduled trip to London and was due to join Spike Milligan and Harry Secombe for dinner when he was taken ill. The hotel Sister, Bridget Siklos, and her assistant, Shirley-Ann Bailey, were summoned from the hotel surgery. Sister Siklos gave Sellers the kiss of life; Dr Arthur Unwin, the hotel doctor, was called. Sellers was taken to Middlesex Hospital by ambulance but never regained consciousness. He died peacefully.

There was sadness when James Mason died. He was always a valuable mirror to the many worlds in which he moved. He was many men. Without being an idealist he wished to be one. Behind a rather cool manner there was a curious intensity. He seldom gave full expression to his feelings unless they could be returned in equal ratio. In this he was fortunate in that his wife, Clarissa, could match his moods with love and understanding. One thing about James, he never aged. He is certainly missed. Their table in the Grill Room seems empty.

234, 235. *James and Clarissa Mason*

Guests of Distinction

Robert Graves

Few English poets of the twentieth century aroused as much interest as Robert Graves, none stimulated so much discussion as this flamboyant, pugnacious eccentric. That in itself was unusual. Englishmen do not habitually oppose poets. They ignore them. Graves refused to be ignored. A day spent with someone who resented authority and enjoyed controversy held promise of being memorable. This one lived up to expectations. It began in St John's College, Oxford, a stone's throw from the room where as a student Graves developed his friendship with T.E. Lawrence. Lunchtime in Oxford was too conventional for Graves. He knotted a colourful silk scarf round his neck, donned a floppy Mexican-type hat, collected a string-bag, and shovelled an untidy mass of note-paper, literally covered with firm classic handwriting, into a brown-paper parcel. That was how one of his books was sent to the publisher. For each page written there were pages of rejects. Not for nothing did he say, 'My best friend is still the waste-paper basket.' A shopping expedition in the Oxford market soon resembled a bazaar outing. In the afternoon we left for London and *The Dorchester.*

His arrival had about it a touch of old English masculinity, heightened by the face of a prize-fighter with a broken nose acquired on the rugby field at Charterhouse. He was in a gritty mood and when tactful questions were raised as to the acceptability of the neckerchief at dinner, we decided a meal in the suite would be more harmonious. It was also the chance of analysing Robert Graves the man without interruption. He was a deliberate extrovert and egotist with a disconcerting habit of criticising contemporaries like Yeats and Eliot. Married twice, Graves had eight children, countless grandchildren, and never concealed the fact that relationships with women had always been a factor in his life. His love poems are passionate, sometimes salacious, but never sensuous. I expressed surprise that he had been able to cope with so many difficult relationships. He

236. Robert Graves

replied that, provided you were self-sufficient, such setbacks were unimportant, adding as an afterthought that he had never engaged in unnatural love or slept with a prostitute. On the other hand, there were many women he still found desirable from afar, one in particular that evening being Maggie Smith.

A jug of iced orange juice and a bottle of vodka encouraged gossip and reminiscing. He dismissed as rubbish the suggestion that the time had come for him to sit in the sun and relax. Some writers die creatively speaking at forty. He could think of some who died at twenty-two. In his seventies he felt at the outset of writing. All he needed was privacy and comfort like this, and embraced the room with a wide sweep of his arms. That was why he lived on the wrong side of the island. He could avoid people, unlike the gregarious Dylan Thomas and Ernest Hemingway. Of the latter he was scornful: Hemingway was not in the same league as Lawrence. He was as phoney as the false hair on his chest, always boasting about the wars he had been in, when he never fought in any real one.

Any verdict of Robert Graves had to accept his own evaluation as a poet. He once wrote. 'A true poet writes because he must, not because he hoped to get a living from the poems.' He was successful, but the income came from historical books. He added wryly, 'There is no money in poetry, but then there's no poetry in money either.'

Somehow Graves did not fit into the Oxford scene or, for that matter, *The Dorchester* setting. Just as Somerset Maugham belonged to Cap Ferrat, Max Beerbohm to Rapallo and Robert Browning to Florence, so this vigorous man with a noble head was more at home on the hot dusty road from Palma to Deya. His life pilgrimage to the sun ended in his ninetieth year. Final tributes were simple. Dressed with the familiar neckerchief, the flat-brimmed Cordova hat by his folded hands, he was laid to rest in the graveyard of Deya church. So passed the greatest love poet in English since Donne.

Dame Laura Knight

An artist who frequently savoured the culinary delights of *The Dorchester* was Dame Laura Knight, whose career bridged many changes, subject-matter ranging from sweating plough horses to raucous sounds of the fairground and the horrors of the Nuremberg war crimes trials. She was devoted to Harold with whom she lived happily ever after until he died fifty years later. Each was a Royal Academician and found fame along separate paths. One of her joys was the Oliver Messel Suite. She loved his seventeenth-century garden scenes with mirror glass behind the latticed frames; the double-doors that he painted with attractive floral sprays; the carpet designed to resemble a garden parterre; the pictures in the exquisite bedroom for *The Sleeping Beauty* ballet at Covent Garden; the mirror-lined bathroom with gold-plate fittings. 'It is too beautiful to be enjoyed by only a few.' Laura recalled her first backstage experience during a Diaghilev ballet season at the Coliseum. It opened up an entirely new world, further stimulated by friendship with Lydia Lopokova and Anna Pavlova. Once before leaving she wondered whether the Messel theme might be enriched by the painting of Pavlova taking her call against the immense folds of the Covent Garden crimson curtains. She felt the memory of Pavlova still lingered, lighter and less substantial than a handful of swansdown, perfectly in harmony with Messel's dream Suite – both were language to the eye.

237. Dame Laura Knight showing her sketch of Anna Pavlova to the author

Sir John Sheppard

Out of hundreds of meals enjoyed at *The Dorchester*, certain guests are remembered by the impact of their personalities. That was particularly true of Sir John Sheppard, a scholar of fastidious taste and Provost of King's College, Cambridge. In appearance a caricature of the traditional don, Sheppard was a superb play-actor, invariably on the look-out for a theatrical effect, noted for personal quirks and fads. Silver-haired, he walked slowly with the aid of a stick, expecting everyone to give him unimpeded progress. This always worked at *The Dorchester.* Arrival at the Grill was aided by support from doormen, porters and waiters until he came to rest on the settee. Sheppard played the role of an old man for so long that, when the years finally caught up, the experience was resented. Only once did I see the bluff called. Cambridge railway station has the longest platform in the country and the morning train to London is always at the farthest end. I went through the barrier with a couple of minutes to spare, followed by the Provost leaning heavily on his stick. A difficult decision had to be made. His usual dignified pace would have meant missing the train. There was no alternative. A sprint did the trick and destroyed a legend.

This time the façade was unruffled. Food came second to the choice of wine that had to be approved. During the meal I asked him to reminisce about the intellectual secrets known as the Cambridge Apostles, which attracted such members as Anthony Blunt and Guy Burgess. He admitted that over the years, that stretched some 170, the Apostles had changed with each generation, but the undercurrent of homosexuality had persisted, becoming almost a hothouse creed at the beginning of the century. The trend declined after the First World War, but revived in the Twenties and Thirties. His own election to the Society was in 1902, the same year as Lytton Strachey. Somehow he became the main recruiter of promising young Apostles between the two Wars. About that time mannerisms and affected phraseology became the vogue and inevitably invited comment, not always flattering.

Sheppard recalled his close friend, Leonard Woolf, who married Virginia Stephen. Between them they formed an inner circle with Maynard Keynes, Strachey, Desmond MacCarthy, Henry Norton and Roger Fry that became known as the Bloomsbury Group. Their sexual preferences were constant, the core of their belief being that the love of man for man outweighed that of man for woman. Virginia Woolf had no illusions. She used to dismiss their activities as the expressions of a group of clever, arrogant men who preferred to be apart from women. In spite of advancing old age, Sheppard still felt there should be such diversity of taste.

My last contact with the Provost was in an unexpected setting – Monte Carlo an hour before the start of the Monaco Grand Prix. Thousands were pouring into the Principality as we walked across Casino Square to a chemist's in the main street. Outside on the pavement, slumped in an upright wooden chair, was a vagrant who had seen better days. Something about the head was familiar. On the way out I stooped down, and recognised the former Provost of King's. I listened to a sorry story. He had motored with friends from Menton and had been left in the chemist's. Nobody had realised that all roads into Monte Carlo would be closed for the duration of the race. He was stranded without money, daren't move, in any case he had difficulty in walking. He looked awful, unshaven, dirty shirt, frayed cuffs and shabby suit. It was a difficult situation. I was due in the pits by the harbour. Back at the Hotel de Paris I arranged for a porter to bring him back to the hotel in a wheelchair, seat him on the balcony with adequate refreshments, and I would look after him when the race ended. Events made it impossible because our car, the BRM, won the Grand Prix. When eventually we returned, Sheppard had gone, presumably collected for there was no message. I never learnt how this venerable Cambridge academic could have become almost an abandoned tramp. Shortly afterwards his death was announced in the papers.

E.M. Forster and Sir David Lean

Another guest, also from King's College, became a legend in his lifetime. E.M. Forster had the reputation of being austere and hermetic, but those who knew him attested to his mildness and courtesy. Talking to him on one of his rare visits to *The Dorchester* was an interesting experience. He induced an atmosphere where conversation could have touched on the evils of child labour, the problems of evangelical work, the 'world mountain' symbolism of Hindu temples, or the state of the West Indian slave market. It was the same in Cambridge. His rooms resembled a time capsule. Nothing changed. The only discordant note would be when he played Beethoven in indifferent fashion. Criticism would be stilled when he recalled how he wrote the libretto for Benjamin Britten's *Billy Budd*. It was the same wherever he went, and the hotel was no exception. It was the temptation to roll back the years. The most modest of men, Forster shrank from identifying with his reputation.

Over coffee he talked of his writings. *The Longest Journey* was his strangest offspring; *Room with a View* seemed to be favoured by the young and businessmen. *A Passage to India* was a fertile topic for discussion. He took the manuscript with him when he returned to India, only to find that what he had written wasn't India at all. 'It was like sticking a photograph on a picture.' He regarded it as a philosophical novel. Salewise it had been an enormous success, being translated into twenty-one languages and gaining the Femina, Vie-Heureuse and James Tait Black prizes. I said it was regrettable that he had written no more novels. He replied that this fact had not affected his standing. In fact, quite the reverse: his reputation as a novelist had grown with every book he didn't write. *A Passage to India* was his most satisfying book. Every aspiring author should find encouragement in his experience. He began the book in 1913; it was not completed until 1924, and there were times when he doubted if it would ever be published. The crux of the novel rests on the brilliant passages describing the visit to the Marabar Caves, where a young woman believes herself to have been assaulted by a Muslim doctor and levels charges against him which could have ruined his life. He is clearly innocent and the young woman retracts her charge when in the witness-box. We are not told what did

238. *E.M. Forster*

happen: whether the young woman had a hallucination or whether she was in fact assaulted. I raised the point and said we would like to know, to which Forster naively replied that so would he.

I have no doubt that Morgan Forster would have approved Sir David Lean's interpretation of his novel that attempted to find the answer. Lean was the ideal director, with a rare pictorial sense and a gift for narrative. Such was its success that the film had eleven Oscar nominations. It was Lean's first picture for fifteen years and by comparison with epics like *Ryan's Daughter* and *Doctor Zhivago* relatively short. The link between this brilliant film director and this gentle scholarly figure somehow captured the English tradition of the novel. Forster was the last survivor of a cultured liberal tradition swept away by two wars. Lean succeeded in capturing the controlled level of his theme in penetratingly beautiful fashion. Another quality in common was patience and exactness of detail.

During a stay at *The Dorchester*, David Lean described in his suite something of the difficulties that had to be overcome in filming Boris Pasternak's *Doctor Zhivago*. MGM spent some £3.5 million translating the 512 pages of the least-read best-seller in literary history into a movie blockbuster. Logistics of preparation give some indication of Lean's search for perfection. It took a year to write the script, cast and decide shooting-locations.

He described how, after a search covering some 30,000 miles, he settled on Spain. A mirage became reality. The acres in the suburb of Canillas became a Moscow look-alike, but the task took 700 workmen six months to build, involving 55,000 hollow bricks, 135 miles of tubular steel and six tons of nails. To find the equivalent of the central Russian steppes in Spain was a headache. Lean described how he selected a dozen locations, reputedly the coldest in Spain, only to have an incredibly mild spring. Such problems were swept aside by the director who had had to cope with physical and climatic difficulties in *Bridge on the River Kwai* and *Lawrence of Arabia*. The association with Sam Spiegel undoubtedly helped to establish Lean as a film director with an international reputation. His interpretation of Forster's novel became an outstanding near-art form with touches of personal vision.

239. *Sir David Lean*

Sir William Reid Dick

Dour Glaswegians tend to be heavy going when it comes to light conversation. Sir William Reid Dick was in that category. This son of a journeyman engine-fitter was a sculptor who had the ability to tackle metal, carve marble, hew granite, and had rare talent that can be seen in the reclining figure of George V on the tomb in St George's Chapel in Windsor, Lord and Lady Irwin in New Delhi, and President Roosevelt in Grosvenor Square. But he is perhaps best known by Lady Godiva's statue. Over dinner I suggested that an attractive young woman at an adjoining table might have been an ideal model for this study. Reid Dick disagreed. There were bound to be irregularities in her figure. He spoke with the conviction of having interviewed many beautiful girls, all of whom had fallen short of what he wanted. Perfection only existed in parts. That is why the shapely Lady Godiva is the composite figure of four women. Tactfully he declined to identify each quarter. In such a prosaic way are illusions shattered.

Sir Frederick Gowland Hopkins

Appearances can be deceptive. The biochemist, Sir Frederick Gowland Hopkins, was in that category. In the Grill he looked unobtrusive and old-fashioned. Small in stature with the delicate fingers of a surgeon, Hopkins' experiments have affected virtually everybody. He concentrated on the nature of the amino-acids and the chemistry of life processes – in brief, he discovered vitamins. He took this revolutionary breakthrough in his stride and concentrated in later years on research into the effect on the human bloodstream of the pigmentation of butterfly wings and its possible use in the treatment of leukaemia. His visit to *The Dorchester* unfortunately had a nearby table occupied by Meredith Frampton, who had been commissioned to execute the official painting of the scientist. Like Lady Churchill's reaction to Sutherland's portrait of her husband, Hopkins felt equally perturbed. Greetings were frigid. It was in part a clash of personalities. He felt Frampton was too self-opinionated and obsessively realistic in style, and produced a photograph to emphasise the point. Too much concentration on detailed rendering of three dimensions with something like *trompe-l'œil* accuracy in two. His gaze had been an almost surrealist intensity like photo-realism. The criticism, partly jaundiced, was justified. Frampton loved a microscopic finish. Any background featuring glass meant the sitter was relegated to secondary importance. In the Hopkins painting attention focused on test-tubes that reflected the varied colours of pigmentation, the scientific ego possibly mollified by the pad on which he had written *Lepidoporphytin* plus some incomprehensible data relating to the experimental stages. Lunch as such was somewhat fragmented. On the other hand, Meredith Frampton had not lost his appetite.

240. *Sir William Reid Dick and his famous work of Lady Godiva*

241. *David Ben-Gurion*

David Ben-Gurion

David Ben-Gurion, the Joshua who established his people in their Promised Land, never relinquished his role as visionary or allowed himself to forget the horror of Hitler's rule in Europe. Nothing blurred the memory of the gas-wagons or the slaughter-houses. Persistent campaigning exacted a toll on his health. Thrombosis symptoms led to frequent visits to England and the calm serenity of the Cotswolds where he could indulge in a mild form of bibliomania. During one stay he came to *The Dorchester* for a private lunch. He greatly admired the amenities, but thought they might have included a private lounge where guests could relax without feeling incarcerated in their rooms. A library might be too ambitious, but it was along those lines. Hotels of international status should try to cater for minority tastes. Two hours searching in the bookshops of Charing Cross Road proved disappointing. He thought their shelves compared unfavourably with Blackwell's of Oxford.

The Dorchester Family

THE DORCHESTER is fortunate to enter the Nineties with a Chairman of rare and diverse qualities. Field Marshal The Lord Bramall has had a very varied career. Born in Kent in December 1923, educated at Eton, he joined the Army in the summer of 1942, being commissioned the following year into the Kings Royal Rifle Corps, now the Royal Green Jackets. In 1944 he took part in the Normandy Landings and saw action throughout the North-West European campaign during which he was awarded the Military Cross. After VE-day he served with Airborne Forces in South-East Asia and then took part in the British Commonwealth occupation of Japan where he lived for nearly a year, returning to the United Kingdom in 1947. Since then, apart from courses and three years as an instructor at the Army Staff College at Camberley, his service has taken him to the Middle East, SE Asia, Berlin, Hong Kong and West Germany as well as the United Kingdom. He has commanded every level of army formation from a company to a Commander-in-Chief Command, including a battalion in the jungles of Borneo, an airportable brigade in Strategic Reserve, an armoured division in Germany, the Combined British Forces in Hong Kong – when he got to know Brunei well – and all the troops in the United Kingdom.

He was knighted in 1974 and made a full General in 1976. He then spent nearly eight years in Whitehall, in the so-called Corridors of Power, first as the Vice Chief of Defence Staff responsible for the Forces' Personnel and Logistics, then as the professional head of the Army (Chief of the General Staff) during the period of the Falklands campaign, and finally the most senior appointment in all the Armed Services, the Chief of Defence Staff. He was ADC (General) to Her Majesty the Queen from 1979–82, promoted to Field Marshal in August 1982 and retired from the services in December 1985. As well as his own Regiment, the Field Marshal has strong connections with the Gurkhas having been Colonel of the 2nd King Edward VII's Own Gurkha Rifles from 1976–86.

On retirement, Lord Bramall was appointed Her Majesty's Lord Lieutenant of Greater London and a year later received a life Barony and was appointed a Knight of the Order of St John. In 1990 he received the Order of the Garter, KG, from Her Majesty. He is a perfectionist as smooth and hard as Perspex, at the same time a more selfless and generous person it would be hard to find. He is a contradictory mixture: quiet in voice and gesture, he has that endearing attribute *politesse de coeur* in such proportion that it is hard, for all but a few, to tell where courtesy ends and heart begins. Essentially a man of action, it never does to underestimate Lord Bramall's determination to get his own way. In a peaceful role this was demonstrated during his year as President of the MCC: tactful handling of friction and distrust among cricketing nations smoothed ruffled nationalistic feelings and eased racial sensitivity.

In controversy Lord Bramall has at command a deadly ironic urbanity. His attitude is that of a man

242. *Field Marshal the Lord Bramall*

who dislikes and distrusts introspection, with more faith in facts than theories. He has gone through life with a casual air that conceals a shrewd brain, probing eye and steel determination. He expects and achieves results, qualities that will mould *The Dorchester* Renaissance.

Lord Bramall has the support of a selective, highly experienced Board of Directors that include Christopher Hanbury, Adriano Versolato, Frank Klein, Anil Tanna and Mohamed Al Fayed. He also has the whole-hearted co-operation of Ricardo Obertelli, who, appointed General Manager in May 1988, was given a unique opportunity to oversee every detail of the major renovation and refurbishment of the hotel. Like the Irish and the Jews, Italians are prone to be the victims of short-range optimism and long-range pessimism. Obertelli, although a true son of Italy, does not indulge in such extremes. He is essentially a realist. I knew Ricci before he came to *The Dorchester* and something of his background. After intensive training in hotel management and catering in Italy, he took a management course with the Savoy Group of Hotels in London, then joined the Ritz in Piccadilly, was later invited by the Four Seasons Group to be responsible for opening and running the Inn on the Park. Results confirmed the expectation that he was a young manager of considerable promise.

The Dorchester presented a daunting challenge to supervise the Renaissance of this famous hotel without changing its outward appearance and always conscious of its traditions. Ricci rose to the occasion and solved inevitable problems in unruffled manner. He set a pace reminiscent of George Ronus's extraordinary vitality. Its completion is a tribute to planning, vision and teamwork.

243. *Ricci Obertelli*

Ricci Obertelli has wit, charm and lightness of touch. He watches with his ears and is extremely popular with guests and staff.

A retrospective montage of six decades not only highlights social changes but is a reminder of well-known faces that have vanished. How rarely do we hear names mentioned of many who over the years played a significant role in making *The Dorchester* one of the world's greatest international hotels. Many have died and, though we tend to forget what they did, the present being so pressing, in our minds when reminded of them the mental picture remains the same. In that sense memories never age. It is certainly true of Sir Malcolm McAlpine.

The McAlpine clan and *The Dorchester* are synonymous. In the words of the lyricist, 'You can't have one without the other.' It all began with Sir Malcolm's ambition to build London's finest hotel, a dream that surfaced in the late Twenties and became reality on 13 April 1931 when the luxurious hotel opened with Sir Malcolm as Chairman, a position he was to hold until his death at ninety in 1967. Although he had residences at Broadstairs and Chobham, the Roof Garden Adams Suite on the ninth floor became home for many years. An indestructible landmark, Sir Malcolm lived through thirty-six turbulent and traumatic years of change. Only an older generation can remember the blackout nights and the shabbiness of London after four war-torn years as a besieged island. The fact that *The Dorchester* was able to maintain such a high standard in those difficult times was due not only to the spirit of loyalty of its employees but the encouragement given by the Chairman.

The self-contained community in the hotel was very much at the heart of affairs. General Eisenhower, Commander of the American Forces and ultimately Supreme Commander of the Allied Forces, used the hotel as his working base. Other guests included Lord Portal, Chief of the Air Staff; Lord Halifax, then Foreign Secretary; Oliver Stanley, President of the Board of Trade. Exiled Heads of State and foreign Royalty found refuge here. Rank and status meant little when falling bombs caused guests to take shelter in improvised bunkers in the basement that had been the gymnasium and the ladies Turkish Baths. Every crisis was met with cosmopolitan aplomb.

It is interesting to recall some of Sir Malcolm's activities outside the hotel. Born on 19 June 1877, the third son of Sir Robert McAlpine, the first baronet and founder of the firm of civil engineering contractors, Sir Robert McAlpine and Sons, he joined the Company on leaving Kelvinside Academy in Glasgow. In 1921 he was awarded the KBE for services to the Ministry of Munitions, and in the Second World War became chairman of

244. *George Ronus with Sir Malcolm McAlpine, first Chairman of* The Dorchester

the committe (which included Professor Sir William Hawthorne, later Master of Churchill College, Cambridge) briefed to construct the huge prefabricated structure known as the Mulberry Harbour. Towed across the English Channel, it provided shelter for supply vessels in the Normandy invasion. Another assignment was leading a government delegation to the United States to assess and report on the American method of open-cast mining, later becoming Chairman of the Open-cast Coal Contractors Committee, supervising coal production in the United Kingdom by this method.

Sir Malcolm's role in horse-racing was recognised by the office of President of the Racehorse Owners Association. The measuring-rod of success in this sport turns on performance in the Classics, an elusive ambition as owners have found, but in the December Sales at Newmarket he bought Zabara, a promising filly that had failed to reach a reserve of 2000 guineas and was sold privately. Trained by Vic Smyth at Epsom, optimism looked justified with wins in the Guernsey Stud Produce Stakes, the Imperial Produce Stakes at Kempton, and the Cheveley Park Stakes, but at three she was beaten five lengths by Lady Sophia in the 1000 Guineas Trial at Kempton. All came well on the day, however. In the 1000 Guineas, ridden by Ken Gethin and starting at 7–1, she was at her best, beating La Mirambule by a neck, a victory that had many backers in the hotel.

Even greater satisfaction came with the sensational Grand National win in 1921 with Shaun Spadah. The recollection of that day never diminished. The weather was brisk and clear, the going heavy. The original entry of ninety-two had been wittled down; fifty owners, withdrawing, had to pay forfeits that increased the first prize to £7060, an incredibly high figure for a steeplechase in those days. There were no past winners in the race. Bookies made The Bore the favourite. The race itself was near disaster, with the field decimated. The favourite led up to the penultimate fence but fell heavily, leaving his jockey with a broken collar-bone. Shaun Spadah came home the only true finisher. The Bore's jockey managed to remount and, with right arm useless, cleared the final obstacle and finished a gallant second. Further back two other horses, All White and Turkey Buzzard, were remounted and eventually finished the course. Sir Malcolm used to say that his win boxed the compass. The horse, who once changed hands for £3, was Irish-bred, Scottish-owned, English-trained and Welsh-ridden. Hardly surprising that the jockey was congratulated afterwards by King George V.

In 1946 Sir Malcolm persuaded the Minister of Works that the repairs needed for the Grandstand at Epsom should not be classified as non-essential. His firm rushed through the necessary work. After six years in exile at Newmarket, the Derby was again at its traditional home, though with sombre overtones. The Stands, course and spectators looked war-weary. Not a single top hat was to be seen in the Members' Enclosure. Strict rationing was still in operation; facilities for eating and drinking were spartan, but it didn't matter. The Derby was back, the King and Queen were present, a virtually unknown horse, Airborne, won at 50–1 by a length from Lord Derby's Gulf Stream, with no challenge from France which, as Sir Malcolm remarked afterwards, 'was just as well'!

When Sir Malcolm died, his nephew, Sir Edwin, became Chairman of *The Dorchester*, a position retained until 1976. Elevated to the peerage in the New Year Honours of 1980, he took the title of Lord McAlpine of Moffat. Like his uncle, Edwin had immense affection for the hotel and the staff, a feeling reciprocated. The extent of his popularity was shown in the annual Christmas luncheon when some 800 guests, from all walks of life including prominent figures of industry, commerce and politics, flooded into the hotel. Only once was the all-male rule waived, so Margaret Thatcher could be invited. The gesture was repaid with a brilliant speech that Edwin took pleasure in playing on tape.

One of Edwin's saddest duties was on 2 July 1976, when the heads of all departments in the hotel were summoned to a meeting in the Silver Room at 3 pm. Precisely on time McAlpine entered with Lord Pritchard and broke the news that *The Dorchester* had been sold to a Middle East consortium. At that moment the same announcement was made in the Stock Exchange. The news came as a shock to the staff, particularly to long-term employees, some with more than forty years service. Lord Pritchard, then Chairman of Allied Breweries and Rothmans, had been approached by Sir Edwin to take the chairman-ship of the hotel. With heavy commitments on time and energy, Derek Pritchard had hesitated before finally agreeing. His introduction as Chairman had a reassuring effect on the staff who felt their interests would be protected. Happily, in spite of the change in ownership, the McAlpines continued to use the hotel much as before.

As with Sir Malcolm, the range of Edwin's activities as head of the family concern were just as varied. Under his direction such London landmarks as the National Theatre and Shell Centre on the South Bank were erected. He exercised great influence on the British nuclear power industry, becoming deputy chairman of the Nuclear Power Plant Company, the consortium representing the north-east group of nuclear contractors.

245. *Lord McAlpine of Moffat with Vida Whitby, Executive Housekeeper*

Later he was made chairman of the company that designed and constructed the Bradwell Nuclear Power Station and obtained the first export power reactor order for the nuclear station at Latina in Italy. Deputy Chairman of the Nuclear Power Group formed in 1959, he was responsible for the design and construction of the nuclear power reactors at Dungeness and Oldbury-on-Severn; in 1973 he was appointed Deputy Chairman of the Advanced Gas Reactor stations. In 1978 the family firm went public through a parent Company, Newarthill, of which he became a Director, a purpose of the flotation being to establish a clear value of the business, though the family retained a controlling interest in Newarthill. For more that twenty years the McAlpine family had controlled *The Dorchester*, through a Company called Development Services of which Edwin was Chairman.

Edwin continued the family interest in horse-racing. Success in the Classics did not come but he bred Oasis, which won the Erroll Stakes at Ascot in 1962, and Golden Leg, which won the Wokingham Stakes. Four trainers looked after his sixteen horses. There was also his stud at Henley-on-Thames. A member of the Jockey Club, and Chairman of the Trustees of the Apprentice School Charitable Trust, he more recently won the Racehorse Owners Award after the successes of Devon Ditty. He had an infectious love of life, thoroughly enjoyed the social scene, and, ever vigilant in watching the work progress, was looking forward to *The Dorchester* reopening. I recall him standing on the hotel steps with Lord Shinwell, gently assuring the Labour peer that he would also top the century mark. Sadly it was not to be. Lord McAlpine ignored his eighty-two years, retained the rare gift of being accepted by people of another generation, and remained to the end a worldly Peter Pan. He is greatly missed. This was reflected by the huge assembly in St Paul's Cathedral at the Memorial Service, attended by the Prime Minister, members of both Houses of Parliament, representatives of industry, sport and every walk of life, who listened to the warm tribute by Lord Colnbrook.

From the outset *The Dorchester* has been fortunate in having a long line of influential directors, each outstanding in his profession, ensuring a rich blending of brainpower and expertise. The past always takes on a certain enchantment. Certainly the directors of the Thirties and the Forties seem in retrospect to have been strong, colourful personalities. Men like Sir Francis Towle, Chairman of Gordon Hotels, who ran *The Dorchester* for the first five years; Lord Wakehurst, Colonel Victor Cazalet, Group-Captain Sir Louis Greig, Sir Evan Charteris, Sir Harry Methven and Sir Robin McAlpine.

In June 1936 a young man joined *The Dorchester* as assistant to Anton Bon, then Managing Director. Three years later George Ronus, at thirty-one, became the youngest manager to hold such a position in London. In 1946 he succeeded Bon as Managing Director with a seat on the Board. His contribution over the next twenty years was significant. As a hotelier Ronus was in a class apart and had mastered every aspect of hotel management. Early training began in a St Moritz bank, followed by a spell in a London chartered accountant's office, before becoming a trainee at Suvretta House in St Moritz. He worked incredibly long hours (something seemed to drive him to accept too much), coped with the problems and difficulties of the war years. His manner was always unruffled. Naturally polite and considerate, he established a relationship with guests and staff that was cordial yet professional. He avoided any tendency to adopt an artificial charismatic approach that seeks personal publicity. Off duty he had a surprisingly shy streak. Sadly he died in October 1970. His influence had enhanced *The Dorchester*'s reputation for elegance and a centre of international flavours. At the Memorial Service in South Audley Street, among the many tributes was an unusual one from Henry Hall. He specially composed 'A lament' that was played with poignant effect. When George Ronus died, the mould was broken.

Other directors who made their mark include Sir Iain Stewart, whose advice was always lucid and informed; he had little patience with procrastination; could be a consider-able artist with verbal mayhem. He had a distinctive brand of Scottish humour not always appreciated south of the Border. It would bubble up without warning. I recall a dinner-party in the Terrace Restaurant. Iain sat next to a somewhat assertive American lady. She remarked that the ageing process had improved his looks. He did not disagree, but added that old age is hardest to ugly women, since it made no difference. Handsome women were the next best served, they at least took on the aspect of picturesque ruins. It was the pretty women who were the real tragedies of old age, since for them there was no alleviation; dimples became ditches. The lady, uncertain of her category, changed the subject.

Christopher Chataway was perhaps an unexpected member of the Board. Like most other people who experienced it, Chataway acquired a taste for fame. Despite the supposed handicap of having short legs, he was a brilliant runner who beat the seemingly invincible Kuts. He then sought fame in a field other than sport. A fluent speaker, politics

*246. George Ronus,
Managing Director of*
The Dorchester
1946–1970

was the natural outlet. *The Dorchester* was fortunate to have the benefit of his thoughts from July 1976 until January 1979. The Earl of Westmorland was a thoughtful, supportive director for several years, with an incisive mind when it came to troublesome issues. Lord Pritchard displayed similar tact after the sale of the hotel to the Arab Consortium. He was succeeded by Christopher Druce, the British financial adviser to Mouaffak al Midani and an excellent Chairman. Christopher is misleading and at first difficult to assess: in repose he has a sad anonymous face. He is always in control; I have never seen him lose his temper or bare his soul – that would smack of nudism. His image is uncontroversial, judgement first-class, always diplomatic. Lord Crowther was different. He had a cold streak and an aloof presence. He reminded me of the truism that the more intelligent people are, the more likely they are to be unhappy. Even his closest friends knew him so well and no further. Many never found themselves wholly at ease in his presence, yet behind the spikes of this cactus was a soft core. He seemed afraid that someone might find he was a kindly man.

The Dorchester ambience is based on unruffled dignity and good taste, an atmosphere sustained by the managerial side that created this image in the first place. The rota of Managers includes names known by generations of guests. When the hotel opened Henri Devigne was appointed by Sir Francis Towle. Three years later he was succeeded by Carlo Cigolini until he retired in 1938. George Marin's nomination was interrupted by the Second World War; he was recalled to France to take up his commission in the French Army. Colin Campbell was the next choice, exchanging the duties of Banqueting Manager for that of Manager. He became ill with tuberculosis and had to enter a sanatorium in Switzerland for treatment. This led to the inspired appointment of George Ronus. In 1946 he became Managing Director with a seat on the Board. He had John Lee as Manager for nine years until he went to the Waldorf Hotel in the Aldwych in 1955. Then came the popular appointment of Jimmy Green, who had gained experience as a cashier and Reception Manager. He was succeeded by Robin Oldland who had been an assistant to Ronus, left to gain experience in Switzerland, Spain and the Gritti Palace Hotel in Venice, before returning as Assistant Manager at the new London Hilton. When Ronus died in 1970, he became General Manager, then Managing Director with a seat on the Board. It was a highly successful appointment that lasted until the hotel was sold by Development Securities in 1976 to a Middle East Consortium. Oldland resigned and went to America to open a new hotel for Trusthouse Forte in New Orleans, later moving to Washington DC to manage the Madison Hotel.

The Consortium's recommendation for replacement was an Australian, Peter Stafford. Born in Brisbane in 1925, he was educated at St Laurence's College and the Teachers' Training College. He joined the Royal Australian Air Force in 1943 and came to England at the end of the war as a navigator. On demobilisation, Stafford went into the hotel trade, gaining experience at the Marine Hotel, North Berwick, the Palais d'Orsay in

247. *A birthday celebration for a former Manager, Mr G.C. Cigolini, in 1960, with George Ronus, Managing Director (left), and Mr H. Sartori (right)*

248. *Jimmy Green,*
Manager 1955–1966

249. *Robin Oldland,*
Manager 1966–1970

250. *Peter Stafford,*
Managing Director 1976–1979

Paris, and the Baur au Lac in Zurich; worked for a time in reception at Claridge's, followed by a post as Assistant General Manager at the Savoy before moving to The Mandarin in Hong Kong. His spell at *The Dorchester* lasted from 1976 to 1979. He was replaced by Albert-Jean Renault from the Plaza Athenée in Paris. It lasted only a year. Differences of opinion with Mouaffak al Midani, the major shareholder of the group that had acquired the hotel from the Middle East Consortium in 1978, meant Renault leaving at the beginning of May 1980. The replacement came in December 1980 when Udo Schlentrich joined as General Manager.

If the word dilettante were stripped of pejorative connotation and used to convey the sense of a gifted versatile personality, then Udo might be so labelled. Life was enhanced by his innate chic. He radiated charm, presence and style with an ingratiating personality that had immediate appeal, and although he swanned around with immaculate courtesy, the veneer hid a fine resolve that everything, just everything, had to match the required standard. His enthusiasms were those of a younger man. As a golfing Walter Mitty he saw himself giving Jack Nicklaus a stroke a hole. For sheer exuberance he reminded me of Stephano Sebastini, the Manager of the Berkeley – both extrovert and first-class at their job. In December 1984 Udo resigned from *The Dorchester* and went to the United States to form his own Company.

He was succeeded by Wolfgang Nitschke, who came from the Melbourne Regent. Born in Berlin, he had more than twenty-eight years experience in the hotel industry in Germany, Switzerland, Canada and the United States. It is always dangerous to judge people by appearance or mannerisms, and Wolfgang had a somewhat cold Teutonic manner with many other signs of a strong protestant outlook – not in an ecclesiastical sense, I hasten to add – but such traits were never shown socially, when he and his wife exuded charm. During his stay at the hotel, he was a perfectionist and expected those under him to have the same standards.

So many Swiss with a Mediterranean complex are never fully understood by Anglo-Saxons. Paul Grunder was not of that company. He spent his youth in Italy and Switzerland, came to England for education, started work at the Ritz Hotel in London where he completed his training, then went to the Hotel Suisse and Majestic in Montreux, and joined *The Dorchester* in 1951. After a spell in the Reception office, he became Reception Manager in 1965, then Deputy General Manager until his retirement in June 1988. Throughout these years Paul was always the same, full of disarming charm. He liked people individually as well as in the abstract, attributes that made him uncontroversial, but behind the carefree exterior was an incredibly hard worker. Using a fluid and easy style, he carried out his duties with tenacity. As an individual Paul could be pungent, innocently sly, superbly explicit in four languages – what one might call 'low-falutin'; had occasional bursts of indignation and a great sense of fairness. He could talk his way out of anything; had a habit of enjoying his own stories that had been heard many times before. Nevertheless he was a welcome antidote to the petty irritations of everyday life. For some reason best known to himself, Paul shied away from the role of Managing Director. Maybe the responsibilities involved were too intimidating. It is a pity for he had all the qualities necessary for success. His phenomenal memory seldom forgot a guest. They in turn liked him enormously. Paul Grunder had everything except ambition for this post. I feel *The Dorchester* was the loser.

The fact that *The Dorchester* was the first London hotel to build a Suite that personified luxury, then went on to add even greater expressions of artistic grandeur, was due in no small measure to the imaginative talents of three men. Oliver Ford, consultant to the hotel, designer of gardens with the Royal Warrant of Queen Elizabeth the Queen Mother, influenced both the appearance and the trappings of *The Dorchester*. With an intuitive feeling for design, Ford is a visionary who makes dreams become reality and has an unshakeable belief in himself as he has demonstrated on several occasions. It began at an early age. Fresh from college, he went by Harvey Nichols in Bournemouth, was not impressed by the window displays, went in and convinced a director of the shortcoming. Ford finished up as director in charge of decoration and display. In Paris there was a repeat performance with Jansen in the Rue Royale; when they opened in London, the ambitious young man was appointed managing director. A decision then had to be made, whether to be employed or set up independently. He chose the latter. Commissions followed in Los Angeles, Nassau and Cleveland from his base in the Bahamas, where he designed the Legislative Council Chamber, the Throne Room and the furniture. Not everything was on such an exalted plane; in a brake-lining factory in Ohio he coded all the machinery in primary colours. Returning to London he joined the established firm of Lenygon and Morant which flourished under his direction.

His role as Consultant to *The Dorchester* from 1962 was so prolific it is difficult to isolate instances. One of his first schemes transformed the hotel corridors. They were prosaic, long and straight with cream walls and carpets beige and brown. He began on the eighth floor, lowered the level of the ceiling at different intervals, added plaster-work with distinctive Spanish lighting fittings. He redesigned the carpet, with a cream background with sprays of rich flowers in sparkling colours, and had it made at the Royal Carpet factory in Madrid. There was a similar treatment on the other floors in varying designs and colours. The overall effect was excellent. Turning his attention to the suites, he was able to vary both colour schemes and furnishing styles. The Orchid Room was highly successful. The original orchid pink and white became blue and white, enhanced with exquisite plaster-work, mirrored doors having blue and white Thai curtains, impressive chandelier, and alcoves with blanc-de-Chine ornaments. The Cumberland stone floor in the Front Hall showed signs of wear; Ford had a marble floor laid, as well as new wrought-iron railings

251. *Oliver Ford used panelling from Dorchester House to decorate the eighth-floor lift lobby*

on the balconies. The Ballroom carpet was designed to his specifications, no mean feat for it contains 1235 yards, 36 inches wide, and was machine-woven in seven shades of grey and blue with a six-foot-square repeat. A section was displayed in the British Pavilion of the Brussels World Fair in 1958. Oliver Ford is an idealist. He has a deep love for fame; success is his fairy wand. His *Dorchester* achievements were those of a realist and an aesthete.

The second name is Alberto Pinto, a brilliant Moroccan-born designer from Paris with an international reputation gained from many commissions, including residences of the Kuwait and Bahrain royal families and the striking offices of Yves St Laurent in New York. Those who knew his work were not surprised at his treatment in *The Dorchester* of the Terrace Restaurant and the Promenade. For size and beauty the last-named was superb. In conception it was an achievement in design, lit by huge Adam-type lanterns, palms, ferns, elegant armchairs and sofas, the epitome of leisured elegance. The Terrace Restaurant was just as effective, with colourings of soft green, peach and yellow, pillars and arches hand-painted and brightened with gold leaf. The floor, raised by three feet above its original level, allowed glimpses of Hyde Park greenery. A gazebo in the centre of the room was an additional novelty. Wherever the changes were introduced in the hotel, the sweep and boldness of Pinto's creations were evident.

The third creative figure was Oliver Messel. As a designer with an eye for the glow of unusual liquid colour combinations his work in *The Dorchester* was outstanding. Born on 13 January 1904, the son of Lt-Col. Leonard Messel and Maud, only daughter of *Punch* cartoonist Linley Sambourne (his sister, now Anne, Countess of Rosse, is the mother of Lord Snowdon), Oliver was educated at Eton, went on to the Slade School, where he found congenial and like-minded students. To escape from the monotony of life-drawing sessions, he found diversion with Rex Whistler in designing masks. The quality of their work impressed C.B. Cochran, who offered Messel a trial commission. The proposal coincided with a request from Diaghilev to design masks for the ballet *Zéphyr et Flore*. This challenge proved more attractive, but Cochran's next offer was accepted, a commission requiring imaginative masks for his annual revues. Messel's next outlet was designing for the stage, work that drew warm praise from the critics, particularly the Lyceum production of *The Miracle and Helen*. Other sets included *The Lady's Not for Burning* and *The Little Hut*; film work had *Suddenly Last Summer* with Elizabeth Taylor. Eye-catching were the costume designs for *The Sleeping Beauty* ballet at Covent Garden and the Metropolitan Opera House, New York. These were of particular interest to *The Dorchester* for the original costume designs are on the walls of the Suite named after the designer, which was opened in June 1953 in time for the Coronation.

He began the task by producing a scale model. His innate theatre sense inspired delightful touches. The setting was ideal, with a vast curved French window. The carpet he designed to look like a garden parterre. His own paintings depicted seventeenth-century garden scenes in latticed frames with mirror-glass behind the lattice. Double doors had painted sprays of flowers. The main bedroom had gold grosgrain on the walls, bedhead and bedcover. *The Sleeping Beauty* ballet designs hang on the wall. A delightful fireplace decorated with acorns and oak leaves was also his design. The mirror-lined bathroom

252. *The gracious setting of the Oliver Messel Suite*

had fittings in gold plate. It was hardly surprising that the Messel Suite became the choice of the rich and famous. It was certainly appreciated by Noel Coward. In June 1957 when he was appearing in cabaret at the Café de Paris he wrote in his diaries: 'I am home in England again installed in the somewhat excessive *luxe* of the Oliver Messel Suite. Apart from the highly coloured décor the rooms are full of flowers from loved ones, and outside, London stretches from Hyde Park to St Paul's. I can see across the grey roofs, green trees, the thick towers of the Chelsea power station, the tall red pencil of Westminster Cathedral, the Abbey and Big Ben "all glittering in the smokeless air".' And again, later that month: 'I gave a "free for all" at *The Dorchester* which was a terrific success. Hugh and Sylvia Foot, Dorothy Dickson, Deborah Kerr, Mike Todd and Elizabeth Taylor, Oliver Messel and Freddie Carpenter. Kenny More came late – very funny and cheerfully disgraceful.'

Such was the popularity of the Oliver Messel Suite that the Board decided that another floor should be built on the roof to provide four more luxury suites. Each suite was the creation of a different interior decorator. John Siddeley, later to become Lord Kenilworth, designed the Harlequin Suite; Eric Giles produced the Adam Suite; Catharine Bray the Audley Suite; and Ronald Fleming the Terrace Suite. The results were outstanding, each showing distinctive fingerprints of style.

Oliver Messel had also been involved in the eighth-floor suite known as the Penthouse, so designed to accommodate luncheon or dinner parties for some eighteen guests. The layout is pure theatre, with a garden balcony and pool, Leda and her Swan the centrepiece among cascading fountains. He repeated the trellis-work effect on the outside walls. This effect is reflected in the Penthouse mirrors, set against a background of interweaving branches and leaves painted light blue and gold with lighting effects from half-birdcages. The door handles were gold-plated birds on twigs. Messel's sculpture of Bacchus was above the fireplace. An adjoining reception room had two choice mirrors, one originally from the old Assembly Rooms in Bath. The Ladies Retiring Room had several of Messel's own paintings including a scene from *Swan Lake.*

253. The Penthouse dining-room

The success of the Penthouse led to a further commission. He was given a completely free hand to design an additional room which could be used either as a larger dining-room or as a drawing-room. The result was an ornate room with *The Magic Flute* theme captured by his painting of all the doors and cupboards. The mirrors in the room and foyer were framed with gold leaves which Messel made from molten rubber on steel wires. Again the overall effect came up to expectations.

Another opportunity for Messel to give expression of his original creative talents came with the invitation to decorate the exterior of *The Dorchester* for the Coronation. He responded by transforming the front of the hotel as the interior of a theatre. The bay windows were draped like boxes; balconies, also draped, became the dress circle. Similar scope for his fertile mind came with the invitation to decorate the Royal Box at the Royal Opera House for the special gala performance of Benjamin Britten's opera *Gloriana* in celebration of the Coronation and in the presence of the Queen, the Duke of Edinburgh, the Queen Mother, Princess Margaret and other members of the Royal Family.

254. The Pavilion Room

For the last fourteen years of his life Oliver Messel lived in the West Indies where the warmth of Barbados sun eased his arthritis. Although cut off from London and New York, he was extremely busy. Assisted by Arne Hasselquist, a Swedish architect, his sketches for buildings in Barbados and the adjoining island of Mustique were made professionally acceptable. He died in 1978. An exhibition of his work covering fifty years in opera, ballet, the theatre and films, along with his painting and designs for houses, was assembled at the Victoria and Albert Museum and opened by Princess Margaret. About the same time *The Dorchester*'s long association with Oliver Messel was marked by a luncheon given by the chairman, Christopher Druce, for members of the Messel family. Among those who attended were the Earl and Countess of Snowdon, Viscount Linley and Lady Sarah Armstrong-Jones, a nephew Thomas Messel and his wife Pepe, Anthony and Penelope Seligman, and Carl Toms, once Oliver's assistant before developing into a theatrical designer in his own right by carrying on the Messel tradition. It was a thoughtful gesture by Christopher Druce and appropriate that it was held in the Penthouse that Oliver had designed.

It is claimed that *The Dorchester* not only has the most satisfied of staff in London but retains more employees for a longer period of time than any other comparable hotel in the capital. The proof is there to see. This spirit of loyalty and responsibility has contributed significantly to its reputation for personal service. The calibre of the clientèle is important, but so is the background of the staff. Each employee has a contribution to make and is part of *The Dorchester Family.*

255. *The Directors with long-serving members of staff:*
SEATED LEFT TO RIGHT: *Robin Oldland; The Earl of Westmorland; Sir Robin McAlpine; Lord McAlpine of Moffat; Lord Crowther; Sir Iain Stewart; Sandy Powell*

Arriving guests are greeted by the Linkmen, an outstanding corps, each man immaculate and courteous, military in mien wearing the green and gold uniform. I recall the massive frame of Bill Williams, who joined the hotel in 1945 after twelve years in the Welsh Guards. At 6ft 4ins, he was not only well known to visitors but a West End landmark. The same could be said of an earlier colleague, even taller with the same Guards presence; unfortunately the winter when London was shrouded in smog cost him his life. This high standard has been maintained over six decades and today is equally pronounced by men like John West who joined in 1974 and Ted Whitcombe nine years earlier. The sight of Linkmen in their familiar uniform is itself a guarantee that all is as before.

Luggage porters are taken for granted. Not so at *The Dorchester* where every man is smartly turned out and alert. Many are long-serving, like Wally Goff, who came from the Metropole in Northumberland Avenue in 1935, served as an infantryman in the Eighth Army during the war, and returned to the hotel after demobilisation. Chris Rubischon joined in 1942 after working as a footman in private service. Instinctively helpful both on and off duty, I remember seeing him in a suburban high street carrying a

256. *Bill Williams*

257. *Luggage Porters: Joe Corkery;*
Ted Whitcombe now Linkman;
Wally Goff; Chris Rubischon

258. *John West*

shopping basket with the same care he exercised when handling suitcases. Denis Kennedy began in 1970 after working as a porter in Eire; he exported some blarney across the Irish Sea. Porter personnel is considerable, but once through the swing-doors there was the welcome from Stanley Willis, the Head Hallporter, who had a long association with the hotel beginning in 1940 as an Enquiry Clerk. Called up for military service in 1943, Willis served as an air gunner in the RAF, posted to India for training, then to 99 Squadron in Calcutta, and completed 300 hours of operational duties in Liberators. When the war with Japan ended in 1945 he was posted to 681 Squadron until demobilisation. He returned to his old job in 1947, becoming Head Hallporter in 1979. He can look back with quiet satisfaction on many years of service.

Leonard Bruce was another long-serving employee. He joined the uniformed staff before the opening in 1931, his first job shifting furniture into the rooms. When he left *The Dorchester* forty-three years later he had become Head Porter and member of the *Clefs d'Or*. Also retiring in the same year was Fred Conway, who began his service in 1946. Philip Simms was another old stager; he joined in 1932 as a mailboy delivering letters to guest rooms, four years later became Assistant Enquiry Clerk, then Head of the department

259. *Philip Simms,*
Enquiry Desk

260. *Leonard Bruce,*
Head Concierge

261. *Stanley Willis, Head Hall-*
porter, with Julian Payne, a former
assistant manager

in 1962. Many of the staff are bilingual like Lj. Milozhovic, better known as Michael; born in Yorkshire, he had ten years' experience as a teacher, became a Head Night Porter at the Basil Street Hotel, staying five years before going to the Hyde Park Hotel, and shortly afterwards joining *The Dorchester*. Christian Sussman had a varied career: born in Düsseldorf, he worked for several years in German hotels, joined *The Dorchester* in 1970 as a commis waiter in the Terrace Restaurant, switched jobs to become a wine waiter, then in 1978 changed to Hall Porter. Jackie Harris was the first woman in uniform in a top hotel: she began on the Enquiry Desk in 1980, promoted to Hall Porter, nominated in 1987 by a German magazine as one of the 'World's Ten Best Concierges'; very efficient and adds a touch of femininity to masculine duties.

Michael Woollen could be described as the Reception Manager *par excellence*; Yorkshire-born, trained at the Westminster Hotel School, he joined *The Dorchester* in 1954, gained first-hand experience in various departments before becoming Head Receptionist, then promoted to Reception Manager in 1976. Since then Michael has been a welcoming figure to guests: never shows surprise or shock; takes everything in his stride; encyclopedic memory when it comes to the whims of the famous; the ideal frontman, typical of a long line of Reception staff who follow the pattern set by Paul Grunder. No better mentor could be found. Their professional approach is that of Said Melaini, fluent in languages: no request is ever too difficult; miracles can take a little longer.

Slightly different was the background of one of his colleagues whom I knew for years as Sam. He must have a surname, but Sam sounds just right. He began as a telephone operator hidden away in an alcove behind the old theatre counter. Unflappable, he coped with the manual switchboard, but sometimes found the hours of inaction so tedious he eased boredom with practising copperwork. After several months an excellent beaten profile of Queen Nefertiti was produced, an unusual extra-mural activity by a telephonist. Shortly afterwards came the offer to join the Reception staff. Poor Sam hesitated long before accepting. A worried man, he had great difficulty in coping with the unfamiliar duties, but made the grade and became immensely popular.

Looking back I recall two lady receptionists. They were formidable in appearance, meticulously efficient; guests who hesitated when filling in the required registration forms were eyed with suspicion. Inaccuracies were frowned on during the war; with the years the stern approach mellowed to the point of being near-skittish off duty. Cashiers are expected to be professional, maybe a characteristic from years of studying cheques with gimlet eyes. I recall Francis Copps, who joined in 1932 after working at the Grosevnor Hotel in Victoria. He used to say that his experience as Sergeant-Instructor of Gunnery during the war was excellent training for the Cashier's Office. Many guests will remember Geoffrey Mattacks, who joined in 1935, served in the Army promoted to Captain, returned to his old job, becoming Chief Cashier in 1961. There have also been a series of efficient, charming young lady cashiers. One in particular a few years ago decided to make a break from working behind bullet-proof glass. With a fellow cashier, she acquired a country inn outside Cambridge and coped successfully with an imaginative menu, rural Mosimann fare.

For many years Charles Davies was a popular figure with guests. A trainee at the Savoy Hotel from 1933–39, he joined *The Dorchester* in 1946 as a receptionist, eventually becoming Deputy Manager. His stock-in-trade was nonchalance, a refreshingly unpretentious personality who exuded charm in rationed doses. In complete sympathy with his duties, Davies was greatly missed when he retired in 1974.

A familiar feature of *The Dorchester* has always been the florist's counter, an attractive layout manned by girls, not only skilled but extremely pretty, a fact confirmed by the number of guests, including Peter Sellers, who claimed them in marriage. I recall Angela Duck, who was Head Florist in 1974. Trained at the Constance Spry School in London, she worked at the Flower Centre in Wigmore Street before moving to the hotel in 1965. The duties of these girls is not always appreciated. It is a world outside usual routine and begins at 5 am in the London Flower Market, always for four hours a scene of great activity, with porters handling trolleys of flower-boxes twelve feet high at great speed. One of the chores of Angela and her team was to arrange floral decorations in all the rooms, often under the supervision of Oliver Ford, the Design Consultant.

No reference to floral displays would be complete without mentioning Frank Holden, *The Dorchester* gardener for some twenty years. It sounds an unusual appointment for Park Lane, but it was no token job. Planting out in the gardens above the Restaurant, Grill Room and on the upper terraces needed some 3000 geraniums, whilst the velvety Cumberland turf by the forecourt pool was always completely weed-free. In one sense he lived a double life: Frank Holden was not his real name. Born in Poland, he responded to Franzizah Zdzenski; unpronounceable, he became Frank Holden and took British nationality. He studied horticulture in Poland and a course in landscape architecture at Heidelberg; served in the Polish Army, captured first by the Germans, then by the Russians; escaped and came to England, joined the British Navy in 1942, demobbed 1946. After a course in agriculture at Glasgow University, came to London 1948, worked as a gardener in the grounds of Dolphin Square luxury flats, finally joining *The Dorchester*. Watching Holden tending plants, it was difficult to realise how varied had been his background.

The new Bar designed by the Parisian interior decorator, Alberto Pinto, was an unqualified success, a harmonious blending of detail on two levels, with windows on one side facing Hyde Park, lined oak panelling on the side walls, mirrors reflecting blue-and-white ceramic-tiled murals made in France and showing exotic birds. It is about three times as spacious as the original Bar opened in the late Thirties. During construction work on the new Bar, a reminder of that decade came to light. Harry Craddock, the Head Bartender, had become enthusiastic about the cocktail cult that was sweeping the United States. At his suggestion a special casket was prepared and built into the wall of the new American bar. It contained this scroll:

'On this Twelfth day of April in the Year of Our Lord Nineteen Hundred and Twenty-Nine, I, Harry Craddock, being at this time Head Bartender at *The Dorchester*, Park Lane, in the County of London, do lay and deposit here five examples of Cocktails, a form of aperitif peculiar to this day and age.

'The Cocktail, which is believed to have originated in America about the year Eighteen Hundred and Six, is a number of drinks so mixed as to form the perfect medicine for cleansing the palate and creating an appetite for the meal to follow. The drink is the most popular before the midday and evening meals, but in recent years had become a drink served at afternoon and evening parties.'

In the Casket were five phials with a sample of the following cocktails: Manhattan, Sidecar, Bronx, Dry Martini and White Lady, which Craddock had invented in 1920. The samples, opened in 1981, were in perfect condition, though today the blending would be slightly different. The Dry Martini was then made from equal portions of dry vermouth and gin, shaken well, and strained into a cocktail glass; today there would be a higher proportion of gin to vermouth, stirred not shaken. During the war cocktail-drinking dropped out of fashion and remained so until a revival of cocktail parties some ten years ago. Cocktail recipes were not only useful as aperitifs but were taken at any time of day or night.

Roy Adcock, who started as a page-boy when *The Dorchester* opened, moved to the Bar in 1935, served six and a half years in the Services, and returned as Head Barman in 1950. David Renton was in charge when the hotel temporarily closed for alterations, and gathered round him an excellent team. They were put to the test in a cocktail contest arranged by the United Kingdom Bartenders Guild. Each team had to submit three original creations – an aperitif, a long drink and an after-dinner cocktail. Their efforts earned third place, two of the entries finding their way into *The Dorchester* list: 'Jade' in the Champagne Cocktails – blue curaçao, fresh lime, Angostura bitters, champagne; and 'Dorchester Royal' in the After Dinner Cocktails – white rum, peach liqueur, pineapple juice, cream and blue curaçao.

In 1988 Renton wrote a useful book in which he describes the secret of making great cocktails, enthusiasm that will serve him in good stead in the new Dorchester Night Club. He is succeeded by Giuliano Morandin as Head Barman. During the closure Giuliano has been Head Barman at The Berkeley Hotel in a bar he helped to redesign and redecorate. Born in Abano Terme, the spa town in Northern Italy, he took a three-year college catering course, spending the summer vacations on the Baltic in northern Germany for the season. Came to London in 1973, began work in the Hilton roof bar, spent a year on the Swedish American Line vessels, then Head Barman at Duke's Hotel in St James's, before joining *The Dorchester*. He resumes with promotion after the refurbishment with a young team, all of whom worked with him before in the hotel.

In some respects the Grill Room has not altered much over the years – with one significant difference. Meals now tend to be prolonged from noon to after three o'clock due to diners being preoccupied with business deals. In that sense many hardly notice what they are eating. Anticipatory pleasure is stirred by visualising the variety of appetising choices on the menu. Percentages and the profit motive ignore culinary delights. Brokers, bankers and executives miss what less pressurised individuals can appreciate at leisure. Their wants have been anticipated by a distinguished line of Grill

262. *Michael Woollen,*
Reception Manager

263. *John Curry,*
Grill Room Manager

264. *Roy Adcock,*
Head Barman

Room Managers. I think of Giessner, surely one of the most dignified to hold the post. A strict disciplinarian, he would stand by his desk and survey the scene with stern demeanour. Any suggestion of a lowering of dress standards was quickly corrected. This was put to the test when a well-known film star dressed in slacks arrived with two escorts. Giessner gravely explained his predicament. Gentlemen without ties or jackets could not be admitted. A similar ruling applied to ladies wearing trousers. Without hesitation the offending garment was whipped off, handed to a waiter, and very scantily clad, she was escorted to the table before appreciative diners. Unfortunately the lifting of such a restriction rules out the possibilty of an encore.

Papavasiliou was another of the old school. He joined in 1934, war years interrupted, resumed in 1946 and remained until 1977. Entirely different were the styles of Charles Kipfer and Walter. Both lacked finesse but were first-class. By comparison with Giessner they were more cryptic, but nevertheless extremely popular. Since 1967 the post had been held by John Curry, who has introduced a style of his own. An interesting career. Served in the Navy during the war, firstly in corvettes on Russian convoys, then in minesweepers in which he took part in the D-Day landings, and finally in a destroyer of the Home Fleet. After the war spent two years in Berne and Basle learning the restaurant business and the French language. Returning to England, he gained further experience at the old Berkeley Hotel, the Colony Restaurant in Berkeley Square, the Chateaubriand Restaurant in Mayfair and the Palm Beach Casino. Joined *The Dorchester* in 1967 as Assistant Manager of the Grill Room, appointed Manager in 1971, spent the closure months in the Far East, and now resumes his *Dorchester* career. Immensely likeable, with a ready smile and distinctive sense of humour. Passionately keen on golf, an activity that has the great virtue of not taking oneself too seriously. An invaluable employee.

As assistants he has had two Cypriot brothers, Shefik Hilmi Ali and Peter Hilmi Ali, whom I remember starting as commis in 1951 and 1954. It would be difficult to match their courtesy and charm. Unfortunately Shefik has retired. Curry had three excellent sommeliers: Luigi Averone, who joined in 1946 as a commis, became assistant Wine

Waiter, then Head Wine Waiter in 1978, a member of the Guild of Sommeliers and serves on their Council; with him Keith Traill and Carlo Fantini, who between them had over eighty years' service.

The Terrace Restaurant has always offered entertainment and a more lavish menu. The clientèle has remained the same though tastes have changed. In the old days five- or six-course meals were the rule, with two or three wines and champagne with dessert. Today the tendency is to settle for an appetiser, main course and dessert, with less wine. Anton Mosimann tried to restore the old order, with gastronomic dinners conjuring up a multiplicity of courses matched by choice wines. I fear they will be special occasions rather than an everyday custom.

As with the Grill Room, the post of Terrace Manager has been held by men of rare experience. I think of Papavasiliou, better known as Mr George, who joined in 1934, worked as a waiter in the Grill Room, returned from military service in 1946, became Head Waiter in the Grill, before transferring to the Terrace in the same position in 1961. Five years later was promoted to Terrace Restaurant Manager. Lorenzo Susini then held the post for fifteen years. As assistant, then Manager of the old Terrace Room, he helped to supervise the plans for the new restaurant. Sadly he died in 1988. Other long-serving staff include the Head Sommelier, Victor Colletta, who worked with Susini for ten years; Chambis 'Jimmy' Anastasi, who was Head Wine Waiter in 1968; Christian Foi who joined in 1970 as commis waiter – experience gained in restaurant business in France, Germany and England led to eventual appointment as Assistant Restaurant Manager. Then there was Kiriakos Thalassitis, whom I knew as Kiri, who worked in the restaurant for twenty-two years. Happily Peter Buderath has returned as the Terrace Restaurant Manager after a spell at Claridge's. His quiet control and charismatic personality is highly sussessful.

The Lounge, or what is now known as The Promenade, has had many long-serving staff. I think of Adelmo Valdini, known as Val, who joined in 1938 as a restaurant waiter, served in the West Kent Regiment, returned 1946 as lounge waiter and was promoted to Head Lounge Waiter in 1977. To mark forty years' service he received the Long Service Award from Lord Pritchard when he was Chairman of *The Dorchester*. Another 'character' was Gordon Richards, whose love of horse-racing almost matched his namesake. In the days of Sir Malcolm McAlpine, he was ever diligent in acquiring anything resembling an inner racing tip. An eternal optimist, Gordon was an excellent Head Waiter, with a service record extending from 1937 to 1977. The new Promenade Manager will be Giuseppe d'Amico, who was for several years in the Bar. A new feature will be The Dorchester Club that promises to be the best private membership club in London, Georgian Township in style, with Bryan Wright as Club Secretary, ably assisted by David Renton and Vincent Dimaio. I remember the lady cashier who, over the years, kept an eagle eye on the lounge waiters, meticulously checked their bills, and had watchful glances at children sitting on the settee by her desk whilst their parents spent a hurried hour in Harrods. In her own way, she became an institution.

Leaving departments and thinking of individuals, there is Stephen Price, a Welshman

265. *Welcome return of Vince and his Quartet, the popular resident band in The Terrace*

266. *'Mr George', Terrace Restaurant Manager until the mid 1970s*

267. LEFT TO RIGHT: *Lorenzo Susini, Terrace Restaurant Manager; Mr Malcolm Watson, Banqueting Manager now Food and Beverage Manager; Mr Muller, Room Service Manager; Mr Warren, Banqueting Ballroom Manager*

originally keen to join the police. After a spell as a cadet at the Police College and a brief introduction to the Force, he became convinced that life as a cellarman would be preferable. Four years at the Café Royal served as an apprenticeship in the trade before joining *The Dorchester* in 1977. I recall Sandy Powell, the Company Secretary, who joined in 1939 as Chief Accountant. War interrupted his career, serving in the Anti-Aircraft Battalion, then in the Infantry seeing action in Palestine, before rejoining in 1962 as Controller and Staff Manager, eventually appointed Company Secretary in 1972. All this was high-powered stuff, but Sandy's interests were not exclusively financial. For many years he was responsible for buying the finest wines for the hotel.

Then there was Joe Muller, Head Floor Waiter known to the guests who have enjoyed the ambience of the Penthouse and the Pavilion. I remember Joe when he worked in the Restaurant shortly after he joined in 1942. Thirteen years later he moved to the Floors and supervised his staff with the efficiency expected from a man trained at Suvretta House in St Moritz. Another popular employee was David Petrie. Born in Middlesex and trained at the Westminster Technical College, he came to *The Dorchester* in 1956 as Assistant Banqueting Manager, an appointment based on experience gained in the Savoy kitchens, a year at The Ritz in Paris, the Berkeley, and the opening of the Westbury Hotel. By 1971 he had become Banqueting Manager. Three years later he set up the Food and Beverage Department. His track record puts him in the same stream as Colombo, doyen of Banqueting Managers – no praise could be higher. A delightful personality, David was immensely popular with guests and colleagues. He is also persuasive: Daphne Bywater, assistant to Marjorie Lee, agreed to change her name to Daphne Petrie, and lived happily ever afterwards. I must mention four other employees. Godfrey Chase, inevitably nicknamed Charlie, joined as a commis chef in 1955, was promoted to Chef de Partie and finally Banqueting Chef in 1978. I must not forget the immaculately dressed Malcolm Watson, for several years a punctilious Banqueting Manager. Getting

268. *Max Colombi* (CENTRE) *Banqueting Manager 1941–1971, with* (LEFT) *Robin Oldland,
Managing Director, and* (RIGHT) *David Petrie, Assistant Banqueting Manager and later
Banqueting Manager and Food and Beverage Manager*

away from food, I think of Bob Gates, the Chief Engineer, whose skills at times avoided
many a crisis; and Bob George, the Garage Manager, who always managed to squeeze a
car into a minute space.

Two ladies of special talents earned respect and affection. Vida Whitby, the Head
Housekeeper, graduated from Acton Hotel School, worked at the George Hotel in
Salisbury, went to North America for further experience at the Lord Simcoe in Toronto,
the Camelback Inn in Scottsdale, Arizona, the Jackson Lake Lodge at Grand Teton,
Wyoming, followed by six years at the Cleft Hotel, San Francisco. When she joined *The
Dorchester* in June 1969, it coincided with the upheaval created by the redecorating
scheme that lasted four years. During that difficult period she had great support from
Marie-José, wife of Robin Oldland, the hotel's Managing Director, as well as working
closely with Oliver Ford.

Many guests do not appreciate the responsibilities involved in the everyday duties of
the Head Housekeeper. In the old days maids were neither to be seen nor heard. When
M'lady left for the day, they were expected to complete their tasks before her return; rush
in again before she left for dinner, then turn down the sheets and dash quickly out again
before being seen. The routine is not so strict today but in essence is the same. Maids still
pack, unpack and repack. Guests with an allergy to linen sheets are given cotton sheets.
There are folding prams, cots and high chairs for the travelling babies. Even a sudden
arrival is anticipated. It is remarkable how many babies have been born in the hotel. One
has spent school holidays in the same suite, married from the hotel, and given cream teas
to his grandchildren. To cope with disabled guests there are wheelchairs, bed boards,
crutches, trained nurses and nannies available, likewise baby-sitters, plus emergency kits
for those whose luggage has been lost. In short, everything was anticipated by the
imperturbable Vida Whitby, her staff of nine housekeepers and ring of twenty-four keys.

As Press and Public Relations Officer no one could excel Marjorie Lee. From that May
day when she joined *The Dorchester* in 1938 it became her entire life, apart from the
occasions when she worked on various assignments connected with the war effort. She
resumed full-time just before VE-Day. Over the years Marjorie established long-standing

friendships with many well-known guests like Elizabeth Taylor, Richard Burton and Peter Sellers, and was appointed by Earl Mountbatten to look after press relations for the marriage of his daughter Pamela to David Hicks. Always efficient, disciplined and feminine, she was greatly missed by staff and guests alike. There was only one Marjorie Lee.

I must not forget the Barber's Saloon that used to be run by the estimable 'H.N. Lawrence, Prop.' His establishment was symbolic of the enduring relationship between the clippers and their customers. The stories of guests who were shaven and shorn are too personal to be repeated, but always good value. Tribute must be paid to the switchboard operators. Over the years these ladies have contributed to the faultless image of the hotel. Ever helpful, courteous and efficient, they have been the beguiling voice of *The Dorchester* for six decades. Now for the Security men whose lot I do not envy, having watched them cope with every kind of situation, problems that called for tact, discretion, immediate action, or sympathy. Wrong judgement could mean trouble; even correct assessment might be embarrassing, like the time when a Middle East gentleman had a series of visits to his suite from adolescent boys. Suspicions were confirmed, but action thwarted by immunity granted by his status. The only option was to request his immediate departure plus habits to a more accommodating hotel.

Another headache is to decide whether an underdressed woman sipping fruit juice on her own is a tart or a bored guest pretending to be a call-girl, a delicate situation calling for discreet action. Not so on the occasion when a guest of Arab extraction rang down to say he was being harassed by a woman in his suite and asked for her to be evicted. Security plus Duty Manager reacted quickly, used a pass-key to open the door and found a furious young woman knocking on the bedroom door. The situation was further complicated by the fact that she was naked. Self-valuation had apparently overpriced her services and the client had turned her out. Without clothes it was an impasse. Security asked for the clothes to be recovered. The door opened, dress and shoes were tossed out, door shut and locked. That was that. Seemingly it was her working wardrobe. Angry at the predicament, the wench refused to dress until she was paid, warning Security if they tried anything, screams would prove attempted assault. Reaction was prompt. The zipless, tight sheath dress was pulled over her head, she was bundled into the corridor and escorted to the Deanery Street exit and handed the shoes. The action had one mistake: the dress had been put on back to front.

There was the instance of a guest complaining of being assaulted in the old Terrace Restaurant by an inebriated woman who had scratched his face. Calming him down, Security went to evict the drunk only to find it was a titled resident who had a flair for making headlines. Soothing noises proved the answer. A quality of naivety hardly applies to Security personnel, down-to-earth street-wise products of Scotland Yard and Special Branch. With sceptical eyes, they have seen it all before. That was why I was surprised when one of their colleagues showed he was susceptible to feminine blandishments. The lady in question was a blonde who had once been good-looking, quite a good figure, nice legs, with a sun-tanned face out of season, snub nose that wrinkled, round blue eyes that looked confidingly at whatever was her choice, be it black, olive-skinned or white, hair ragged as if cut with nail-scissors. The impressionable Security officer felt she deserved better companions, particularly the corpulent gentleman once banned from the premises. As a hotel resident, the lady had convinced Security that her business was a self-employed commercial activity. It was just that. She laughed her way to the bank. Even so Security refused to be disillusioned. One point I concede. She was pretty.

Another area closed to security action is common to all big hotels. I refer to the countless instances of petty larceny among guests. However rich and elegant, there is a tendency to take anything that is not nailed down. The range is wide. Ball-point pens by the hundred, notepaper and envelopes, towels, silverware, embroidered sheets and blankets, bathrobes, and of course matches and soaps. None of the items are really wanted. If accused, the guests would be mortified. The habit has to be accepted as a psychological blip. Another category are those who leave everything behind. The assortment is full of surprises, apart from the usual eye-glasses, contact lenses, pyjamas, dressing-gowns, trousers and toys. Whenever possible they are mailed back; even that has led to complications, as when an elderly peer summoned to the Lords when every Tory vote was precious did his duty and returned home. The item forwarded was lingerie found in the bathroom. A member of the House of Bishops was equally forgetful. A box of unmentionables was forwarded to the Palace that posed a question-mark against his celibacy. Most indignant was the actress who denied ownership of a set of dentures, an unwitting insult to her near-perfect image of thoroughbred limbs, pointed bosom, porcelain complexion, but certainly not artificial teeth. It is impossible to please all of the people all the time.

269. *Ricci Obertelli and his team before the closure in 1988*

The Renaissance

Now that *The Dorchester* lights once again beckon across Park Lane, it is appropriate to describe some of the changes that have taken place during the refurbishment, to give an indication of major alterations completed and the imaginative way in which the latest technology has been incorporated into the existing structure without affecting the essential qualities and atmosphere for which this hotel has earned international fame.

It all began in 1984 when discussions took place to explore ways of modernising that would not alter its style. Increasing sophistication of the industry over the previous twenty years made such changes a top priority. With that in mind, John R. Harris Partnership, Architects, were asked to put forward suggestions. It was not easy for, whilst there was recognition of the type of new facilities required, the snag was shortage of space. Over the years the hotel had been altered by using every conceivable piece of space. Many possibilities were considered. Some did not survive close scrutiny; others are best forgotten. Gradually an ambitious series of proposals hardened into this firm brief:

New lift cars throughout and some entirely new lift shafts.
New mechanical, electrical and plumbing installations, including state-of-the-art air-conditioning in all rooms.
Remodelled marble bathrooms and bedrooms.
Entirely new kitchens and staff areas, including escalators.
New windows virtually everywhere and general improvements to roofs and elevations.
A new Night Club.
A new Health Farm.
A new Oriental Restaurant.
A new Business Centre.
A new Shopping Arcade and remodelled Foyer offices.

A new goods delivery and refuse system.
A new centralised Room Service system.
A new luggage-handling system.
Increased fire exit stairways and sprinklers.
High-technology Security systems and computer Guest Room locking systems.

Theory had become reality, though still only on paper. Record drawings were studied along with such detailed inspections as were possible without disrupting the life of the hotel. Gradually, like the traditional jigsaw, the pieces began to fall into place. It was agreed that a new lift could be inserted between the old lift shafts and the adjacent staircase. The old Room Service hoists could be replaced by full-size lifts to all floors. The kitchens and laundry in the basement had been planned in the Twenties and by using the latest technology sufficient floor area could be reclaimed for the Night Club and Health Club. Satellite kitchens on the ground floor could be regrouped in the basement. Escalators to the ground floor were planned to improve waiter service.

The biggest headache was replacing the entire floor slab in the basement. It was essentially a concrete tank with drainage and other services built on the bottom, with the second floor rising over the pipes. To renew the pipework the entire floor had to be taken up and all the walls removed because of the replanning. Space was found along the Park Lane elevation to create a new entrance leading directly down to the Night Club, while the main lifts could be extended to serve the Health Club. Along the Park Lane front, the old Chinese Room was selected as the site for the new Oriental Restaurant. Advantage was taken of the Mezzanine to form a large light well with an internal staircase to tables on two levels overlooking Hyde Park. A number of private dining-rooms were also provided off the two main storey space.

The new shopping facility close to the guest-lift lobby emphasises the importance of having strong visual links between the shops and the Foyer–Promenade area, a connection emphasised by flanking display cabinets. This area meant relocating the Guest Cloak-rooms by rearranging the fire escapes from the staff offices on the Mezzanine and extending the old staircase adjacent to the Queen Mother Entrance in Deanery Street to a further three floors. This staircase provides a new route privately connecting all staff areas in a way that had not previously been possible.

The Basement reorganisation meant losing two small private function areas known as The Stanhope Rooms, but the hotel association with Stanhope Gate was retained by transferring the Stanhope name to the major stair alongside the Queen Mother Entrance. The Park Lane delivery chutes were finally abandoned, all incoming goods being controlled from a new Secure Loading Bay complete with turntable located alongside the Garage. A Business Centre at Mezzanine level linked via the Foyer Gallery with the prestigious Park Suite, with all conference and business support services.

Every bedroom floor was scheduled to be refurbished. Bedrooms and bathrooms were to have their own entrance lobbies, jacuzzis, deep baths, personalised tap heads, every-thing supported by the latest guest computer technology. A complete sample bedroom, created like a stage set in a small riverside warehouse near Chelsea, was available for experiments in advance of the main project.

With initial design appraisals complete and the scheme concept generally established, the project was gathering momentum. Consultants were invited to assist the architects in the specialised fields of structures and services. It was essential that the décor and fabrics chosen be in harmony with *The Dorchester* ambience and atmosphere. Refurbishment, like cosmetic surgery, must enhance the patient's original appearance, not render him or her unrecognisable to those who know them. The project was costed several times. From the outset it became obvious that a task of such magnitude could only be tackled if the hotel was closed for the duration of the work. This decision was finally approved by the Board in December 1987. Considerable preparatory work had to be done: interior design developed with the team; competitive tenders obtained; contracts awarded; building work managed. By 14 January 1988 a report was put to the Board of Directors summarising the overall project to date, plus the various methods suggested and tentative timetables for completing the work. The Board had hoped to close the hotel in the summer and open again in time for the following spring. It was wishful thinking. It would have meant building at a rate of £10 million a month, even if all the necessary drawings, consent, tenders and contract management provisions could be achieved in time, let alone the points of design detail about which the Board would need to be consulted. Also to be tackled was the no mean feat of emptying one of the world's most luxurious hotels of all its furniture and equipment; the departure of guests, many of whom had looked upon *The Dorchester* as their home for years; and the hundreds of employees who had faithfully maintained the special standard of *Dorchester* service.

It was agreed there should be a series of separate contracts to teams of highly specialised, traditional craftsmen, under the overall control of a Specialist Management Contractor. All work was competitively tendered to ensure best value for money. The project was officially announced to the Press, but the search continued for a Management Contractor with the skill and sensitivity to do justice to the brief. Short lists were drawn up, tenders sought, interviews conducted and the merits of each assessed. Finally the hotel decided that the key role should go to Sir Robert McAlpine (Management Contractors) Ltd, the family that built the hotel originally and had been its owner for many years.

Management Contractors confirmed that the craftsmen required could begin their work in the hotel by the beginning of 1989 and hopefully complete by the following year. Over fifty different contracts were envisaged, each tendered by at least three firms, which required over 150 bids to be arranged, checked and narrowed down to some fifty or so awards. Summer turned to autumn as the paperwork proceeded; guests moved out; fleets of removal vans took the furniture; the goldfish departed. After the Christmas Party of 1988, the lights of this historic Grade II listed building of special Architectural interest went out for the first time in its sixty-year history. Discussions which began with John R. Harris Partnership Architects some five years earlier had come to fruition.

As is the case with many major refurbishment projects aimed at creating a range of ambitious new facilities, the progress seemed painfully slow. It was necessary first to

270. ABOVE: *The Grill Room – famous for its distinctive English cuisine. The Spanish-style decor has been carefully retained, including the magnificent gilded ceilings*

271. LEFT: *A corner of The Grill Room, showing details of the elaborate regilded architectural features*

272. *Musicians in The Ballroom, which has been refurbished with new carpet and festooned curtains but retains its original decorative features, including 850 diamanté bows and 1,250 crystal heads on the wall mirrors*

protect the empty structure that was about to become a building site; to put cranes in position; to liaise with neighbours over whose property the cranes had to rotate and overhang; to undertake a survey of the condition of the building when handed over to the Management Contractor; to erect temporary offices for hundreds of craftsmen, managers, consultants and others; to erect temporary hoardings, scaffolds; to make arrangements for thousands of tons of rubbish to be removed from the basement demolition work; to form temporary openings; to work in conjunction with the Police and the Highway Department; to investigate any areas where access had to be restricted.

The building had always been known for its strength. The first-floor slab, over which rose all the eight bedroom floors, was some three feet thick, a fact that made the hotel a refuge for many during the air raids of the Second World War. The slab was to test the ingenuity of all in threading through the additional drainage. Bathrooms, which in the Thirties consisted of the usual facilities, now had to take double-bowl vanitory units, showers and jacuzzis all requiring vertical pipework. Despite its strength, the building

273. *Detail of restored metalwork motif on the doors to The Boardroom Suite.*
The Suite incorporates all the latest business facilities

was fully loaded by the various extensions carried out over the years. The introduction of marble into the bathrooms would not lighten this load, a fact that influenced the decision to use high-performance dry-wall construction in many of the replanned bathrooms. Early in the project it became apparent that the main partitions on the bed-floors would not withstand the various cutting and chasing work necessary to conceal new electric services. These walls were a mixture of wafer-thin hollow blocks and pots. It was decided to remove all these walls except at the top of the building where the other tradesmen were already well advanced, replacing them with similar high-performance dry walls as in the bathroom construction.

All the old floorboards were removed and with them went one of the unique *avant-garde* innovations of the original building. This was seaweed insulation, very progressive in its

274. *The Promenade, which was redesigned by Alberto Pinto in the late 1970s, restored to its full glory. Objets d'art, tapestries and striking hand-tufted carpets all contribute to stunning effect*

275. A corner of The Dorchester Bar, where magnificent blue and white tiles dominate the room, completely refurbished but architecturally unchanged

day, which had been used in the three-inch gaps between the old floorboards and the main structural concrete floors under. As the work progressed and the internal structure was increasingly revealed, adjustments had to be made to reconcile the findings with the exacting requirements of new ducts, pipes and ceiling levels. The meticulous design-brief had an additional extra to form a prestigious new reception room to the private Roof-top Suite looking south to the Thames and east towards the City and Westminster.

The Ballroom had to be extensively refurbished and the external works increased. Dialogue continued with the hotel regarding the colours of the marbles, ceramic tiles, wall decorations, taps, doorknobs, and so on. Televisions were chosen; marble quarries in Northern Italy visited and hundreds of tons of marble selected while still part of a mountainside; craftsmen produced their own drawings from those prepared by the architects and interior designers, setting in motion the approval of these drawings, visiting their factories and checking samples of the vast range of materials specified for the project.

The timber panelling salvaged from the original Dorchester House and about a hundred years old went back into the building, along with such of the other salvaged panelling, a few basins and taps originally used in the hotel, to form what might be called a Nostalgia

276. *View of The Promenade from the Entrance Hall, showing detail of the repainted and regilded dome*

277. *The Duke of Edinburgh with Lord Bramall, Chairman of* The Dorchester*'s Board of Directors, unveiling a plaque to commemorate the reopening of* The Dorchester *on 26 October 1990. The Hotel reopened on 19 November 1990*

Suite, though it lacked the authentic seaweed insulation touch. All bed-floor windows were replaced with special glass ranging from bullet-proof to shatter-proof and heat-retaining; double and triple glazing was also used. Before the hotel could be recommissioned, a mass of restrictions had to be settled: fire certificate reactivated; liquor licence reinstated; massage licence obtained for the Health Club; entertainment licence reissued; licence for the Garage, first granted in 1939 for the storage of petroleum during the War, had to be renewed; plus final clearance of all installations from the District Surveyor, the Fire Officer and Environment Health Officer – chores that marked the completion of an incredible refurbishing operation creating an hotel unparalleled in luxury and modern sophistication. The word 'unique' can seldom be used with its full implication: that claim can rightly be applied to *The Dorchester*, a great English institution that exudes an air of immense reassurance as befits a tradition and social history second to none.

278. *HRH Prince Michael of Kent cutting the ribbon for the opening of The Dorchester Ride.*
6 November 1990

Somerset Maugham once wrote, 'When you sit down to dinner at the very same table you sat at the year before, and the year before that, and when you see that your bottle of Soave is in the ice pail waiting for you, as it has been year after year, you cannot help but feel very comfortable and very much at home.' Future guests will enjoy the same experience, of seeing familiar faces, and being cosseted by the same staff who are like old family retainers. The glorious days of *The Dorchester* have returned, with the same impeccable service appreciated by the rich, the beautiful, the eccentric and the famous against a background of sheer loveliness. All those involved in this monumental task of its renaissance are to be complimented on their superb achievement. The results are there for all to see and savour.

Acknowledgements

Photographs are reproduced by kind permission of the following:
Associated Press, plate nos. 61, 162, 164, 182; Camera Press Ltd, 49, 108, 121, 122, 139, 142, 151, 153, 154, 158, 167, 188, 190, 194, 203, 204, 208, 218; Express Newspapers, 77–9, 92, 93; Hulton-Deutsch, 33, 37–41, 43, 44, 66, 76, 81–3, 117, 126, 129, 136, 145, 149, 150, 169, 171, 174, 175, 177, 181, 195, 197; John Harris, 20; John Hillelson Agency, 233; A.H. Jolly (Editorial) Ltd, 1; Mail Newspapers plc, 234; Mansell Collection, 2, 9, 36; Mary Evans Picture Library, 7, 10, 11; Popperfoto, 34, 35, 47, 72, 86, 87, 133, 141, 144, 146, 156, 163, 200; Press Association/Topham, 73, 89–91, 125, 147, 152, 159–61, 189, 192, 205, 209, 211; Reuter, 56; Sincroflash Ltd, 215, 216; Wallace Collection, 3 (Crown copyright).

The following photographs were supplied by the author: 19, 21, 48, 50–2, 67–71, 75, 80, 84, 85, 88, 100–2, 104–7, 109–11, 130–1, 143, 148, 155, 157, 165, 166, 168, 170, 172, 173, 176, 178, 179, 186, 187, 198, 199, 201, 202, 236–41.

All other illustrations come from *The Dorchester*'s own archive.